Spiritual Letters

MAHARAJ SAWAN SINGH

Spiritual Letters

Baba Jaimal Singh Ji

RADHA SOAMI SATSANG BEAS

Published by:
Sewa Singh, Secretary
Radha Soami Satsang Beas
P.O. Dera Baba Jaimal Singh
Dist. Amritsar, 143204
Punjab, India

1st Edition	1958	(as Part I of *Spiritual Gems)*
2nd Edition	1960	(as Part I of *Spiritual Gems)*
3rd Edition	1967	(as *Spiritual Letters)*
4th Edition	1973	
5th Edition	1976	5,000 copies
6th Edition	1984	5,000 copies
7th Edition	1998	15,000 copies *(new translation, unabridged)*

Printed at: Baba Barkha Nath Printers, New Delhi.

Contents

Contents

Preface to the Seventh Edition

This edition marks the first complete English translation of the letters of Baba Jaimal Singh to his disciple, Babu Sawan Singh. Extracts of the letters were first translated in the early fifties under the instructions of Maharaj Charan Singh and published in 1958 as part of a larger work, *Spiritual Gems.* Two years later, additional translated material was added, and in 1967 the third edition was published as a separate book called *Spiritual Letters.*

Much of the front matter from the earlier editions has been retained as it provides valuable material for understanding the letters in context. The beautiful Foreword, written by Maharaj Charan Singh in 1958, explains how the book came to be; Rai Munshi Ram's History was written at the same time and talks of the early years of the Radha Soami Masters; the letter by the Great Master, Maharaj Sawan Singh, written in the thirties and retained as the Introduction, gives the reader an overview of the spiritual teachings and the life of both his own Master, Baba Jaimal Singh, and his Master's Master, Soami Ji Maharaj.

As in earlier editions, the letters from Baba Jaimal Singh to the sangat in Bhandal, and miscellaneous letters to Baba Ji and to Maharaj (Babu) Sawan Singh from the Agra sangat have been included after the main body of letters.

The main portion of the book consists of the letters Baba Jaimal Singh wrote to the Great Master when he was grooming him as his successor. Written a century ago, between 1896 and 1903, they must surely rank among the world's great devotional guides, revealing a rare level of spiritual insight and practical guidance on the inner path to God.

Prof. K. S. Narang, head of Publications at the Dera from 1975 to 1995, used to tell how he had visited Maharaj Charan Singh in the intensive care ward of a Delhi hospital in 1971, when he had just had his first heart attack. The Master was reading *Spiritual Letters* in Panjabi. He commented to Narang Sahib that if he had to choose one book from all the books on the teachings, it would be Baba Ji's letters to the Great Master.

It is a privilege for the Society to be able to bring out this first complete translation of the letters in English.

Sewa Singh
Secretary
Radha Soami Satsang Beas
21 April 1997

Foreword

It was early in 1948 when the Great Master called me to his sick-bed and handed me a silk-lined jewel chest.

Before parting with it, Maharaj Ji pressed it against his bosom and then, with his eyes moistened with two big pearl-like drops, kissed it with devotion and humility, for it contained letters which his dearly beloved Satguru had written to him from time to time. I was told that this was the rarest and most precious gift in his possession, which was being passed on to my care as an heirloom.

I little realized at that time how precious the gift was and what a fund of esoteric knowledge on Sant Mat it contained. As I went through the letters in later years, however, I was deeply impressed with their profundity and practical character, and felt that this great gift must be shared by as many satsangi brothers and sisters as possible, not only in our country but also abroad. Most of the letters were written in Panjabi but, with the effort and zeal of Professor Jagmohan Lal and Miss Louise Hilger, now appear in English translation, extracts of which are in this book. These extracts are not chronologically arranged, as in a number of cases either the letters bear no dates or the dates are not legible.

As is well known, Baba Ji himself went to the Murree Hills to seek the Great Master who was to carry on his mission, and initiated him there on the 15th day of October 1894. The period between his initiation and the assumption of duties and responsibilities at the Dera is, almost in its entirety, covered by these letters. A great soul was being groomed for the highest spiritual achievement by another great soul.

The letters were primarily meant for the Great Master. Though we cannot generalize on all matters, we can profit by them in many ways. Some may think there is a lot of repetition in the letters, but it should be remembered that the sole object of the saints in life is to bring us in contact with the audible life stream, i.e., Shabd. Therefore they take advantage of every situation and opportunity to press home this all-important point.

I shall be very happy if these letters enable readers to grasp the basic teachings of Sant Mat and help them to mould their lives after this pattern.

Charan Singh
Dera Baba Jaimal Singh
1958

Extract from

"History of the Beas Satsang"

Written in 1958 by Rai Sahib Munshi Ram, who served as personal secretary to three Masters—the Great Master, Sardar Bahadur and Maharaj Charan Singh.

Radha Soami Mat or Sant Mat—the teachings of the saints—was propounded in Agra in July 1861 by Soami Ji Maharaj Seth Shiv Dayal Singh Ji. Soami Ji was born on the 25th August 1818, meditated for seventeen years in a secluded apartment of his house at a very young age and departed from this life on the 15th June 1878. His father's name was Seth Dilwali Singh Ji. Soami Ji was married but had no children. A few hours before his death, he issued some commandments which are detailed below.

Last commandments of Soami Ji Maharaj
The words that Soami Ji Maharaj uttered with his own sacred tongue on the last day before he went in forever, for the guidance of sadhus, satsangis and satsangans (male and female followers). Date, 15th June 1878 A.D., corresponding to Asarh, Badi Parwa, Sambat 1935, Saturday, early morning.

1. Soami Ji Maharaj called Chandar Sen, a satsangi who used to come from village Kursande every full moon day for the darshan of Soami Ji Maharaj, to come near, and said: "Sit down, look intently and let this form dwell in your mind, for you will not have darshan on the next full moon day. Your devotion (*bhakti*) is complete."

2. At eight o'clock in the morning Soami Ji Maharaj said: "Now I am preparing to leave." After that Maharaj took his *surat* up and drew up all the consciousness; only the whites of the eyes were visible, and the body began to tremble. After fifteen minutes he brought his *surat* down and then said: "The will *(mauj)* is now changed. There is yet some time." Then Lala Seth Pratap Singh (Chacha Ji) asked: "When is the *mauj?*" On which he replied: "Sometime this afternoon."

3. Then Sadhu Bhara Singh and satsangis began making offerings and performing obeisance. Thereupon Lala Jagannath Khatri, a neighbour, said: "Let the *dhyan* (attention) of Maharaj be fixed inwards; this is not the time for such offerings." Then Soami Ji Maharaj turned to him and said: "To be able to send the *surat* up whenever you like, at will, and to bring it down whenever you like, this is called *dhyan*. As for me, I had already taken myself up last night and put the *surat* into the lap of Sat Purush, but have come down to say a few things to you people."

4. Then he said: "You know I was six years old when I applied myself to spiritual work *(parmarth)*; thus I have been able to perfect this practice of meditation *(abhyas)*." And he gave this analogy in its support: "Tell an imperfect swimmer to swim when he is about to drown. He will not be able to swim but will sink. Whereas if you throw one into the river who has learned swimming from boyhood, he will not drown. As for the body, it is only a skin cover. In no case has it lasted. Lifelong bhajan and simran is only for this reason, that one should not forget at this time [at the time of death]. Therefore practise Nam in such a way

that you do not forget it even while moving about and talking."

5. Then, turning to Rai Saligram and all sadhus and satsangis, male and female, Soami Ji Maharaj said: "Look upon Radha Ji [Soami Ji's wife] as you look upon me, and consider Radha Ji and Chhoti Mata Ji [wife of Soami Ji's younger brother, Seth Bindraban Singh] as equal."

6. Then he told Radha Ji Maharaj (his wife) not to turn her back on Sibbo, Bukki and Vishno.

7. About Sanmukh Das, he said that he was appointed the *mahant* or head of all the sadhus, and explained: "Not that type of leadership *(mahanti)* that is current in the world. That is, Sanmukh Das and Birmal Das are appointed officers over the sadhus, and the arrangement for and the adminstration of the sadhus will be their responsibility. They will stay in the Bagh (garden) and Partapa (Seth Pratap Singh) will be the owner of the Bagh."

8. Then he said that persons with families (householders) should expect no devotion from the sadhus.

9. Radhi Bibi then asked who would be appointed for them. Soami Ji replied: "Radha Ji for householders *(grihasthi)* and Sanmukh Das for sadhus."

10. Soami Ji Maharaj said that women living a family life *(grihasthi)* should not go to the Bagh to offer service or devotion to any sadhu. "They should all go to Radha Ji to have darshan and to offer devotion." He then said: "It is I

who have made the tiger and the goat drink from the same pool. It is not possible for anybody else to do it."

11. Then Bibi Bukki entreated that Soami Ji take her also along with him. Whereupon he said: "Do not worry. I shall call you soon. Emphasize your attention on the Lotus Feet inside."

12. Then Lala Pratap Singh requested that he also be taken along, to which Soami Ji Maharaj replied: "I have still to take a lot of work from you. You will live in the Bagh, hold satsang and make others hold satsang."

13. Then Sudarshan Singh (Soami Ji's nephew) asked: "Whom shall we ask, if there is anything to be asked (if there are any questions to be answered)?" To this he replied: "If anyone wants to ask anything (wishes anything to be explained), he should ask Saligram."

14. Turning to Lala Pratap Singh, he said: "My teachings (*mat*) were of Satnam and Anami, whereas Radha Soami Mat was started by Saligram. Let this also go on. Satsang should continue and satsang will flourish more than before."

15. Then he said: "No satsangis, whether householder (*grihasth*) or sadhu (*bhekh*), should in any way feel perturbed. I am with every one of them and in future they will be looked after even more than before."

16. He continued: "No other effort (*karni*) will be successful in Kaliyug. Dhyan or contemplation of the inner form (*swarup*) of the Satguru, simran of Nam and contemplation of Nam will be successful."

17. Lala Pratap Singh then requested that Shabd be opened. Soami Ji replied: "To hear the Dhun and to enjoy its bliss is the equivalent to the opening of the Shabd."

18. Then Soami Ji Maharaj turned to Radha Ji and said: "I have practised both spiritual work and worldly work (*parmarth* and *swararth*). Therefore, follow the worldly rule also and let the sadhus too follow their own customs."

19. Soami Ji Maharaj then moved out of the courtyard into the inner room and breathed his last at about 1:45 p.m.

~

Baba Jaimal Singh Ji Maharaj was one of the foremost disciples of Soami Ji Maharaj. Whenever Baba Ji would get any time, he would spend it in the satsang of Soami Ji Maharaj and his darshan. In October 1877, when Baba Ji came on leave, Soami Ji Maharaj said to him:

"This is our last meeting. Now I shall go away to Param Dham (the eternal home), after completing my life's pilgrimage. I have made you my beloved and my own *roop* (self or form)."

Bhai Chanda Singh then requested that satsang be started in the Panjab. Soami Ji replied: "This request has been accepted by Akal Purush, and this task has been allotted to Baba Jaimal Singh." Then Soami Ji Maharaj gave his own turban to Baba Ji as parshad and ordered him to go and preach Nam in the Panjab.

Bibi Rukko used to reside in Agra in the service of Mata Radha Ji. One day, sometime after Soami Ji Maharaj's death, Mata Ji asked Bibi Rukko to return to the Panjab. Bibi Rukko replied that she had no work there and she did not want to give up her satsang and go to the Panjab. She further suggested that some sadhu be sent there, who should preach Soami Ji's teachings (bachan). Mata Ji replied that for satsang and the spreading of Nam in the Panjab, Soami Ji's orders had already been given.

Next morning Mata Ji asked Bibi Rukko to go to the railway station and receive the Satguru who had been appointed by Soami Ji Maharaj for the Panjab. "He is our beloved son, and Soami Ji Maharaj has to take both worldly work (swararth) and spiritual work (parmarth) from him," Mata Ji further said.

When Baba Jaimal Singh Ji arrived, the elder Mata Ji [Radha Ji] and the younger Mata Ji [the wife of Seth Bindraban Singh] as well as Chacha Ji [Seth Pratap Singh] and Bibi Bukki gave Bibi Rukko some money and ordered her to accompany Baba Ji to the Panjab. Mata Ji said that his service was the service of Soami Ji Maharaj. Bibi Rukko entreated in the following words: "Mata Ji, this body is not capable of doing any service and the mind is not within my control, and wealth I do not possess. What can we mortals do?" Mata Ji replied that she should consider the money given to her as grace (daya) and that Soami Ji would himself get the work done in the best possible manner.

Then Mata Ji reminded Baba Ji that Soami Ji Maharaj had left orders for him to spread Nam in the Panjab; so now, according to his orders, he should continue to hold satsang and give Nam.

Thereafter, Baba Jaimal Singh Ji came and settled down on the banks of the river Beas, between the villages of Balsarai and Waraich, and started satsang there.

Baba Jaimal Singh Ji was born in 1839 in a village called Ghuman in the district of Gurdaspur (Panjab). He had spiritual inclinations from his very childhood and moved from place to place, for enlightenment. At the age of seventeen, he came to Agra, as advised by a sadhu in Rishikesh (Hardwar) and was initiated into the spiritual practice of Sant Mat by Soami Ji Maharaj. He joined the army in pursuance of the orders of his Master and retired from service on pension in 1889. This colony, which was named after him 'Dera Baba Jaimal Singh', was founded in 1891. It was a veritable piece of wasteland and had a peaceful and quiet surrounding, situated on the banks of the river Beas. It was a general belief that the place was haunted by evil spirits and therefore it had remained uninhabited. The place has since grown into a flourishing colony but still retains its serene and peaceful atmosphere. Baba Ji Maharaj did not marry and remained a bachelor throughout his life. He left his mortal body on the 29th December 1903. He was succeeded in this great task by Hazur Baba Sawan Singh Ji.

Hazur Baba Sawan Singh was born in 1858 in village Jatana, near Mehmansinghwala, District Ludhiana (Panjab), his ancestral home, and was initiated into Surat Shabd Abhyas on the 15th of October 1894. He was responsible for the development of the colony and for the uplift of many a soul, and proved himself to be worthy of the words uttered by his great Master about the work which was intended to be entrusted to him.

Maharaj Sawan Singh Ji initiated a large number of persons of all shades and walks of life and from all countries, including Europe, America, South Africa, etc. He died on the 2nd of April 1948 and was succeeded by Sardar Bahadur Jagat Singh Ji, by a registered will, executed on the 20th of March 1948.

Munshi Ram (Rai Sahib)
Retired District & Sessions Judge
Chairman, Executive Committee
Radha Soami Satsang Beas
1958

Introduction

A letter by Maharaj Sawan Singh
translated into English in the 1930s.

Radha Soami is not the name of a religion. It is the name of the Creator of the universe, whom we also call Wahiguru or Akal Purush. Every Satguru has praised Soami. If in this world there is any highest region of spirituality, that is Soami. When a saint has gained that region of Soami, he is called *param sant*. And there are numerous names of that supreme Lord.

The sages who gained the region of Radha Soami lived in different nations, belonged to different religions, and have called Him by some name in their own language. Similarly Guru Gobind Singh in his book *Jap Sahib* had mentioned about twelve or fourteen hundred names for the supreme Creator, which names are not found in any Veda or Shastra. In the same way other sages in their own language mention the names of the various internal spiritual stages. The sages of the Panjab or of India as a whole named these regions in Sanskrit, while those in Persia or Arabia used Persian or Arabic names for them.

In the same way Hazur Shiv Dayal Singh (Soami Ji), Param Sant of Agra, gave the name 'Soami' to the supreme Creator and called the soul 'Radha'. Therefore in his *Sar Bachan Poetry* he has said that Radha was the name of the primal soul, while Soami was the name of the highest region and sound current called Shabd. Therefore Radha Soami and Surat Shabd indicate the same thing. Radha (soul) Soami (Creator), Surat (soul) Shabd or sound current (Creator), mean that the

xix

soul is to merge with the supreme Creator, just as a drop which joins the ocean becomes the ocean.

Sant Mat is common to all the sages of the world who attain the highest region. It is a natural science. It is complete in every human being no matter to what country, tribe or religion he belongs. When the supreme Creator is One and the structure of human beings is the same everywhere, then how is it possible that there should be a different way for Hindus, a different way for Mohammedans and a still different way for Christians?

The sages who went to the highest region had the same ideal or goal and although their writings were in different languages, they were not bound by any religion or creed. They come to the world under the orders of the Supreme Being and their mission is not to create a new religion. Their mission is only to release the prisoners (bound in the cycle of births and deaths) by means of Shabd or sound current and take them to the highest region.

If we read their teachings with care, then we shall find that they are above all religions; that they liberate us from the shackles of religion and give us everlasting bliss. There is no doubt that the teachings are explained in some language or other in their books, but the real path on which they take their disciples is beyond speech and writing. As is said by Guru Nanak in the holy *Granth*, "It is seeing without eyes, hearing without ears, walking without feet, working without hands and dying a living death after recognizing the sound current." This means that the Reality cannot be seen with these material eyes. It cannot be heard with these material ears. It cannot be explained with this physical tongue. It cannot be described.

The Word which gives salvation is unwritten and unspoken. Or in other words, it can be said that the Word or sound current is not contained in any holy scripture or any religion. The holy scriptures of every religion sing the praises of Nam or sound current and induce us to work on That, and they cite the advantage of Nam. And though there is a mention of Nam in them, yet the Nam itself is not in them. That Nam is within the human being. Says the holy *Granth:* "Nam lives within the human body. It is the immortal Creator. Nam is a treasure and lives in the mind of Masters. Everything is contained within the human body. Those who seek outside are in error."

The teaching of the Masters aims to release the souls which have been imprisoned for innumerable ages and births, to free them from the shackles of religion and castes, to take them to everlasting bliss and to merge them back in their source, the Supreme Being.

Now I speak about Soami Ji Maharaj. Soami Ji Maharaj was born on 25th August 1818 in Panni Lane, Agra City. His name was Shiv Dayal Singh and he belonged to a well-known family of Baikal Seth Kshatriyas which had migrated from Lahore to Delhi about two hundred years previously, and then had moved from Delhi to Agra. His father's name was Seth Dilwali Singh. His grandfather, Seth Malik Chand, was a Diwan (a judge or some higher officer) of Dholpur State. Bani *(Granth Sahib)* was read in his family from the very beginning. All the family members used to recite some portion of *Guru Granth Sahib* each day with great love and devotion.

In his satsangs Soami Ji Maharaj used to read the poems of Guru Nanak, Kabir and other Masters, of which the most prominent was especially *Guru Granth Sahib.* As Agra and U.P. people could not understand Panjabi language—and it is no exaggeration to say that the language of holy *Granth* is so difficult that even Panjabis cannot understand its mysteries—therefore many prominent disciples of Soami Ji Maharaj, both men and women, humbly requested him to explain his teachings in their own language and in easy terms. The result was that about three years before leaving the world, he dictated the poems called *Sar Bachan,* in which the mysteries of Sant Mat are explained in detail in very easy language. Yet it is not easy for anyone to understand fully either the holy *Granth* or the writings of Soami Ji Maharaj until he is initiated into the secret of the five shabds.

The great Master, Tulsi Sahib, had given up the kingdom of Pune and Sitara shortly after the year 1800 and had taken up his residence in Hathras near Agra. His writings are very powerful and well known, and clearly describe the internal regions as well as the way of gaining them. He often visited Soami Ji Maharaj at Agra and used to stay with him and both were on very affectionate terms with each other.

Although the disciples of Soami Ji Maharaj reached to thousands in number, yet three of them were most prominent. They were Rai Bahadur Saligram Ji at Agra, Baba Garib Das Ji of Delhi and Maharaj Baba Jaimal Singh Ji in the Panjab.

Baba Ji Maharaj was born in 1839 in the village of Ghuman. His father was named Sardar Jodh Singh and belonged to a Jat Sikh family. From his childhood Baba Ji was fond of the society of holy men and used to read Vedant with a Vedantic holy man, Baba Khem Das, who lived in his village and with whom he also read the holy *Granth*. When he read it with careful attention, he found that the holy *Granth* mentioned again and again the words 'Nam' and 'Shabd', also 'five shabds'. He also concluded from reading this scripture that the Shabd was not a song capable of being sung or played but was the essence of all creation. He began to enquire from Baba Khem Das but as the latter was a Vedantist, he was not acquainted with the secret of the sound current and he expressed his ignorance on the point.

Shortly afterwards Baba Ji's father passed away and he began to roam about in search of sages. He would go to every place where he learned there was some sage and would question that sage about the five sounds, but none could satisfy him. His quest led him to Lahore where there were many Mohammedan and Hindu sages and still he could not find the answer for which he was searching.

Becoming desperate he went to Nankana Sahib (where Guru Nanak was born and passed his childhood). While there Bhai Mota Singh praised to him one Baba Balak Singh of Hazro, District Attock. When he talked with Baba Balak Singh Ji about the five shabds, Baba Ram Singh Ji of Bheni Sahib (the founder of the Namdhari sect of Sikhs who also believe in a living Guru) was also there serving Baba Balak Singh. As Baba Balak Singh was a sage of a very clean conscience, he told Baba Ji Maharaj that his method was to repeat the word 'Wahiguru', but that he was not acquainted with the secret of the five sounds. Thereupon Baba Ram Singh Ji told Baba Jaimal Singh Maharaj not to return empty-handed when he had found such a great sage as Baba Balak Singh. On hearing this Baba Balak Singh said, "No, he is seeking a very high thing. Do not dissuade him. Let him go and search for his high ideal."

Baba Ji continued his search and on passing through Nowshara, Peshawar, reached a village in the district of Mardan. While there he met with a *granthi* (one who reads *Granth)* in a dharamshala. This *granthi* was an *abhyasi* (one who performs spiritual practice). When Baba Ji talked with him, the latter said that his guru had revealed to him the secret of two shabds and that he was working on them, but the remaining three he did not know. Thereupon Baba Ji was very happy. Due to previous failures, he had begun to believe that the five sounds might merely be a fancy of his brain but now he had found that his idea was correct. He then left the *granthi,* saying that the Almighty Lord who had arranged to give the *granthi* the secret of two sounds would also arrange to give him the secret of five sounds.

From there he was starting home via Beas when he met a group of sadhus going to Hardwar. He accompanied them to that place of pilgrimage, met many different mahatmas and stayed there for several months but could not find that for which he was searching. While there he came to know that there was a very old sadhu living by himself in a solitary place in the forest about fifteen miles away, that the sadhu never came to any habitation nor did he allow anyone to stay with him. He lived on whatever vegetation and fruit he could find in the forest.

Then Baba Ji went to him and found that he was a great devotee who was engaged in *abhyas* (spiritual practice) day and night, that he always remained standing, and when he became tired he would use a piece of cloth to support himself. The two ends of the piece of cloth were supported by ropes tied to the branch of a tree. When Baba Ji met him he threatened him, asking him why he came and telling him that the place was haunted by tigers and bears and they would devour him. Baba Ji replied that if they did not eat the sadhu, why would they eat him? On hearing this the sadhu was pacified, began to talk in a better mood, and Baba Ji enquired from him about the five shabds for which he was searching. The sadhu sighed and replied that Baba Ji was after the same thing which he was seeking, and continued: "By doing *abhyas* in this place I have acquired miraculous powers yet I know there is no salvation without the five sounds. And through my internal vision I have discovered that a great sage at Agra who had been engaged in *abhyas* for the last seventeen years has emerged from his secret place to teach the world. You should go to him. My legs have become very heavy because I have remained standing for years. I shall come there, but sometime after you."

Thereupon Baba Ji left the place and went straight to Agra but in his haste he had forgotten to enquire from the sadhu the name of the lane or quarters in which the saint was living. Therefore he searched in many temples and other holy places in Agra but found no man corresponding to the description given by the sadhu. At last he went to the Jamuna to have a dip. When he was taking off his clothes and thinking what he should do next, where he should search, as good luck would have it two disciples of Soami Ji Maharaj arrived there for bathing and began to talk about Soami Ji. Baba Ji at once came to them and enquired the address of the mahatma about whom they were speaking. They gave him the address of Panni Lane.

It was time for Soami Ji's afternoon satsang and Baba Ji reached the place when Soami Ji Maharaj was holding satsang. Baba Ji bowed at his feet. Soami Ji enquired: "From where have you come?" Baba Ji replied: "From the Panjab." Thereupon Soami Ji Maharaj said: "He has arrived—my old friend!" Baba Ji was surprised because he had never seen Soami Ji before, so why was he saying that they had met before?

He passed a few days there attending satsang and was satisfied that there could be no greater Master than Soami Ji. But then he hesitated, thinking that Soami Ji was a non-Sikh while he was a Sikh. On the fourth day it happened that all the people left the place after satsang had finished but Baba Ji and Soami Ji remained there. Soami Ji enquired of Baba Ji whether he had yet decided the question of Sikh and non-Sikh. Seeing the all-knowing character of Soami Ji Maharaj, Baba Ji could not help having tears in his eyes. Then Soami Ji described Sant Mat to him at length and said that it was not a question of Sikh or non-Sikh but that the philosophy of Sant Mat was quite beyond both. Soami Ji Maharaj then initiated him. Baba Ji stayed for some time in Agra and remained engaged in *abhyas*.

One day Baba Ji was engaged in meditation *(abhyas)* in the garden of Soami Ji Maharaj, which was outside the City of Agra, when Soami Ji Maharaj arrived there; but as Baba Ji's attention was inside, he did not get up nor greet him. Soami Ji, with his own power, brought down Baba Ji's attention and enquired: "Are you satisfied that what I have given you is the path of Guru Nanak?" Baba Ji Maharaj replied that it was perfectly true and his soul went into high regions but there was some obstacle. Then Soami Ji said: "You have already done it in the previous birth when you were with me. All this was already done by you." Then Baba Ji asked, "What is the proof of what you are saying?" And Soami Ji replied: "Well, if you want proof then take your attention in." On Baba Ji's doing so, Soami Ji Maharaj removed the obstruction which was in Baba Ji's way internally.

When Baba Ji's attention came out he said to Soami Ji: "My life's work is finished. Yet let me know, please, at which place of pilgrimage I should sit and engage in *abhyas*?" Soami Ji replied: "In this world we should take up both worldly and spiritual work *(swarath* and *parmarth)* and try to adapt ourselves to both. If one gives up worldly work, then he would have to depend on others for a living and his meditation *(abhyas)* would suffer because of those who serve him or worship him, as people do when they see a sadhu who has renounced the world." Soami Ji advised: "You should take up some work in the world. One's spiritual progress depends upon living on one's own income."

The result was that Baba Ji joined the army, in the Twenty-Fourth Panjab Infantry, and remained at Agra for three years in military service. He would conscientiously perform his military duties and attend the satsang of Soami Ji. After that his regiment was transferred from one cantonment to another but he remained in service and carried on his devotions.

He retired after serving for more than thirty-two years, but during all this period of service he was engaged in devotion. And as he had taught Gurmukhi (Panjabi script) to the Commanding Officer and Major Sahib, they had great regard for him.

Whenever he took a few days leave from his army unit, he would spend it in seclusion, engaged in devotion.

After retirement, as he was living in solitude, he made a small hut near the banks of the river Beas and was engaged in spiritual practice. This happened in 1891. From then on until his death, he continued to live there and the place is now called Dera Baba Jaimal Singh. He left this world on the night of 28th-29th December 1903.

Translator's Note

It was in the summer of 1987 that Hazur Maharaj Charan Singh, acceding to the Western readers' requests, commissioned a new English translation of Baba Ji's letters that would include everything in the published Panjabi version. The translation, while not literal, would remain faithful to the original letters and try to retain their flavour, especially their sweetness and simplicity. After nine years of continuous effort by many individuals, this book is the product of that charge.

These are the personal letters that Baba Jaimal Singh wrote to his disciple, Baba Sawan Singh. The general reader of course can receive much benefit by reflecting on their contents, the words of the Satguru to his gurmukh, but it is well to bear in mind that those contents are the specifics of a personal and purposeful dialogue between Baba Sawan Singh and his Master: in the words of Maharaj Charan Singh, "A great soul was being groomed for the highest spiritual achievement by another great soul."

During the course of work on the translation, a few hitherto-unpublished letters of Baba Ji were discovered, some of which are included in this edition. Also, while studying these letters and their originals, some of the dates were found to be questionable: some originals had firm dates—day, month, year—others gave only the day and month, while a few, almost invariably by scribes, had no dates at all. Square brackets have been used to indicate that the information was incomplete but deduced through research. Internal evidence suggested that at least 41 letters belonged to different places in the sequence, and these have now been relocated with an appropriate adjustment in their dates. It may be mentioned that the word 'letter' in this Note includes both letters, enclosures in envelopes, as well as some 41-odd postcards that Baba Sawan Singh received from Baba Ji.

It was customary for Baba Ji to sometimes address one letter to several persons, so many letters contain replies and messages to two, three, or more individuals. At the same time, he would remind his correspondents, not to write separately, but to include all their messages in the letter from Baba Sawan Singh. The letters that came from Baba Sawan Singh were also sometimes read to the whole sangat at the Dera (vide letter 113).

The main purpose of this work is to give the reader a rich flavour in English of the full contents of the letters of Baba Jaimal Singh. The only materials left out are a few interpolatory lines inserted occasionally by the writers of the dictated letters, or some names and brief matters that were of a sensitive nature. In such a holistic undertaking some compromises had to be made in order to access some complicated syntax and to deal with the archaic, pro forma and repetitive expressions that were normal in Baba Ji's days but that appear odd and confusing to a modern reader. This Note documents some of the important changes.

To provide an unimpeded flow of reading, it was decided to keep the textual footnotes to a minimum and to use them only where crucial to understand the text. The explanatory and background information that would clarify or underline the text, and the scriptural and other scholarly references, are placed in the Endnotes and the Glossary.

In the letters Baba Ji uses both Indian and Western calendars interchangeably and sometimes together. Western equivalents of the Indian months are not given in the text but can be consulted in the Glossary. The old Indian weights and measures, such as seers, maunds, hand-length, palm-length, etc., that Baba Ji uses in his letters have been converted to their modern equivalents in kilograms, feet and yards.

The text consists of 180 letters: 155 from Baba Jaimal Singh to Baba Sawan Singh—including a few addressed to others but with messages for Baba Sawan Singh as well—6 from Baba Ji to his disciples of Bhandal, and 19 letters from Agra in two sections that provide a perspective on the events at the Dera. The 155 letters from Baba Ji to Sawan Singh Ji in this book are three more than in the Panjabi edition. These are the hitherto unpublished letters of Baba Ji, discovered during the course of research on the project, that have now been included in the text. The letters fall into two categories: 112 letters in Gurmukhi, written by Baba Ji himself, and 49 in Urdu (4 with some writing by Baba Ji as well), written by various scribes under dictation from him. In the text, the latter are identified as '[Dictated]'.

Dictated Letters

Letter-writing by scribes was a common feature of village life in Panjab in Baba Ji's times since few people could read or write. Both amateur scribes and itinerant writers (Baba Ji mentions the latter in letter 19) performed this service—the local postman who brought the mail was one such handy resource. In Baba Ji's letters, of the four identifiable scribes, two, Ganda Ram and Ram Dhan, were postmen from Sathiala, the post office for Dera, a third, Milkhi Ram, was a satsangi, as was probably also the fourth, Kahan Singh. Occasionally, to curry favour with Baba Sawan Singh, a scribe would interject his own material in the letter, with a consequent interruption in the flow of the letter, which would also occur since not all of the letters were dictated line by line, and some took more than one sitting to finish. So in some of the letters there are breaks in the syntax, sudden shifts in the subject-matter, and occasionally even a mixed-up message. When reading the dictated letters, it would be well to keep in mind Baba Ji's caution to Baba Sawan Singh: "Try to understand it well even if a word is missing here and there" (Letter 124).

In general, in the dictated letters a reader misses the depth of feeling, verbal richness and politeness of the letters that are in Baba Ji's own hand. Baba Ji's gentle *Ji* and the blessings from his Guru, Soami Ji, are missing from most of the dictated letters. While the translation has smoothed out some of their rough edges it has retained the basic syntactical structure that informs these letters.

Baba Ji's Language and Style

Language, among other things, reflects a culture's priorities. In the Indian context, in matters spiritual or worldly, relating and relationships assume great importance.[*] In fact, Sant Mat itself is a way of relating with the Lord—of the self with the Self. It is a relationship expressed through terms of endearment and eulogy for the singular attributes of the One that cover a vast span of vocabulary, from the ungraspable Agam Anami [the Unreachable Nameless One] to the earthly *lālnā* [sweet little babe]. There are literally thousands of expressions that address that relationship— in the end the vocabulary runs out but His attributes continue on. This is true also of the fifty-odd attributive and descriptive epithets that Baba Ji uses to define both the Lord and his Satguru, Hazur Soami Ji, in such a way that ultimately, for the reader, the two become one. Translation of some of these expressions may appear a bit odd because of the excessive use of adjectives, but in the spiritual context the flow is smooth and constant, with an understanding that is reached gradually through feeling.

In spiritual terminology, words often merge into each other, because the inner states are fluid and not locked in and the mind comes to the basically-indefinable inner reality from many direc-

---

[*] For instance, compare the relationships defined by the English word *aunt* with the five or six terms that Panjabi uses to locate the relationship: the aunt who is father's sister, or mother's sister, or mother's brother's wife, father's older brother's wife, his younger brother's wife, and so on.

tions. Verbal terms flow into each other—*Shabd* into *Dhun*, into *Nad*, into *Nam*—and yet retain their palpable contours. The translator's problems become aggravated, on the one hand, by a lack of precise words for some basic spiritual terms (*hukam*, for example), while on the other hand some key terms, such as *Shabd, shabd, surat, nirat, dhyan*, are so generic to the culture, with broad applications grasped only contextually, that even detailed explications can give only educated proximities and not their soft feel, which is essential in order to access them. English tends to move the words toward a preciseness in definition that, in spirit, is the opposite of the Indian response to the word forms. The translation, in addition to the Notes and a detailed Glossary, has tried to respond to this problem by keeping the text fluid so that, for instance, the context determines whether *surat* is experienced as soul, attention, concentration, or consciousness, or how, on the other hand, *surat, nirat* and *dhyan* constitute different aspects of the same inner attention, depending upon the angle of view that is being emphasized.

Basically, the translation has not strained to reproduce Baba Ji's thought in syntactically correct English, but rather has tried to capture and simplify (where that was possible) his ideas even if at times it meant compromising the language. Thus where a choice could not be avoided, the specifics of Baba Ji's thought and expression were privileged over the grammatically correct form of the English idiom.

The translation has kept as close as possible to Baba Ji's language without becoming literal. His style alternates between a simplicity of expression in mundane and worldly matters and a delightful richness of metaphor and precise syntax in matters that are spiritual—letter 77 is a good example.

Baba Ji's terminology for individuals is full of love and respect. The mother and grandfather of Baba Sawan Singh are always *Mai Ji* and *Baba Ji* (literally, respected elderly lady or gentleman). *Mai Ji* is also Baba Ji's term for his own mother. To preclude any confusion, it was decided to use for Baba Sawan Singh's mother the term *Ma Ji*—as she was affectionately called—and 'my mother' for the mother of Baba Jaimal Singh. The affectionate term *Baba Ji* has been retained for the grandfather of Baba Sawan Singh in the letters written by Baba Ji himself (the reader can understand that Baba Ji is not self-communing!), but substituted by 'grandfather' for the letters written under dictation.

Similarly, the term *Bibi*, a Panjabi word of respect for any lady, is retained in all the letters in the translation. Baba Ji invariably uses it for Bibi Rukko and also both for the wife of Baba Sawan Singh, the elder Bibi Ji, and for Baba Sawan Singh's daughters-in-law, the younger Bibis.

A problem arose with the term 'master' that Baba Ji uses, for instance, for Gajja Singh. In the Indian context it could mean either that Gajja Singh was once a schoolmaster or that he had received training to become one. In a straightforward use, 'Master Gajja Singh' could be mixed up with the Master as the Satguru, so it was decided to replace it with the term *Babu*, an equally honorable word that Baba Ji always uses for Baba Sawan Singh.

The letters contain many old, archaic and formal expressions—*bhayia ji, likhtum, jog, barkhurdar, vachna,* etc.—for some of which modern equivalents ('dear brother' for *bhayia ji*) or approximations ('obedient son' for *barkhurdar*, a psuedo-Persian Indian word) are given, while others that are purely formulaic—traditional opening and ending of letters—have been either condensed, as the invocation, 'Radha Soami', which appears three to seven times at the beginning of each Panjabi letter; or discarded, as the word, *jog* (worthy), that invariably appears after Baba Ji's name in all letters; or replaced by modern expressions, as 'From Jaimal Singh' for *az janab* (from the direction of)

Jaimal Singh; or rationalized, as with 'Convey Radha Soami', or simply 'Radha Soami from', for the old formulaic *Radha Soami vachna* or *vachni ji* (say or read out aloud, Radha Soami).

The language that Baba Ji uses is metaphorical and highly colloquial, reproducing in writing the patterns of speech from rural Panjab, specifically of the Ravi-Beas Doab, Baba Ji's own region. As the same word in this dialect could sometimes denote a meaning different from the standard Panjabi, occasionally his meaning had to be teased out. For instance, in an important section in letter 60 (No. 5 in Panjabi ed.) Baba Ji describes the omnipresence of Shabd in this way:

Antar Sachkhand kaa Naam hai te

<u>*baahar jo Sachkhand thoŋ thaaŋ hai so baahar hai jee*</u>

ਅੰਤਰ ਸੱਚਖੰਡ ਕਾ ਨਾਮ ਹੈ ਤੇ <u>ਬਾਹਰ ਜੋ ਸ'ਚਖੰਡ ਥੋਂ ਥਾਂ ਹੈ ਸੋ ਬਾਹਰ ਹੈ ਜੀ॥</u>

He is telling how Shabd is all-pervasive both inside and outside Sach Khand. Now, *thanh* in standard Panjabi means *place*, so the underlined part at first did not make sense—"the place that is outside Sachkhand is outside it!"—and threw the whole sentence off, until it was realized that Baba Ji was using this word in a regional sense, in which it also means *lower than, below* or *beneath*. Immediately, the sentence began to make sense: "The reality inside is the Nam of Sach Khand, and all that is below Sach Khand,... is perishable (because not inside Sachkhand, the imperishable home)".

The sweetness in Baba Ji's writings comes basically from his general tone, outlook and attitude in these letters, in which a key element is the choice of words with which he addresses Baba Sawan Singh and other disciples. His continuous use of the untranslatable *Ji* in almost every sentence is one such word. Along with the polite, plural grammatical forms which he invariably uses in his letters, *Ji* is at the core of the sweetness in his syntax. It was decided to retain its use with the individual names where it serves as an honorific, but otherwise to find substitutes that would serve the translation well. The problem is that English has no substitutes or close approximations to match *Ji*. 'Sir' was rejected right away: it seemed to beg attention, and could even be ironic or sarcastic. 'My son' worked for some expressions but its overuse tended to create a religious overtone. 'Please' was politely pleasant, but sounded a bit cold and formal. Finally, it was decided to use a judicious combination of 'please' and 'my son', which do somewhat soften the translated syntax—but nothing of course substitutes for *Ji*.

This sweetness, however, is not created by *Ji* alone. An important contribution is also made by his choice of the polite, plural forms in the syntax and vocabulary. He invariably prefers the soft sibilants, with their gentle and full-bodied feel, against their more functional equivalents: for instance, using *tuseen* and *tusanoon*, over the curt *toon*, the condescending *tum*, or even the polite but aspirated *tuhanoon*. Since we could see no way to reproduce this in the translation, it was decided to stay with the standard English in this regard. We have also replaced Baba Ji's 'we' with 'I', and not used words like 'thee', 'thine', etc., that look archaic and feel affected.

Acknowledgements

It is a pleasure and a privilege to acknowledge the contributions that have made this translation possible. It would not have appeared in the finished form it is in now without the close personal touch of the present Master, who supervised the project during the last seven years in order to see that the book was shaping up as the best that could be offered. The editors and reviewers of this work laboured long and incessantly to create an accurate match between the original and the translation. The finished book is a testimony to their dedication, hard work and patience.

In the end what remains is a long-deferred tribute to the one whose magnanimity gave life to this project. This book is in the hands of the reader because our Master, Hazur Maharaj Charan Singh, acceding to the Western readers' perennial requests for a translation that would give them all of Baba Ji's writings, gave charge to the project—and this is its result. So in all humbleness and love this translation is presented to him:

ਪ੍ਰੀਤਮੁ ਭਾਈ
ਬਾਪੁ ਮੋਰੋ ਮਾਈ
ਭਗਤਨ ਕਾ ਓਲ੍ਹਾ
(ਸ੍ਰੀ ਗੁਰੂ ਗਰੰਥ ਸਾਹਿਬ, ਆਸਾ ਮ:੫, ੪੦੭)

My love, and brother,
Father and my mother,
The refuge of his devotees.
(Adi Granth, p. 407)

Nirmal Singh Dhesi
Dera Baba Jaimal Singh
June 1997

Letters from
Baba Jaimal Singh Ji

~ 1 ~

Ik Onkaar Satgur Parsaad.[*]

"There is but one God. By the True Guru's Grace He is obtained."

Wahiguru Ji ki Fateh[†] and joyful Radha Soami greetings from Jaimal Singh to my obedient son, Babu Sawan Singh Ji. We are all well and happy in every way, and always pray for your health and happiness to the compassionate Lord, Satguru. Your 10 rupees were duly received: 5 were sent by draft from Sathiala post office to Agra on 12 August for the bhandara, and 5 have been spent on the free kitchen for the sangat here. A large satsang is held here every Sunday. Satsangis from all around—from across the river as well—come here for the satsang on Sunday. Bhandara and free kitchen, etc., are all held here with food being distributed right into the night. All your money has been spent for spiritual ends, in seva—you have done much too much.

As no letter had come from you for some time, I started to inquire about where you might have gone. This thought had just come to me when that very day your money order for 10 rupees arrived. Now please send me the exact address of your residence and also write about your well-being. Do your bhajan and simran regularly every day. Read Hazur Soami Ji's holy books attentively, and whenever you have time listen daily to the Shabd-dhun.

Your letter has arrived and I am very happy to read it. You write that you do not hear any sound distinctly. Do not worry,

---

[*] Traditional Sikh invocation. From *Sri Guru Granth Sahib*, English and Panjabi translation, trans. by Manmohan Singh (Amritsar: Shiromani Gurdwara Parbandhak Committee, 1993), vol.1, p. 53.

[†] *See* Glossary for clarification of spiritual and other special terms, unusual usage of English words and information about some of the frequently mentioned people, places and Indian months.

3

my son. When you listen to the Sound, focus on the bell-like sound—first comes the sharp chirping sound, like that of a cricket, next will come a deep and full sound like that of a conch. Do not worry at all about reaching Sach Khand. Hold on to the five-fold melody of the Shabd, the Shabd-dhun, that has been given to you—one day, it will take you to Sach Khand because it emanates from there. The Sound comes only to take the soul up with itself. The soul of whosoever finds a Satguru, custodian of the five shabds' secret, and learns from him their whole mystery, will certainly ascend as it gradually becomes pure. Do not be in a hurry, my son.

I have not left the Dera since coming back in the month of Phagun. You should not have listened to anyone else because you could have received the information by writing a letter to me at the Dera. I am very happy with you. You should continue just as you have been instructed to do and you will assuredly go with me. Do not have any worry in this respect.

Do your bhajan daily; the soul will become purified, my son. One should not become perturbed by pain or pleasure, which come through his command.

Radha Soami greetings from Bibi and Ganda Singh. You have received the fruit of darshan since you felt deep regret at not having had darshan. You write that I should come to your place for a visit. Well, at present I am unable to do so as satsang is now held regularly at the Dera. But we will see in the winter.

18 August [1896]

∼ 2 ∼

Radha Soami. Radha Soami Ji is the Comforter.

From Jaimal Singh: Sri Wahiguru Ji ki Fateh to my obedient sons, Babu Sawan Singh and Pritam Singh. May the grace and mercy of the compassionate Hazur be upon you all the time. Your letter has been received and I am absolutely delighted to learn that you are fine and that all has gone well with your return to work. Earlier, because of the hot weather I was worried about your return, hoping that it had gone well. However much work there may be, please keep writing to me regularly. All work, official or otherwise, is being done by the merciful Hazur himself. In his Shabd-dhun form, he is ever present in each hair, in each and every part of the body. Inside and outside, he is always with us. The Satguru is ever present within us. Listen with love to the Shabd-dhun, which is resounding in our bodies with every breath. Whether for an hour or two, or for fifteen minutes, or ten, or five, whatever free time you have, you must listen to it regularly. Do your simran mentally while carrying on your worldly activities. Walking or moving around, it has to be done every day, my son.

The news of the well: everything is ready; we are trying to arrange for the bricks urgently. Everyone is anxious that the well be sunk, and you are urging it too. Therefore, send whatever you wish—whether 100 rupees or more—but send it immediately upon receiving this letter. Others have written to say that they too will send money and that we should sink the well. So I am trying to move quickly. You too should reply quickly because the brick supplier wants 100 rupees in advance. The work, my son, will be done by the Lord himself. We are not capable of doing anything—the doer of everything is the compassionate Hazur himself. Whatever is his will and grace, that will come to pass. He will do as it pleases him, and I, too, am content and happy in his will. The name of the young man has slipped my mind; please convey my Wahiguru Ji ki Fateh to him. We will have all the satsangis contribute to the well, but things are not quite ready yet. So now make an effort—all your other work has been done by the compassionate Hazur.

Please accept Radha Soami from Bibi; also Radha Soami
from Dasaundha Singh and all the other satsangis. Whatever the
compassionate Radha Soami does will be all for the good. Every
instant he is with us. One day he will take us to Sach Khand, his
real and true home. Even now he is with us—he is bestowing his
gracious mercy upon us all the time. Please write about yourself
more frequently. I will come when you send me a letter, but now
is the time to concentrate our efforts on the well. We are not capable of doing anything, the compassionate Radha Soami Ji will
be doing it all himself.

31 August [1896]

~ 3 ~

Radha Soami. Radha Soami Ji is the Comforter.

Sri Wahiguru Ji ki Fateh and Radha Soami greetings from
Jaimal Singh to my obedient son, Babu Sawan Singh Ji. May
the grace and mercy of the compassionate Hazur be upon you all
the time, my son. This is to inform you that your 100 rupees,
sent by money order, were received on [9] September 1896. As
for the well, money is now coming in. When all the contributions
have been received, I will send you a letter about how much has
been collected. Everyone is looking forward to the sinking of the
well. The owner of the brick-kiln has gone to Amritsar. As soon
as he returns, I will give him the 100 rupees that he asked for as
an advance.

You should write about yourself, my son, and every day,
whenever you have time, keep doing bhajan and simran. Radha
Soami from Bibi and Pal Singh. For the time being, no more
money is needed here.

9 September 1896

~ 4 ~

[Dictated]

Radha Soami. Radha Soami Ji is the Comforter.

Radha Soami greetings from Jaimal Singh to my obedient son, Babu Sawan Singh. This is to let you know that we are all well and happy here, and shall always pray to Radha Soami Ji for your health and happiness. Your letter arrived, informing me of your whole situation. My beloved son, the Satguru is always with you—have absolutely no worry in this regard. You will go to Sach Khand (Sat Lok) in my company. You should look upon everything as the Satguru's: body, mind and wealth, all belong to him. Do not consider anything as your own.

You had mentioned coming on leave on 20 December 1896. Whenever you come on leave, it would be good to let me know beforehand about the date of your arrival. Someone can then go to the railway station to pick you up in a tonga. Dear Pritam Singh did stay with me for five or six days. I had to go to Ambala, so he accompanied me up to Ludhiana.

As regards darshan: in six months' time—not possible before then. This was his command. Please understand that all worldly work, everything, is the Satguru's; that the Satguru is the doer of everything, you merely provide the name. When all official and domestic responsibilities have been fulfilled, the attention (*surat*) will not part from the Shabd. Hazur is very pleased with you—have no worry of any kind. Listen to the Shabd-dhun every day when you are free. The more you listen, the purer you will become, and the soul will reach Sach Khand. So fix the attention inwardly in the Shabd—the Satguru's form is with you all the time.

27 December 1896

~ 5 ~

[Dictated]
Radha Soami. Radha Soami Ji is the Comforter.

From Jaimal Singh: May happiness, grace and mercy bless my
obedient son, Babu Sawan Singh; may grace and mercy be upon
him all the time. Dearly beloved Babu Ji, the following articles
have arrived here from the railway station: twenty straw stools
and one tied-up bundle of rope. Why did you take so much
trouble, my son? Was there ever dearth of anything from your
side? Earlier also it was you who have always been doing such
seva.

Your letter was received earlier but no reply could be sent
because we had no information regarding your permanent address, as to where you were posted. Since now I have come to
know that you work in the Barrack Master's Office in Murree
Hills, so this reply is being sent. Therefore have no worry or apprehension of any kind. Keep doing bhajan and simran all the
time when you are free, and work diligently in the service of the
government—the doer in everything is the Lord himself.

Anoop Singh came here, stayed for four/five, or perhaps six
or seven days, and then left after hearing the Sunday satsang. He
probably met Basant Singh at Amritsar—I had gone to Ambala
Cantonment at the time—as he left for Amritsar saying that he
would visit young Basant Singh there. He mentioned that everything at home was fine, that the whole family was well and
happy.

Please accept Bibi Rukko's Radha Soami and also Radha
Soami from Lambardar Dasaundha Singh of Dhaliwal. The
situation regarding the brick-kiln is that 18,000 bricks are now
ready. The bricks will be prepared like this every day. Indeed, in

a month the kiln will be ready and the bricks baked. Further news will be sent in the next letter. All is well otherwise.

By order of Maharaj Jaimal Singh Ji
At Waraich
March 1897

∼ 6 ∼

Radha Soami. Radha Soami Ji is the Comforter.

From Jaimal Singh: Sri Wahiguru Ji ki Fateh to my obedient son, Babu Sawan Singh Ji. I have received your telegram in which you request: "I am very sick. Please come immediately." My son, I am unable to come. The reason is that the brick-kiln is loaded up and about to be fired, and it is hard to find labour. Also, the rains are continuing and there is no one here at the Dera to look after the place. I can find absolutely no way to come. Twice I tried to leave, but both times the brickmakers called me back. The work here comes to a standstill in my absence. So I will come in ten to fifteen days when the bricks in the kiln are baked. Do not worry; the compassionate Hazur with his grace and mercy will forgive you. The karmas that are left over from the past are to be settled in this very life—he who is in the company of a saint is not born again. So, as misfortune befalls, endure it patiently; pain and pleasure will then pass away by themselves.

Whenever you become conscious of the pain in your body, immediately put your attention in the Satguru and try to listen to the Shabd-dhun. Then, through the Sound, the Shabd Guru will at once send you his grace and mercy. Only the pain of the karmas you have to go through will then remain; all other karmas will be forgiven.

The Shabd-incarnate Satguru is beyond birth or death;
Behold him in the body—a fixed truth, O saint.

Shabd swaroop satguru haiŋ, jaa ḳaa aadi na ant;
Kaayaa maaheeŋ dars haiŋ, nihche maano sant.[1*]

Nothing has happened without his will *(huḳam)*. Send me the information again, and immediately. The Satguru in his Shabd form is always with you, my son. I must soon receive your news—the Satguru is now with and within you. The compassionate immortal Lord will shower you with abundant grace and mercy. Since everyone has to leave the physical body, why be apprehensive about it? The Shabd-dhun is not going to leave you. Your home is the Shabd, so have no worry. But you must write to me again very soon.

Please accept Radha Soami greetings from Bibi Ji. I am unable to come at this time, my son, because I am utterly helpless to find a way to visit you. The kiln has been stacked with 100,000 bricks; there is no need to make any more now as these are sufficient.

8 May 1897

∼ 7 ∼

Radha Soami. Radha Soami Ji is the Comforter.

Sri Wahiguru Ji ki Fateh from Jaimal Singh to my obedient son, Babu Sawan Singh. May the grace and mercy of the compassionate Lord always be upon you, dear son. Your letter, fully describing your condition, has arrived, and I now feel somewhat relieved. In all, two telegrams and two letters have come from you, and previously I wrote to you one letter and one postcard, and

---

[*] For sources of scriptual quotations see Endnotes. The special character 'ŋ' indicates a nasalized 'n' sound.

now this letter. You have not mentioned whether you received my previous letter or the postcard. You should always write to me whether or not a letter has reached you.

My son, please do not mind this suffering. Since both pain and pleasure result from our past actions, they are bound to happen. You write that you are experiencing great distress. That is indeed so: the body is a house of pain and pleasure, and in it both will certainly come to pass. So endure the pain as it is good for you—it will last only a few days. Years and years of a satsangi's sufferings are paid off within a few days. So do not worry about anything. The body is a covering that we change many times. Even in your present condition, hold fast to the Shabd-dhun all the time. For one, the sensation of pain will decrease, and secondly, the mind and soul will not become distressed. Also, the sins which cause the suffering will continue to be erased. The Satguru in Shabd form is always by your side; he is protecting you at every breath.

When the broken bone of your leg is being set and bound, do not move at all, even though a lot of pain will be felt at the time. But no matter how much pain you feel, the leg is not to be moved—the bone will then set quickly. Be brave, you will get well.

When the second telegram reached me at 9 p.m. on the night of 11 May, I set out alone on foot immediately to come to you. On reaching the railway station at 11 p.m., I had the telegram read by the clerk, who said that Babu Sawan Singh writes, "I am well now." At this I turned back, otherwise I had started from the Dera to come to you.

The brick-kiln is now ready to be charged on Sunday, 16 May. After the kiln has been fired for six days, I shall leave here to come to your place. My intention is to reach there by 24 or 25 May—the rest is up to the will *(mauj)* of the compassionate almighty Lord. My thoughts are with you day and night, beloved

son, and I keep imploring the compassionate Lord for mercy—
the rest is his divine will, for whatever he does will be for our
good. I shall send you a postcard before I come.

Radha Soami greetings from Bibi; Wahiguru Ji ki Fateh to
Hari Chand. Wahiguru Ji ki Fateh also from Dasaundha Singh.
You should send me a letter daily about your condition. Your
last letter was received on 13 May. Please reply soon.

14 May 1897

≈ 8 ≈

Radha Soami. Radha Soami Ji is the Comforter.

Radha Soami greetings and Sri Wahiguru Ji ki Fateh from
Jaimal Singh to my obedient son, Babu Sawan Singh Ji. This is
to let you know that I received your two letters in Urdu the same
day. From these I have come to know the whole story of your injury, right from the beginning. In fact, I waited endlessly for your
letter during the month of Vaisakh, so that in reply I would explain the misfortune. But no letter or note came from you. Even
if delayed, the letter should not have taken more than fifteen
days. However, no news or letter came from you during the later
part of Chet and the entire month of Vaisakh.

The pain you have gone through this time is a fifth of the
destined suffering—four parts have been forgiven. A bound-up
broken leg should not be moved. You should eat more ghee, but
only fresh ghee. The compassionate Lord himself will forgive
you. You are to have no worry; his will was like this. Since pain
and pleasure are sown with the body itself, it is the body which
has to harvest them. This body is a field, my son, within which
they grow. You will become strong again.

About the bricks and the kiln: the kiln was stacked with
100,000 bricks and fired on the 5th of Jeth. I shall send you

details of the bricks and their expense in the next letter. The kiln will be completely baked in eight to ten days.

I shall come after you have left the hospital for your residence and rejoined service. Whenever you feel pain, engage immediately in simran and then listen to the Shabd-dhun. You will not feel the pain in the body once the attention attaches itself to the Shabd-dhun. My son, fate *(pralabdh)* karmas cannot be erased without being gone through. But when the soul loses itself in the rapture of love for the pure melody of the Sound, then the fate karmas also keep on getting erased. Fate karmas are erased to the extent that love is experienced. I shall explain it all personally when I come to visit you.

Bibi's Radha Soami to you, her brother. Radha Soami from Dasaundha Singh Lambardar and all the other satsangis. The horse was not at fault.[*] Later, I shall explain personally to you what really happened—this was his will, never to be erased. Please convey Ram-Ram to Hari Ram.

19 May 1897

∼ 9 ∼

Radha Soami. Radha Soami Ji is the Comforter.

Sri Wahiguru Ji ki Fateh from Jaimal Singh to my obedient son, Babu Sawan Singh. May the grace and mercy of the compassionate Radha Soami be upon you all the time, my son. Your two letters arrived here on the same day with the news of your health; my heart is full of joy to know that the merciful Hazur has showered his grace on you. His grace was always there, but this was his will. You will become strong. "Look upon the hour of

---

[*] Baba Sawan Singh broke his leg when he fell while mounting his horse. The incident is described in *Heaven on Earth*.

pain as a blessing" (*Dukh kee gharee ganeemat jaano*),[2] as pain
or pleasure comes from the Lord himself. Since it comes by his
command, why should we treat it as bad? The Lord, ever
present, always watches over us, and if our good lies in suffering
he sends us suffering, if it lies in happiness he sends us happiness. Both, beloved son, are within his will. So now you are not
to have any worry; the suffering will come to an end very soon.

When the body forms in the mother's womb through the
union of the mother's ovum and the father's sperm, it develops
there for three months in the heat of the primal fire. The inert
being keeps lying there on one side—the bones in the body come
from the father's seed; they have 1,600 bonds and joints. The
being continues to lie on one side for three months (ninety days)
as the bones are formed and tempered by the torrid heat of the
primal fire. The pain and suffering endured at that time cannot be
described. But a blessing also reaches there: with each breath,
the being remembers the Lord and cries out: "Save me, save me!
Mercy! Mercy! I have no one." His absolute trust rests in the Lord,
and no harm comes to him there because of the power of Nam.

The body's flesh comes from the mother's blood; it has
formed through baking. Outside the womb then, whenever a
bone is broken, it will join together if the individual stays motion-
less in the same way. So have no worry—at this stage there is
not that much pain.

Do your bhajan and simran. If the attention gets distracted,
bring it back again. Nothing except bhajan and simran can eliminate suffering. The Lord is pleased with you in every way, so
you are not to have any worry. When a bone in the body breaks,
it repairs itself in three months by joining together—and yours
will heal quite rapidly.

The news about the brick-kiln: 100,000 bricks are now
baked and ready; the heat in the kiln will die down substantially
in a couple of months. The construction of the well has started—

we were only waiting for the bricks. The cost of the bricks came to 350 rupees. We will give out the contract as soon as I return from your place. The firing of the bricks has come out well: a couple were pulled out and found to be nicely baked.

Lambardar Dasaundha Singh and the satsangis here wish you Wahiguru Ji ki Fateh. You write that you did not inform the people at home about your injury. I was also of the opinion that such news should not be sent to them. So you have done well.

I had left a book for reading at Mehmansinghwala when you were visiting your home. So far no one has come from there. Anoop Singh did come here once, in the month of Phagun, and stayed for four or five days, after which he left for Amritsar to visit Basant Singh before returning home. No news has come from him since then.

Please accept Radha Soami from Bibi and convey Ram-Ram to Hari Ram.

23 May 1897

~ 10 ~

Radha Soami. Radha Soami Ji is the Comforter.

Sri Wahiguru Ji ki Fateh from Jaimal Singh to my obedient son, Babu Sawan Singh Ji. We are all well and happy here, dear son, and always pray to the compassionate Lord for your health and happiness. Two letters from you arrived here on 24 May, and I was very happy to read the good news in both. I see in this the grace and mercy of Hazur, who has forgiven you with his glance of mercy *(drishti)*. The hardship was for a few days; it will now come to an end.

You have probably received my previous letter in which I wrote to you about the brick-kiln. Now write to me every week, my son, as the Lord himself has forgiven you. Most likely you still feel some discomfort when you write. In that case, write after you rejoin the service. I shall then come and personally explain everything that lies hidden in this body: the manner in which Kal has accumulated karmas in the body; actions that have tied down the being; the karmas that result from taking a physical birth, and which are discharged in the body itself—all will be explained, because only after the karmas are cleared does the soul, catching the Shabd-dhun, reach Sach Khand.

One type of karma is entirely disposed of and forgiven by the Satguru; however, some karmas are such that they are paid off only by being worked out in the body. Those who have surrendered themselves to a perfect Satguru, who have received from him the full teaching of the five shabds, who have developed love and devotion for the Satguru, and to whom a firm conviction has come that the Satguru is not a mere man but has assumed the human form for the good of others—never, my son, should it enter the mind that the Satguru is a man—they have all the karmas of the gross body taken care of. That leaves the karmas of the subtle (suksham), astral body—in Sahansdal Kanwal, they too will be finished; and on reaching Trikuti, the karmas due to the causal maya—the divine energy that gives birth to both man and gods—will also be taken care of. Then the soul (surat), that is, the individual being, having become pure, will catch the Shabd-dhun and become absorbed in it, and the Shabd-dhun, which comes from Sach Khand, will take it to Sach Khand, into which that soul will then merge. So there is nothing to be afraid of; that home is our own. Now no more births lie ahead. All and everything is to be worked out in this very body.

You write:

The gurmukh redeems millions of people
by giving a droplet of Nam.
Gurmukh kot udhaardaa bhaaee, de navai ek kanee.[3]

That is correct, my son, but it is important to remember that Nam comes through his grace and mercy. Whether the gurmukh bestows not even a particle of Nam, that is, Dhun, on anyone or, with his gracious and merciful glance, takes the whole creation with him, no one can stand in his way. So have no fear. We are going to our home, Sach Khand itself.

Bibi's Radha Soami to you, her brother. Please also convey Ram-Ram to Hari Ram. You write, "I also keep hoping." Well, whatever is the will of the Immortal One will happen. You also mention that you are to stay in bed for six weeks. That is right; this is how a broken bone is treated. You will have no discomfort. Keep your attention fixed in the Shabd-dhun and you won't even know about the pain.

25 May 1897

≈ 11 ≈

Radha Soami. Radha Soami Ji is the Comforter.

Sri Wahiguru Ji ki Fateh and Radha Soami greetings from Jaimal Singh to my obedient son, Babu Sawan Singh Ji. May the infinite grace and mercy of the compassionate Lord be upon you all the time. I have received your two letters in the same cover, which also included a verse in Gurmukhi from the *Granth Sahib*. Also received was a postcard in Urdu about meat and alcohol. I was very happy and pleased to receive your news. I also always entreat Hazur to cancel all the bad karmas of satsangis: some of these will come to an end by being worked through; others he will forgive.

You wrote that the doctors asked you to take meat and alcohol in order to get well and that you replied, "Only if my Satguru says so shall I have them." Well, the Satguru's word is one, my son, not two or three. The rest I shall explain personally when I come to visit you.

About the brick-kiln: it has been well baked and will cool down in a couple of months. The construction of the well will start then. Also, I have to visit you, so work will start after I return. Money, my son, is not yet needed—it is you who are needed; so may Hazur soon have mercy on you. You should write to me every week. Hazur will be merciful—do not worry about it. Please ask the person who writes your letters to do so in Gurmukhi. The shabd in Gurmukhi from *Sri Guru Granth Sahib* was very well written. Do not worry about anything; the Lord can instantly forgive innumerable *khattas* of sin. One lakh sins constitutes an *aggh*, and one lakh *agghs* equals one *khatta*. Thus he forgives millions upon millions of sins in an instant.

Beloved son, I am extremely pleased with you. Do not be afraid to keep lying in one position, as a broken bone mends in this way. The compassionate Lord is protecting us at every moment; he will forgive you in every way. When you send a letter home, write of your well-being and happiness, for indeed you are well. Why bother to write home if the body suffers for a few days? Those at home will worry unnecessarily. No, simply inform them that you are well and happy.

Be attentive to the Shabd-dhun every day. Try to increase the intensity of effort—and listen! Listening to it repeatedly will purify the soul and mind. Bodily suffering cannot affect you for our real home is Sach Khand where there is no body. The Shabd-dhun, too, is an aspect of that home, just as the sound that issues from the tongue is not separate from the body. When the soul is caught by the unstruck melody of the Shabd, it automatically ascends to Sach Khand by remaining absorbed in the music of the Shabd-dhun. The Shabd-dhun comes from Sach Khand, and it will transport the soul to the same place. A verse from *Sri Guru Granth Sahib* says:

The inner music sounds; my mind is rapt.
Vaajai anahad meraa man leenaa.[4]

The soul will definitely reach Sach Khand—the body is a mere cover. So have no apprehension of any kind.

Radha Soami from Bibi to you, her brother. Please convey Ram-Ram to Hari Ram. As in so many letters you have written that an intense longing for darshan persists, the fruit of darshan keeps accruing to you and your mind is becoming greatly purified. My son, no practice of any kind can measure up to the mind's longing for the Satguru's darshan.

                                                    28 May 1897

                          ∾ 12 ∾

        Radha Soami. Radha Soami Ji is the Comforter.

Radha Soami greetings and Sri Wahiguru Ji ki Fateh from Jaimal Singh to my obedient son, Babu Sawan Singh Ji. We are all well and happy, and always pray to the compassionate Lord, the ever-benevolent, ever-merciful forgiver of all sinners, for your health, happiness and well-being. Beyond everything is the Anami Radha Soami Ji. Through his grace and mercy he looks after millions upon millions of worlds. May he always be merciful, loving, and the saviour of sinners. This is how his goodness is always there. My Satguru, dear son, is Soami Ji whom I always implore for your well-being.

I was very happy to receive your two letters enclosed in the same envelope, which also included a verse in Gurmukhi from *Sri Guru Granth Sahib* that I was very pleased to read. You write that it would be good if you left government service to stay at the feet of the Master because there is not much free time in the service. Well, you are always with me, my son, not far away. Until the account of debit and credit with others is settled, it is not possible to break free from worldly ties.

When the Lord bestows his grace and mercy on any individual—that he will join with him the soul whom he has forgiven, that it is not to be given a birth again—then incarnating himself as Satguru, he blesses that individual with Nam-dhun, that is, the sound of the Shabd, within the body. Innumerable karmas of the individual are cancelled when the Satguru gives the teaching of the five shabds, but the balance sheet itself is not cancelled. Through the strength of his spiritual wealth, the Satguru has the power to instantly connect the soul of an individual with his own soul and carry it immersed within the Dhun. But that person's soul cannot blend into the Dhun; it will stay below Daswan Dwar. It cannot merge into the pure Dhun above Daswan Dwar. Only after meditating upon the Dhun for many ages will that soul become pure. However, at that stage also there are many enlightened souls (hansas) with high achievements. The soul will reside among them for many births. Then whenever the Satguru comes again from Sach Khand and again imparts the teaching of the Shabd, that soul will reach Sach Khand. The promise, however, is that the soul will never come below Sahans-dal Kanwal but will remain in the higher regions.

As regards the individual whose karmic account (including the subtle karmas, the bad karmas of past births with roots above Trikuti) the perfect Satguru is to settle within the body itself: the Satguru detaches him from all desires and expectations of worldly pleasures, all hopes and expectations from son, daughter, mother, father, wife, and maya, that is, from the whole creation of the five elements [tattva]; strengthens his love and devotion for the Satguru's Holy Feet; and then by attaching him to the Shabd-dhun purifies him day by day. As the disciple's love for the Shabd-dhun Guru grows steadfast, the soul, becoming absolutely pure, merges into the Shabd Guru, which is the real form of the Satguru. That soul thus becomes superconscious. The perfect Satguru then bestows upon it the power to ascend from the body, by way of the five shabds, to Sach Khand, passing from one shabd to the next, and then by the same path to descend from Sach Khand to the body. Thereafter, whenever the soul desires, it can at once ascend to Sach Khand by the same way.

But this power belongs to a gurmukh, and not to everyone in spiritual pursuit. Therefore, to settle a karmic account, the perfect Satguru separates the devotee from his physical form but not from the Shabd-dhun. So you are serving me in every way. The work that you do for the government or in your house is Satguru's work, and doing bhajan and simran is also Satguru's work. "All occupations, mind, body and wealth, whatever exists, all and everything belong to the Satguru. I am nothing." Realize and understand that "I am merely the one who carries out his work." The self should be totally surrendered. I have written out this point briefly here and shall explain it in more detail when I come to visit you. Please read this letter again and again in order to understand it. The letters that I write to you are never to be torn up—recount them to me when I come to visit you.

You wrote to ask if money was needed. There is no such need at the moment. We shall see when the need arises later on.

Keep your attention in bhajan and simran every day, for then you will feel much less pain in the body. Please write your letters to me in Gurmukhi; you should send one every week. Also write when you rejoin service, I shall then come to visit you. You write that the longing for darshan persists day and night. This, too, is bhajan, and the fruit of darshan keeps accruing to you. To experience true love for the Satguru is bhajan. You will reach Sach Khand without delay.

Bibi sends Radha Soami greetings to you, her brother; the other satsangis also send Radha Soami greetings to you, Babu Sawan Singh Ji. Ram-Ram to Hari Ram; please write about Hari Ram in Gurmukhi. Which place does he belong to and what is his caste? What work does he do? Is he married? Does he have children? Write all this and also if he has previously received any spiritual teachings from a sadhu of some faith or some brahmin pandit? Does he practise simran of *Gayatri Sandhya*? Whatever he does, write about it to me in Gurmukhi. What does he read: Urdu, Gurmukhi, or Devnagri? Write to me on all these points.

2 June 1897

∼ 13 ∼

Radha Soami. Radha Soami Ji is the Comforter.

Radha Soami greetings from Jaimal Singh to my obedient son, Babu Sawan Singh Ji. May the grace and mercy of the compassionate Lord always be upon you. Your letter arrived on 7 June and I was extremely happy to read it. You mention that in two weeks' time you will send me a letter in Gurmukhi. There is no need to do so, my son; you may continue to write to me in Urdu. Do not worry at all about the leg; it will neither become short nor remain useless. In a short while it will become normal again. Please eat plenty of fresh ghee. The affected bone will then toughen up so that you won't even remember which part of the leg was broken.

No doubt there is some pain from being bedridden, but how can we appreciate suffering unless it shows its power? Nam is our support in pain and pleasure. In other words, the Lord sends us suffering in order to test us. When the mind does not waver in pain or pleasure, but realizes his will in both and welcomes them equally, then the Lord blesses us with Nam. The individual who learns to assimilate Nam, that is to say, does not get entangled in pride, pomp, or miracles, nor fall into any attachments, and believes absolutely that the Satguru alone is the Lord—in no way does his mind waver—for that individual the Satguru becomes everything. And when the Satguru sees that that person has become one with him, he at once bestows his grace and mercy from Sach Khand by way of the Shabd-dhun. Whatever happens, my son, will be beneficial. So keep on doing your bhajan and simran every day; that is, hold on to the Shabd-dhun, which is our real form. The body is a mere garment: neither can it last, nor can anyone keep it permanently. I am very pleased with you; you are here in fact with me.

The Shabd-incarnate Satguru is beyond birth or death;
Behold him in the body—a fixed truth, O saint.
Shabd swaroop satguru hain, jaa kaa aadi na ant;
Kaayaa maaheen dars hain, nihche maano sant.[5]

Hazur is all-forgiving. Also, there is another point: whatever we do in keeping with the Satguru's will is karmaless action. But the Satguru, the loving friend of the individual, must be perfect. Then the individual is forgiven the very moment the Satguru gives the instruction. For the rest, the Satguru is the Lord himself: if he so wishes, he can burn up millions upon millions of sins with a single glance.

Bibi sends her Radha Soami to you, her dear brother, and Ram-Ram to Hari Ram. I asked about him in the previous letter; a reply will be sent when you respond to it.

8 June 1897

~ 14 ~

Radha Soami. Radha Soami Ji is the Comforter.

Radha Soami with lots of grace and mercy from Jaimal Singh to my obedient son, Babu Sawan Singh Ji. Your letter has arrived and I am absolutely delighted to know that your leg has healed. I am very happy and gratified at the news. You write that your family has come to know about the accident—so now inform them of your well-being. May the grace and mercy of the compassionate Hazur always be upon you. Whatever he does will be for our good. In pain or pleasure, may our faith always abide in his Lotus Feet.

Pain and pleasure, my son, are the consequences of our own actions, and the karmas from the past, the fate karmas, will certainly produce their consequences. So in pain or pleasure one should not become unduly perturbed. Fix your love in the Shabd-dhun all the time. Rather, let your devotion for it be so deep that both pain and pleasure appear as equally good. The attention *(dhyan)* in the Shabd-dhun is to be fastened with such a deep love that even the awareness of pain or pleasure ceases to exist. There is not a touch of pain in the land of Shabd-dhun. Pain and pleasure are felt due to the love of the body, while in Shabd-dhun not even a hint of the body exists. Here's an illustration of this: the body is like a village—that is, a collection of all kinds of dwellings—whereas the Shabd-dhun is like our own home in the village. When there is a misfortune in some other house, or someone dies, great grief is felt there, but in our own home all is quiet and peaceful. Similarly, the limbs of our body are like the houses in the village, while the Shabd-dhun is our own home. So we are to maintain our love with it all the time. Whatever we love, that is where we will reside.

I have written the above in reply to the grave concern you expressed in your letter about your inability to do bhajan—whatever we love, into that we merge. When the Satguru gave the command to attach the attention to the Shabd-dhun, that very day the disciple became entitled to the Shabd-dhun. Now he will not go elsewhere. Whatever spiritual work I had to do for you has been done. Please do not worry about that. Worry, however, that you do nothing outside the instructions of the Satguru. For a gurmukh, everything he does is bhajan. The rest of his bhajan has been done by the perfect Satguru. The perfect Master has the authority for three hundred and thirty million: he will take three hundred and thirty million souls to Sach Khand. As it says in a hymn of *Sri Guru Granth Sahib*:

> The gurmukh may laugh or he may weep;
> The gurmukh's actions become devotion deep.
> *Gurmukh hasai gurmukh rovai,*
> *Ji gurmukh kare saaee bhagati hovai.*[6]

We should understand this so that we may also become gurmukhs. Another line from *Sri Guru Granth Sahib*:

> The gurmukh recites Nam but once.
> *Naanak gurmukh naam japee-e ik vaar.*[7]

Now when is that once? It is the time when the perfect Satguru met the disciple and gave him Nam-dhun—everything happened at that very moment. The Shabd-dhun may sound loud or low, or disappear at times, or the disciple may not even hear it, but it remains the same. The blessing conferred by the Satguru cannot be undone by anyone. So what is left now for you to worry about? You reached Sach Khand the very day you were initiated—

that is the place for which you are destined. Who can take away the gift bestowed by the Satguru? Because the karmic account of worldly give-and-take is still to be finished, he cannot take you there. Once it is fully settled, he will take you there at once. The rest I will explain when I come to visit you.

Bibi's Radha Soami to you, her dear brother; Ram-Ram to Hari Ram. Hari Ram's time on the spiritual path began to be counted from the very day he placed full faith in me. He will receive the grace and mercy of initiation through the Satguru's benign inner glance *(drishti)*. Even if life now departs from his body, he will again receive a human birth and will not re-enter the cycle of eighty-four.

17 June 1897

~ 15 ~

Radha Soami. Radha Soami Ji is the Comforter.

Radha Soami greetings with gracious blessings from Jaimal Singh to my obedient son, Babu Sawan Singh. May the grace and mercy of the compassionate Soami Ji be upon you all the time. The news is that I was not at the Dera as I had gone towards Kasur for twelve days. That's why there has been a delay in writing to you. I have received your two letters and the postcard, and a letter in Urdu from Hari Ram. I was extremely happy to read them. I came back to the Dera on 29 June, at which time these letters were given to me.

I have followed in detail the account of the unbandaging of your leg. You should not be in a hurry to move around so that the leg bone can set and heal well by bonding firmly. It takes three months (ninety days) for a broken bone to mend. Right now your knee-joints are swollen from being bandaged. The ligaments that move the bonded joints have become compacted and because of the leg's long inactivity are now stiff from dryness. When the leg gets aired, the swelling will go down and the thickened ligaments that prevent the joints from moving easily will slowly and gradually become normal again. Do not worry, my son. The leg, after removing the bandage, should not have been rotated vigorously since a joint takes three months to toughen up properly. Also, do not massage it much, nor force the knee to bend. It will heal by itself. Do not worry at all, for I am by your side all the time. I shall come to visit you as soon as you get well. Do not be in a hurry to start working; you will now get well soon. "Look upon the hour of pain as a blessing" (*Dukh kee gharee ganeemat jaano*),[8] because it is through pain that the mind gets deflated.

You write that you have received a postcard from a satsangi, Nihal Singh, who has given no address. I also do not know who this Nihal Singh is, because there are many satsangis of that name. Also a postcard has come from your village—it is not clear whether Pritam Singh or Bachint Singh wrote it—informing me that Bapu Ji (grandfather) has been gravely ill. They are asking me to visit the village soon.

Please start sitting and walking only gradually. The compassionate Soami Ji is merciful and forgiving; everything will be all right, have no apprehension. The body belongs to the Satguru, as also do pain and pleasure. All activities, occupations, households, service, money, shops, mansions, lands, wealth, sons and daughters, all belong to the Satguru—as also do the Shabd-dhun and the soul—everything is the Satguru's. Then why should you get perturbed in pain or pleasure? He will do whatever is beneficial for you. He is ever the loving friend of the individual. You should regard yourself as nothing. Let only the Satguru remain; leave it all to his will. Listen to the Shabd-dhun every day and hold fast to it. Erasing all your sins and karmas, it will take you to Sach Khand. At that place, not even a hint of pain or tension exists. That is the home of the Satguru, my son, and you, too, will go there. Have no worry; he will take you there after all the worldly activities are complete. Such is his divine will.

Please convey my Wahiguru Ji ki Fateh to Hari Ram. Your letter has been received and I am very happy to know its contents. I have understood your situation. Infinite grace and mercy will reach you, my son. Everything will be completed when I come to visit you. You should also call your wife to your place. It would be good if she were with you. However, if social conventions are such that a wife may not leave home, then she should not be called. Social conventions are not to be broken.*

[1] July 1897

~ 16 ~

Radha Soami. Radha Soami Ji is the Comforter.

Wahiguru Ji ki Fateh and Radha Soami greetings from Jaimal Singh to my obedient son, Babu Sawan Singh Ji. May the grace and mercy of the compassionate Lord abundantly be upon you all the time. I have received your letter and am extremely happy to read about your health. Do not worry about the leg, my son, it will not become short. You should have taken a good deal of ghee. The swelling in the leg and the knee will keep going down as they continue to be exposed to the air. In a month's time all the swelling will be gone. Please do not walk too much, nor put much weight on the leg or massage it too much. Do everything in moderation and take a lot of ghee. It would be good if you could eat about 200 grams each time. If it is difficult to take it all at once, eat at least that much every day. The leg and the knee will then begin to function freely.

---

* This paragraph is addressed to Hari Ram. See Translator's Note.

You write that for darshan you are writhing like a fish out of water. His will is like that. When true love for the Satguru is felt inwardly, only then does true yearning for darshan develop. Please understand that even with hundreds of years of bhajan one does not become so pure as one does with true yearning for the Satguru's darshan. That is why the disciple is separated from the physical form of the Satguru: because he does not become pure so quickly through doing bhajan as through true love for the Satguru and true longing for his darshan. In fact Sat Purush himself is the Satguru. So in the Shabd form, my son, I am always by your side. The disciple, however, cannot discern the Satguru's Shabd form. And why can't he do so? Because he is unclean, his intellect is also unclean, and highly unclean is his mind as well. In this age, my son, to attain liberation, to meet the Lord, to become pure in a short time, the only way is to have true love and faith for the Satguru and never to regard him as merely human. True yearning for darshan is the key for meeting the Lord. The mind's dirt is shed only when these means become fully ingrained in the mind. Only then can the disciple perceive the Shabd-dhun form of the Satguru. So please try to listen to the Shabd-dhun— then the Dhun itself will take you to your home. He who has true longing for the Satguru in his mind has accomplished everything. The Satguru has the authority to take him at once to Sach Khand, the land of saints. Please do not feel apprehensive; he who attaches himself to the Shabd-dhun will not be born again.

However, until the disciple realizes that the physical-form Satguru is the same as the formless Shabd-dhun, he cannot get support from the Shabd-dhun. Your spiritual work is now complete—so have no apprehension.

You asked for news of the well: the well has been delayed because of the rainy season and the bricks still being warm, and also because I have to come to see you. When I return after visiting you, I shall finish the well before going anywhere else. So all

is ready for the well. I have received two letters from your village.
They were from Pritam Singh who invited me to come to Mehmansinghwala. I have replied in the negative. He was saying that
the people there remember me a lot. I wrote back that I would
come when Babu Ji visits there. The rest I will do as you write. If
you say so, I will go.

Bibi's Radha Soami to you, her dear brother. Radha Soami
from all the satsangis. Ram-Ram to Hari Ram.

7 July 1897

~ 17 ~

Radha Soami. Radha Soami Ji is the Comforter.

Radha Soami greetings with grace and mercy from Jaimal Singh
to my obedient son, Babu Sawan Singh; blessings of the Lord's
peace on you. Your letter has been received and I feel extremely
happy to read of your well-being. I shall visit your village, Mehmansinghwala, when you go there on leave. You write that you
do not expect to receive even a single pice this year. My son, you
have become despondent over nothing. No! Have faith. No obstacle will stand in your way; all your affairs will work out well.
You should not worry like this—the Lord has all the money in
the world. "The person substituting for you has been awarded
the fruit of your year's hard work, and orders have been passed
to stop your pay—that you are not to be remunerated." No. The
Lord will give to you as well, my son. You just keep watching
what he does. It is all his doing that he takes the money away
from one person and gives it to another. This is his play. Only a
gurmukh can understand it. Do not worry about how your family will be fed, or how you will be able to carry on. The Lord
will take care of everything. Our house belongs to the Lord, as
also does our wealth—family, shop, mansions, land, body, soul,

village—everything belongs to him. He will look after everything to the end. You will receive as much wealth as you want, my son, and all the promotions you desire. At present this is his will.

Your leg will get well and you will feel normal as before. Please do not worry about anything except doing your bhajan and simran. Whatever else the Lord had to do has been done once and for all. Throughout one's life only that will happen which is written on the forehead. Nothing new is going to come about. Be patient. Nothing will remain wanting, my son. Do not keep any attachments within yourself. Our home is Sach Khand. He whose hope is attached to Sach Khand has absolutely nothing to fear; he whose heart is steadfast in love for the Satguru is always wealthy. Whatever else was to happen to you at this time will be described when I come to visit you.

You write that letters have come from home asking about the nature of your illness. If you like, you may give them the information; or, if you so desire, you may withhold it. But the letter you send there should contain good news only, so that it does not cause them any distress.

Bibi's Radha Soami to you, her dear brother. Radha Soami also from all the satsangis and from Dasaundha Singh.

Whatever karmas are written on your forehead cannot be erased by anyone. Have firm faith and remain content in your mind. Nam itself is the wealth and the Lord has already given you the whole wealth of Nam. Listen to the Shabd-dhun each day and attach the mind and soul firmly to the Dhun—you will then enjoy its bliss and the mind will never be distracted by desires. Always keep the Satguru's form in your mind. Then the mind, becoming pure, will receive the full rapture of the Dhun. Worldly hopes, desires, and attachments, which are the root of all suffering, will then immediately leave the mind. They will never stay where the perfect Satguru's form is present.

13 July 1897

Radha Soami. Radha Soami Ji is the Comforter.

Radha Soami and Sri Wahiguru Ji ki Fateh from Jaimal Singh
to my obedient son, Babu Sawan Singh, to Babu Hari Ram,
Babu Kahan Singh, Ishar Das, and to all the other satsangis.
May the infinite grace and mercy of the compassionate Soami Ji
be upon you all the time. Dear son, if a letter, postcard, or
money order for me arrives at your place, please redirect it to the
Dera after correcting the address. With the grace of the compassionate Soami Ji, I arrived safe and sound at the Dera on Monday at two o'clock in the afternoon. On the day I left you, I
reached the railway station at nine o'clock at night and boarded
the mail [fast] train at 1 a.m....

We are trying to find pipal tree gum, but have not had any
success so far. The genuine product is not available. Plenty of
imitations are on offer, but we are not buying those. I will send
you some when it is available. Apply fomentation to the leg, if it
gives some relief, and also have it massaged occasionally. Hazur
will now, day by day, improve your leg, so please do not have
any worry.

Do your bhajan and simran daily, and be sure to send me a
letter once a week about your condition as it improves. Write
every Friday. Hazur Soami Ji is with you in every way. May the
Lord's grace be upon Chanan Singh and Basant Singh.

Please convey Bibi's Radha Soami greetings to everyone.

12 August 1897

∼ 19 ∼

Radha Soami. Radha Soami Ji is the Comforter.

Radha Soami greetings from Jaimal Singh to my obedient son, Babu Sawan Singh. May the grace and mercy of the compassionate Lord be upon you all the time. Your letter has arrived informing me of your condition and I am delighted to know that you are well and happy. You write that you are under orders to go to Khairagali. Whatever orders are given will be all for the good. You are not to worry about how the Lord makes you work—just do the work. You may use a sedan chair to do your work till such time as you are able to walk well. In a short while—in a couple of months—you will be completely well. When you are at Khairagali, drink one kilo of sweetened milk every day, and also continue to take ghee daily as both are useful for purifying the blood.

It was my plea to Hazur Soami Ji to let you go to work in your own area. Even lame and limbless persons go around for many miles to work in their areas as scribes and readers, whereas your body is whole. So what does it matter if for a few days work is an effort for you? Hazur will do all the work. In any case, I would like you to go to your own area. Also, please continue with your bhajan and simran every day.

You write that you feel apprehensive because of the rains. There is nothing to fear, my son. If the Lord wishes, he will heal the leg in an instant; and if he wills it otherwise, he will have you work without the leg. Just continue to do your work with the attention fixed in Hazur. Do not be afraid; just keep observing how he himself does whatever has to be done. Just as you have written now, my son, send me the news of your condition every fifteen days in a letter in Gurmukhi.

Bibi's Radha Soami to you, her dear brother. She is sending you a *rakhi*. An affectionate Radha Soami to Basant Singh Ji and Chanan Singh Ji. Also Radha Soami greetings to Ishar Das, Labhu Ram, Natha Singh Ji, Narain Das Ji, Munshi Ram Ji, and to all the other satsangis. Remind them all to do their bhajan and simran every day. May the grace and mercy of the compassionate Hazur be upon them all. Heavy rains are falling all over Panjab. Please convey Radha Soami from Machhar to all the satsangis there.

24 August 1897

∼ 20 ∼

Radha Soami. Radha Soami Ji is the Comforter.

Radha Soami greetings from Jaimal Singh to my obedient son, Babu Sawan Singh. May the grace and mercy of the compassionate Anami Lord always be upon you, my son. Your letter has arrived, giving me all your news. I am glad to know that you are well and happy.

You are not to worry; the Lord himself is the doer of everything. Let me know when your new officer arrives. If free, I will then come and stay at Khairagali for four or five days, provided you feel at ease with the arrival of the new officer. Regarding the money, I will write to you later as to when you may send it. Please do not do so now, because I intend to visit you after you write about the arrival of the new officer. Also, by then it will be cool enough to travel by train. I am definitely of a mind to come—the rest is up to the will of Hazur Soami Ji. My son, please do not send any money; do so when I write to you.

Please convey my Radha Soami to Chanan Singh and ask him why he wishes to go back home. He should write to me in detail. I may allow him to go home after I see how desperate his need is. He is definitely not to leave now. When I come I will look into his situation and tell him if he may go. Please let him know this. His mind is wavering because there is a hardship hanging over him. It will be dispelled by the grace and mercy of the compassionate Hazur; that is, he will be forgiven. He should do his bhajan and simran every day. Please keep me informed about Chanan Singh.

Continue with your bhajan and simran every day whenever you are free. At work or moving about or sitting around, keep your thoughts fixed in simran all the time; always from everyone, and from you, at all times, simran is accepted at the court of Hazur. Listen to the Shabd-dhun and remember that whether or not your mind is in it, or scarcely feels for it, your effort at all times will be acceptable. This was my supplication to the compassionate Hazur. You are not to worry; one day he will merge your soul in the Shabd-dhun and take it to Sach Khand. Believe this firmly, my son: he is himself carrying out all the affairs of the world by being in it. Everything that he does is for our good.

Please convey my Radha Soami to Babu Hari Ram, Babu Mohan Singh, Basant Singh, to the elder and younger Bibi Jis, and to all the other satsangis there. May the compassionate Soami Ji always bless all of you. Radha Soami greetings from Bibi to you, her dear brother, to the family, to the other satsangis, and to the satsangi sisters. All of you are urged to engage in bhajan and simran every day. You will receive whatever you wish. Everything is secondary to bhajan. Where there is bhajan, all other things will come automatically. Make room for the current of the Shabd-dhun within your mind, and then experience its bliss.

Please accept Radha Soami from Sukhdayal Singh and all the other satsangis at the Dera. From Mehmansinghwala, Bhai Dasaundha Singh has written that Pandit Ji had gone to Agra and brought back the books from Rai Sahib Saligram Ji. So far

Pritam Singh has not come here either. He wrote a postcard
saying that he would be going via Dera to see his dear brother,
but nothing has been heard since then.

29 August 1897

~ 21 ~

Radha Soami. Radha Soami Ji is the Comforter.

Radha Soami greetings from Jaimal Singh to my obedient son,
Babu Sawan Singh. May the grace and mercy of the compassionate Hazur, of the immortal Anami, the True Lord, always
be with you, my son. Your letter has been received and I am very
happy to know of your well-being. I have written a postcard to
your home to Ma Ji,* addressed to your Baba Ji [grandfather],
that they should not worry. Babu Hari Ram and Babu Mohan
Singh both wrote in a letter that the books from Agra had not
yet arrived.

You write that you go to the office on crutches. That is all
right, but don't be in a hurry—you are going to walk on your legs
all your life. The grace and mercy of the compassionate Hazur
will come by itself. You will be well in a month's time. Do not
put much weight on the leg; it will get better slowly and steadily.
Also, when you are in Khairagali, do not strain the leg—either
walk or ride in a sedan chair. Do as your strength permits, but
go soon to your post at Khairagali as the water there is better
than at your present station. Besides, you will recover properly
only when you work there day and night in government service.

Hazur, the Master himself, is always with you: he has the
power to do everything. Do your bhajan and simran every day
whenever you are free. Also, read four or five shabds daily and

---

* *See* Glossary.

keep the Satguru's image in your mind and soul all the time. While walking or moving around, sitting or sleeping, or during any activity, it should always remain there. Then neither pride for anything you do nor any thought of self-importance will enter the mind. Listen to the Shabd-dhun every day; listening to it repeatedly will purify the soul. The source of everything, the root of every practice, is having complete faith in the Satguru; that there is no doer other than him.

> The Shabd-incarnate Satguru is beyond birth or death;
> Behold him in the body—a fixed truth, O saint.
> *Shabd swaroop satguru hain, jaa kaa aadi na ant;*
> *Kaayaa maaheen dars hain, nihche maano sant.*[9]

My son, the compassionate Hazur has taken care of all your spiritual work, so now attend to your worldly business without apprehension. Do nothing outside the instructions of the Satguru. You write that you would like to send some money for the bhandara from the first salary after your promotion. You may do as you wish. Your seva has already been done. We will see to it after you go to Khairagali.

Please convey Radha Soami greetings to Ishar Das, Natha Singh, Labhu Ram, and to all the other satsangis there. Tell everyone to listen daily to the Shabd-dhun. Repeated listenings will purify, and one day they will reach Sach Khand.

Radha Soami from Bibi to you, her dear brother, and to all her other satsangi brothers. I shall write about the well later on. It is raining very heavily these days. Please give my love and lots and lots of grace and mercy to Chanan Singh and Basant Singh. My son, always remember your bhajan and simran.

8 September 1897

Radha Soami. Radha Soami Ji is the Comforter.

Radha Soami greetings from Jaimal Singh to my obedient son, Babu Sawan Singh, Babu Hari Ram, Babu Mohan Singh, Ram Piara, Chanan Singh, and to all the satsangis and satsangi sisters there, and also to the satsangis of Murree Hills. May the grace and mercy of the compassionate Hazur, and of the beloved Lord, always be with you. The Master in his Shabd form, my son, is always with us—he is protecting you with each and every breath. Your letter giving an account of your moving to Khairagali has been received. I am delighted to read about your health. It is my wish that you proceed immediately to your area, where you will get better as you become more active. Continue as before to daily take the fresh ghee sent by Ma Ji. In my previous letter I had written that at Khairagali you should start drinking milk as well. Please see if it suits you. If digesting both becomes a problem, give up the milk but continue to take the ghee every day.

In your letter to me you have asked for mercy. My son, you are already forgiven. To do nothing outside the instructions of the Satguru—that is called forgiveness. You also write that you do not ask even for Sach Khand, that you always beg only for love and faith in the Satguru and devotion for his Holy Feet. This, my son, is the foremost spiritual task. He who has an unshakeable love and devotion for the Satguru, who has surrendered to him with a true heart, and whose heart is always imbued with love for the Satguru's Holy Feet—that is, his mind has realized that the Satguru is not a mere man, but is the doer of everything, that he is Sat Nam, Sat Purush, Alakh, Agam, Anami, the Master of all and everything, and that there is no one greater than his Satguru—such a true devotee will reach Sach

Khand. He will merge in Alakh, Agam, and Anami, in the ultimate realm of wonder, Radha Soami. So listen to the Shabd-dhun every day. By listening repeatedly, becoming purified, love and devotion for the Satguru will become fixed in your mind and soul. Thus one merges into that which one loves. So take the self out, my son, then only the Satguru, the doer of all worldly and spiritual activities, will remain. There is always grace and mercy upon you.

A letter has come from Pritam Singh in which he writes that he has taken alcohol. He asks forgiveness and says that he will not drink again. He also mentions that he will be going to see brother Sawan Singh. So now I will request the compassionate Hazur to forgive him.

Bibi's Radha Soami to you, her dear brother, and to all the other satsangis. You write that the rains are very heavy. That is good. The Lord will do all the work, my son. Have no apprehension, do the work fearlessly as Hazur Soami Ji will have you do it.

Please convey Radha Soami greetings to Kaka Ram and Gali Ram. Tell them to do bhajan, and also to do simran and always keep it in mind while working or moving around. Of course, this has to be done when free, but they should not forget it even while moving around—because the breaths we take and the morsels we eat are all numbered.

11 September 1897

∼ 23 ∼

Radha Soami. Radha Soami Ji is the Comforter.

From Jaimal Singh: Sri Wahiguru Ji ki Fateh and Radha Soami greetings to both my obedient sons, Babu Sawan Singh Ji and Pritam Singh Ji. May the grace and mercy of the compassionate

Hazur always be upon you. I received your letter and was very happy to read it and know of your well-being. About the well, all the satsangis here have decided that the expense of the well should be shared by everyone, and they are now getting ready to sink it.

You write that you will get leave and come in December. I am very happy and gratified to know this. But ten days must be spent at Beas in spiritual practice (abhyas)—of course, it should be done every day as well. As the physical body gets more involved in outside pursuits, the mind should be kept absorbed in simran. Listen to the Shabd-dhun every day—even if you do it only for ten minutes, it should be done every day. And understand undoubtingly that one day the Satguru will take you to Sach Khand. Read daily from the sacred writings, even if you read only one verse. And whatever work you do, believe in your heart that the Satguru is doing it all: "I am not doing anything. Worldly or spiritual work, all is the Satguru's. I am nothing; you are everything." Then the Satguru alone will be all-in-all.

A postcard from Pritam Singh has come in which he says that he does his bhajan and simran regularly, but that I have never written a letter to him. But I always mention Pritam Singh in every letter or postcard. How far does he live from you? I am very happy and pleased with him. He should do his meditation daily and listen regularly to the Shabd-dhun every day.

Radha Soami from Bibi to her brother, Babu Sawan Singh, and to Pritam Singh. She has sent a rakhi and also some parshad for her brother, Babu Sawan Singh—the parshad is from the bhandara held at Agra during the full moon. Radha Soami from Dasaundha Singh also, and from all the satsangis here as well. Have no apprehension, my son, the Satguru will take you to Sach Khand after finishing all your worldly affairs. Now you will not have to take birth again, but will stay above Sahansdal Kanwal—there will be no more coming below that region. I could find no one to write this in Urdu. This letter contains some parshad. Do not be in a hurry and scatter it—open it carefully.

22 September [1897]

∼ 24 ∽

Radha Soami. Radha Soami Ji is the Comforter.

Radha Soami greetings from Jaimal Singh to my obedient son, Babu Sawan Singh. May the grace and mercy of the compassionate Hazur be upon you all the time. Your letter has been received and I feel very happy to know that you are doing well. You have written that you are unable to ride a horse to go around with the other officers. This condition is only for a month, after that you may start riding the horse. Have no fear. You have done well in going around in a sedan chair. You have also written that your supervising officer is being transferred and that his replacement is a strict person. A strict officer is good, because the government work is then done with care and concern. The Satguru is with and within us—"Kings and emperors are all made by the Lord" *(Saah patisaah sabh hari kaa keeaa).*[10] Keep the Shabd-dhun always in mind. It alone does all the work by being present in everything. It is the ever-present protector, my son.

You asked about the well: work on it has started. The wooden sill of the masonry chamber is now being constructed. So the work is underway, but labour is hard to find. Still, we are determined now to carry it through. Twenty rupees have been sent for the awning. One person has been sent to personally handle it. So once the material arrives, the stitching will start upon Issar Das's return. At that time sixty-yard-long ropes will also be ordered.

Dear son, please convey my Radha Soami greetings to Babu Hari Ram, Babu Mohan Singh, Ram Piara, Chanan Singh, Kaka Ram, Gali Ram, to the elder Bibi Ji and the younger Bibi Ji. May the blessings of grace and mercy from the compassionate Hazur be upon them all. Convey this to everyone: listen to the Shabd-dhun every day, and always keep simran in your mind when working or moving around, sleeping or sitting. The younger Bibi Ji is suffering from a karmic illness; it will disappear by itself after a short while. Keep giving her some medicine, because without medication, the sufferer harbours a suspicion of not being treated at all. She should listen to the Shabd-dhun every day—that is her real medicine. In the course of time all her illness will disappear. Believe this firmly in your mind that man can do nothing. As the Lord's command continues to unfold, the individual keeps on acting accordingly. Whosoever is posted as your superior will be all for your good. Try to listen to the Shabd-dhun every day, because whatever is happening is being done by the current of the Shabd. Satguru is the creator of all: he will give that which he thinks to be good. If our benefit lies in pleasure, he will send us pleasure; if it lies in pain, he will send us pain. So look upon pain and pleasure as the same.

Please accept Bibi's Radha Soami to you, her dear brother; Bibi's Radha Soami also to all the satsangis. Also Radha Soami from all the satsangis at the Dera to you, Babu Ji, and to the other satsangis there. May grace and mercy be upon Basant Singh. Please accept Radha Soami from Dasaundha Singh.

My son, please do not decrease your intake of ghee since it alone is good for you—you may, if you like, cut down on the amount of milk.

26 September [1897]

~ 25 ~

Radha Soami. Radha Soami Ji is the Comforter.

Radha Soami greetings from Jaimal Singh to my obedient son, Babu Sawan Singh. May the grace and mercy of the compassionate Lord always, in every way, be with you. The news is that I have received your money order of 21 rupees and 4 annas. A good deal of your money has already been spent in seva, my son, you need not have taken the trouble. This amount will be spent on the bhandara. You have not, however, written to me. So long as your leg is not fully healed, you should write a letter every ten days. Of course, you may take your time to write when you are able to ride a horse. Radha Soami greetings from Bibi to you, her dear brother, and from Bibi and myself to all the other satsangis.

16 October 1897

~ 26 ~

Radha Soami. Radha Soami Ji is the Comforter.

From Jaimal Singh to my obedient son, Babu Sawan Singh, and to Babu Hari Ram, Babu Mohan Singh, Chanan Singh, Basant Singh, Kaka Ram, Gali Ram, the elder Bibi Ji and the younger Bibi Ji—Radha Soami greetings to everyone. May the grace and mercy of the compassionate Anami Lord always be upon all of you. Your letter has been received and given me your news. I am delighted to read that you are all well and happy. It was a very well-written letter: whatever heartfelt requests you have made at the Lotus Feet of the compassionate Hazur have all been accepted at his court. All the bonds of worldly hopes and desires and the pains and pleasures of the past twenty-one lives are cast aside once one has the darshan of a perfect Satguru.

When the perfect Satguru, out of his grace and mercy, bestows the gift of Nam, the Shabd-dhun, that very moment the karmic record of birth and death with the lord of justice is torn up and the cycle of eighty-four terminated; and when the individual's faith in the Satguru gets to be absolutely firm, he becomes a resident of Sach Khand.

As yet, however, the mind is soiled, and the worldly account of debit and credit is still to be settled. The mind, still soiled, yearns for the false things of the world. As the disciple develops full faith, love and devotion for the Satguru and does not look upon any of his actions as merely human; does not do anything outside the Satguru's teachings, but keeps his image continuously in the mind and attention, and listens daily to the Shabd-dhun—the Satguru, severing all the earthly ties of that disciple, one day takes him to Sach Khand, his home and true residence. Slowly and steadily, in this very body, the Satguru cuts away all the karmas and everything that has to be settled with others, including the karmic account of the past twenty-one lives, and then takes the disciple to Sach Khand by merging him in the Shabd-dhun. But other than the Satguru's Holy Feet, the disciple should not have faith in anything. Then consider such a disciple to be already in Sach Khand. He who has love and faith in the perfect Satguru, who does not transgress the Satguru's instructions, and in whose inner mind the love for the Creator has firmly taken root—never allowing any other thought to enter his mind—such a one will be merged in the Dhun and taken up at once by the Satguru himself.

It does not matter, my son, if Pritam Singh has gone away. It was his own decision; you didn't say anything unpleasant to him. Bibi has been asking whether or not you have eaten the mung preparation (moongi). Do write about this as well.

Please convey my Wahiguru Ji ki Fateh to Bishen Singh. You have written that your project will be completed by 10

December. Well, wherever the compassionate Hazur keeps you will be good for you. Understand this absolutely, my son: you are to listen daily to the Shabd-dhun by attaching your mind to it with love and devotion. I am very pleased and happy with you. Radha Soami from Bibi to you, her dear brother, and to all the other satsangis; also Radha Soami from Bibi to the elder and younger Bibis. This letter has been delayed because I was absent from the Dera. I had gone to Majha, from where I returned after fourteen days. I am now back at the Dera. You are not to worry at all; please continue with your bhajan. You will one day reach Sach Khand; there will be no more births now. Please accept Radha Soami from all the satsangis at the Dera. Dasaundha Singh the priest has written a letter from Mehmansinghwala, in which he says: "I have not agreed to any salary. I am doing bhajan. Kindly shower your grace on me." To this I have not yet sent a reply.

10 November 1897

~ 27 ~

Radha Soami. Radha Soami Ji is the Comforter.

Radha Soami greetings from Jaimal Singh to my obedient son, Babu Sawan Singh. May the grace and mercy of the compassionate Lord be upon you all the time. I have received your postcard and the letter and am happy to read of your well-being. Hazur Radha Soami Ji is with you in every respect; he is protecting you at every moment.

Regarding the well, the masonry chamber has been lowered to a depth of thirty feet. During excavation, sand was struck at around twenty-five feet—the wooden sill [of the masonry chamber] has reached a depth of thirty feet. Today, Saturday, the 30th of Kartik, the first water from the well was drawn by a waterskin *(baaraa)* pulled by many people. Every day, workers costing 4 and sometimes 5 rupees, are being employed. I still have 50 rupees left. It is expected that, in addition to the previous 200, we will need 50 more for the well, so you may send it from your salary for November. You wrote that you had bought some morel mushrooms. There are still plenty left over, so there was no need to buy more. Just bring half or a quarter kilo when you come, but do not send them by parcel.

Listen to the Shabd-dhun every day whenever you are free, and continue with your simran even when moving around. All your worldly business will be taken care of by the Lord, the Satguru himself. The work on the well is very time-consuming— that is why a reply to your postcard was not written earlier. Do not worry in any way. You are not going to take birth again but will always remain with me.

Bibi's Radha Soami to you, her dear brother, and to all the other satsangis. Blessings of grace and mercy upon Chanan Singh and Basant Singh. They should keep on doing their bhajan. I have not understood about Roor Singh, as to who he is. Write about him again, whether or not he is a satsangi. Write also about where your office will be located. Please tell Basant Singh to study wholeheartedly. And gradually you should start riding your horse.

14 November [1897]

~ 28 ~

Radha Soami. Radha Soami Ji is the Comforter.

Radha Soami greetings from Jaimal Singh to my obedient son, Babu Sawan Singh. May the infinite grace and mercy of the compassionate Lord be upon you all the time. Satguru in his

Shabd form is always protecting you, my son. Your letter has been received and I am very happy to know that you are well. You write that Mata Ji has given you darshan and also the blessed water three times. Please understand that it was my request that Babu Sawan Singh should be taken across the three regions—because he who gets across the three regions is not born again—and that he should receive a visible sign of this. That is why Mata Ji has taken you beyond the three regions. From now on when you are separated from the body, you will immediately step across the three regions. Do not have any worry, my son. Hazur's grace and mercy will also be showered upon Bibi Ji at your home.

Regarding the well: the masonry chamber has been sunk to a depth of forty-eight feet. First sand appeared at about twenty-two feet, and then clay along with water. The excavators are digging every day. They said that sand would be struck again at six feet more. Please also write about how much money you will receive this year; treat the salary and allowance as the same, but write about the latter separately. Then I will write to you about budgeting your income for this year. You are the very breath of my life, my son. Listen to the Shabd-dhun every day, whether or not your mind likes it. Undoubtedly you will always remain with me.

Bibi's Radha Soami to you, her dear brother, and also to Basant Singh and Chanan Singh. May grace and mercy always be upon Chanan Singh and Basant Singh. They should both do their meditation regularly. This letter has been written in a hurry because there is a lot of work to be done here. Please consider it, though brief, to be substantial. You will receive his grace and mercy in abundance.

25 November [1897]

∾ 29 ∾

Radha Soami. Radha Soami Ji is the Comforter.

From Jaimal Singh to my obedient son, Babu Sawan Singh, and to Babu Hari Ram, Babu Mohan Singh, and to all the other satsangis: Radha Soami greetings. May the grace and mercy of the compassionate Anami Lord always be upon all of you. You are indeed my truly beloved ones. Wherever my Satguru Ji sends me, there you will always remain with me. I received a money order for 50 rupees on 6 December and have used it for the expenses of the well. I also received a letter with the news of all three of you, and was delighted to read about your well-being and about your family matters.

About the well: sand was struck today. After reaching the water level, the excavators bored into the subsoil for nine feet more until they struck sand. They will now go down three or four feet further in the sand so that the overall water column is twelve to thirteen feet in depth. The work on the well is expected to be finished in ten to twelve days. A small pitcher of the first water was sent to Agra, where most likely it has been distributed to the whole sangat. The well is now in place: it has about ten feet of water, which is enough. A day back, the well was run for half a day, with a waterskin *(charas)* pulled by oxen, but it did not run dry. A little sand came up, so the well was set right there. It was finished on 8 December, the 24th of Maghar. Its inauguration ceremony will be performed after you come.

What I wrote above about the well being finished in ten to twelve days was written three days ago—because I can't find time even to write. Two or three lines one day, a couple of lines another day—that's how this letter has been written. So consider this account, though short, to be substantial. Bibi has made some spiced bean-dumplings *(warian)* for you, so let us know whether you will be coming to collect them or if we should send them by parcel. This account has been brief because of lack of time. Bibi's Radha Soami to you, her dear brother. And please convey my Radha Soami to the elder Bibi Ji, the younger Bibi Ji, and to all the satsangis. Bibi's Radha Soami also to the elder Bibi, the younger Bibi, and to her two brothers.

Please convey this to everyone from me: listen to the Shabd-dhun every day, and always keep simran in the mind. Consider it your good fortune that you are not to be born again. You will now go to Sach Khand from above Sahansdal Kanwal. Whatever words of advice the Satguru gives, always treasure them in your heart. Then the Satguru will do all your worldly and spiritual work—you are not to worry at all.

Due to lack of time, I have written this one letter for all of you. May his grace and mercy shower plentifully upon Chanan Singh and Basant Singh. Bibi's Radha Soami to both of them. Grace and mercy in abundance upon them from my side.

9 December [1897]

~ 30 ~

Radha Soami. Radha Soami Ji is the Comforter.

Radha Soami greetings from Jaimal Singh to my obedient son, Babu Sawan Singh. May the grace and mercy of the compassionate Lord always be upon you. I have received your letter and am glad to know that you are doing well. I am sorry to read, however, that you have been injured again. But do not worry, my son, the karmas are being worked out in whatever is happening. We do not want to be born again so it is better to go through these karmas now. However busy you might be, do keep me informed about your condition, even by a postcard, until your leg gets better. Listen to the Shabd-dhun every day whenever you

are free. You write that you did not want to leave, that you did
not wish to be separate from me. You are never separate from
me, my son, because our real form is the Shabd-dhun, which is
never separate, and the Shabd-dhun has been bestowed upon
you. Because of the physical body, the business of the world has
to be carried out. So you are always with me, my son.

Regarding the durbar hall: five masons have been employed
at 6 annas plus two meals per day—they work every day. The
wall on one side has been built up to a man's height. For timber,
I have selected an 18 by 3 foot deodar log. They were offering it
at 3 rupees per foot, but the official who could sanction the
sale—it is government timber—was on tour somewhere, and I
was told that he'd be back in two or three days. I shall let you
know when it has been purchased. For the scaffolding planks,
five beams of pine wood were bought for 10 rupees, and each
has been sawn into three planks of three feet each. Also, we have
three labourers working at 3 annas each per day. For the rest, my
son, whatever is the will of Hazur will happen.

May the grace and mercy of Hazur always be upon Chanan
Singh and Basant Singh. Please convey my Radha Soami to
them. Chanan Singh should sit in bhajan every day, whenever he
is free, and Basant Singh should study wholeheartedly—that is
his bhajan. Radha Soami from Bibi to you, her dear brother.
Bibi's Radha Soami also to Chanan Singh and Basant Singh.
All the sadhus at the Dera send their Radha Soami to Babu Ji.
Please have no worry; the Satguru, in his Shabd-form, is always
by your side. He is the one who is doing all the work. Every moment he is calling us within and showering us with his protection
and grace. Please accept Radha Soami from Dasaundha Singh.

You write that while some people recite the scriptures, and
others engage in penances or do noble and charitable deeds, you
are without any of these good works. My son, all this work you
have already done. The fruit of such work is meeting the perfect

Satguru. For you no other practice or pious, good or noble deed remains to be performed—all these you have already done.

Please convey Radha Soami greetings to Babu Mohan Singh when he comes there. So long as the leg is weak, you should definitely use the support of a stick to walk around. Once the leg becomes normal and the healed bone is firmly in place, you won't need a crutch or support. The leg will then be as it was before.

30 January 1898

~ 31 ~

Radha Soami. Radha Soami Ji is the Comforter.

Radha Soami greetings and Sri Wahiguru Ji ki Fateh from Jaimal Singh to my obedient son, Babu Sawan Singh. May the grace and mercy of the compassionate Lord be upon you all the time. Your letter has been received and I am glad to know that you are well and happy. You should write about your leg and your health more frequently. As long as the leg is weak, use the support of a crutch to walk around. This will help it to become normal as before—do not feel any apprehension. You write that someone is about to come on a promotion to replace you. It does not matter. No one can take away what is in your destiny. The Lord will give you everything. Do remember to eat the pipal tree gum again for seven days.

Regarding the durbar hall: the building has been constructed to a height of eight feet, and today the framing of the doors has also been started. We have engaged four masons and four carpenters for the job: two of them receive 7 annas a day each, while the other six are paid 6 annas each per day—all of them receive their meals also from us. One deodar log has arrived and now the sawing has started. I intend going out today to buy a second

18-foot log. A 112-foot log to provide five beams was also selected for a price of 130 rupees. If more wood is needed, I will
buy it after these two pieces have been sawed. I will then write to
you about how things are here. We are also employing three
labourers at 3 annas each per day.

Your money order of 100 rupees was received today, 14
February. Some of this money has been used to pay for the
wood, the remainder is still with me. I have also borrowed another 100 rupees from someone else. The remainder of the 100
rupees from your salary will be spent as you wish. I would like to
see the hall completed by Baisakhi, as it starts to get hot after
that time. For the rest, whatever is the will of Hazur will happen.

Listen to the Shabd-dhun every day. I want you to regain
normal health within this year. Illness in your household was destined to last for two years; Hazur has reduced it at my supplication. Please do not worry about anything—all will be well with
Hazur's grace.

May his grace and mercy be upon Chanan Singh and
Basant Singh. They should do their meditation. When you write
to Basant Singh at Rawalpindi, give him my love and Radha
Soami greetings and tell him to study with his whole heart.
Radha Soami from Bibi to you, her dear brother; also Bibi's
Radha Soami to Chanan Singh and Basant Singh. Please con-
vey my Radha Soami greetings also to Babu Mohan Singh and
tell him to listen to the Shabd-dhun every day. Listening to it
repeatedly will purify him. Bibi's Radha Soami to Babu Mohan
Singh.

My son, you should write your letters or postcards more frequently. Also please send the money about which I wrote. If it is
available send it immediately, or drop me a line if there is some
delay. I also have a lot to do and so have not been able to write
this letter properly. Just understand it this way: more precious to
me are you, my son, than even the breath of my very own body.

Never again will you have to take a birth. Wherever I am, there
you also shall reside with me. I am very pleased with you indeed.
Radha Soami from all the satsangis here to you, Babu Ji.

14 February 1898

~ 32 ~

Radha Soami. Radha Soami Ji is the Comforter.

From Jaimal Singh to my obedient son, Babu Sawan Singh Ji:
Radha Soami, Radha Soami, Radha Soami—due to an over-
sight it got written three times. May the grace and mercy of the
compassionate Lord be upon you all the time.

Regarding the durbar hall: the deodar log that cost 80 rupees has been used for the frames and panels. All the panels for
the doors, windows, and wardrobes will be made from it. The
log costing 130 rupees will be sawn into five beams and some
wood will be left over—but it has not been sawed yet. The
arches have all been fitted; the walls have reached a height of
eight feet. We hired three carpenters to work at 7 annas each per
day, another carpenter and three masons at 6 annas each, and
three labourers for 3 annas each per day. In all, there are seven
masons and carpenters; the total of their daily wages comes to 3
rupees and 6 annas.

Listen to the Shabd-dhun every day, my son. Even if there
is little progress, it will add up to a lot. When listening to the
Sound, first inwardly visualize the Satguru's form—indeed, the
inner focus *(dhyan)* should be on the Master in everything we
do. Whatever form the Dhun has, the same is that of the Shabd,
the same of the gross *(sthool)* physical form, the same of the eternal Lord (Sat Purush), the same of the Lord of Alakh, Agam,
and the same also of the Anami Lord, Radha Soami. When all
these forms are blended together as one in the mind, only then is

one's whole work complete. Then the thought that the Satguru is merely a human being will never come.

About the money order: on 28 February, 100 rupees were received along with your letter. I was very happy to read the contents of the letter. If you get leave for Holi, please let me know the date of your arrival; someone will be there at the railway station to receive you. Two letters came from Babu Mohan Singh with good news which I was very happy to read. May the grace and mercy of Hazur be upon Babu Mohan Singh all the time. Listen to the Shabd-dhun every day. Listening repeatedly, you will become pure and one day reach Sach Khand. I am very happy with you, my son. Radha Soami from Bibi to both her brothers, and to Chanan Singh and Basant Singh. Please also convey Radha Soami on my behalf to Chanan Singh and Basant Singh. The reply to both of Babu Mohan Singh's letters has been given.

The most precious jewel of love are you, beloved son, as dear to me as my very own body. A day is coming when I will take you to Sach Khand. I am not going to Peshawar now, but shall do so in the month of Vaisakh.

1 March 1898

∼ 33 ∼

Radha Soami. Radha Soami Ji is the Comforter.

Radha Soami greetings from Jaimal Singh to both my obedient sons, Babu Sawan Singh and Babu Mohan Singh. May the grace and mercy of the compassionate Lord be upon you all the time. Babu Mohan Singh's postcard has been received and I am happy to read it and know of his well-being.

Pritam Singh came and stayed here for two days. He left today. I bought another piece of timber for 37½ rupees, plus

1 rupee for freight. We now have all the cross-ties and boards that are needed. If anything runs short, there is some wood left over that can be sawn and used. The beams for the roof will be set at twelve feet—construction of the building now has gone up to that level. One side is still to be built up a little, after which the work on the roof will start. Please write soon about what colour the building should be painted, and remember to send the paint soon. The builders say that the building must be painted. Reply to this letter as soon as you arrive in Khairagali. Even if you are short of time, write a few lines about your well-being. This letter has been written to inform you about the progress on the durbar hall.

Listen to the Shabd-dhun every day. Keep simran in mind all the time—no pain will then affect you. The Satguru's form should always remain before you, then it is Shabd all the time. While walking or working, sitting or sleeping, or doing your official duties, always remember: "I am nothing; all is Satguru's work, I am merely an instrument." No matter what happens, always remain cheerful.

Radha Soami from Bibi to her brothers. Also Radha Soami from all the satsangis and the workmen here. Sri Wahiguru Ji ki Fateh from myself and from all others. I am extremely pleased with you, beloved son. You are my very own son in essence. You will always remain with me—but do not stray outside the teachings. This letter is written on 16 March. Do send a reply.

Please send a copy of the Tenth Guru's *Granth Sahib* by parcel. Send both volumes at the same time. A letter of well-being was received from Babu Hari Ram; he wrote that he was unable to have darshan.

16 March 1898

~ 34 ~

Radha Soami. Radha Soami Ji is the Comforter.

Radha Soami greetings from Jaimal Singh to my obedient son, Babu Sawan Singh. May the grace and mercy of the compassionate Hazur and the Anami Lord always be upon you, dear son. Your letter has arrived and I am pleased to receive your news and to learn that you are doing well. You write that lust and anger are still with you as before. Do your bhajan and simran every day, my son, and from time to time, leaving aside the desire for worldly work, contemplate on the Satguru's form in the higher mind. If his form is seen clearly, then put the mind and soul at his Holy Feet and offer this supplication: "O Lord! Please merge my soul into your Shabd form, your true and real being." Make this plea repeatedly for a quarter-hour (fifteen minutes), and then connect the soul slowly and gently to the Sound. Listen to the melody as long as the mind remains absorbed in it, but do not allow any worldly desire to arise. The form of the heart centre lies below Sahansdal Kanwal at the left corner of the right eye—at a spot between the two eyes, but more toward the right eye—having settled there after descending from Trikuti. Its reflection is found at the throat, and then again at a third place, the area of the physical heart and navel. Concentration on these lower centres is forbidden. The true heart centre lies only above the eyes, in the left corner of the right eye. The Satguru's form is in Trikuti; its duplicate, a complete form, lies above the eyes. The heart centre lies there. That is where the contemplation on the Satguru's form is to be done, as I have described above. If the form of the Satguru's image appears at that place, his darshan will be enjoyed every day. Because the being is very weak, totally unclean and surrounded by maya, he becomes pure through the darshan of the Satguru's form and by following his teachings. The Satguru's intrinsic form is Shabddhun. The disciple becomes very pure by listening to it, and exceedingly pure when he receives the Satguru's full darshan within. The Satguru then observes whether the disciple's worldly hopes and desires, both gross and subtle, are all gone, and if he is now a supplicant only for the Satguru's form, pleased with the Satguru's will, happy with however tough a command the Satguru may give, and saying honestly that whatever has happened is very good. The Satguru's command is meditation, my son. When such an understanding has been achieved, the Satguru will at once take the disciple to Sach Khand. Thus there is no delay but that the being lacks the strength to go there.

You ask in your letter what sin has denied you darshan. My son, there is no sin from the past hanging over you that would hold you back from the spiritual path. It was the Satguru's wish that you should go to your place of work. No news was received from you. You had not requested earlier on that you wanted to come for a night to have darshan. The fruit of Satguru's darshan has reached you, my son. If we request the Satguru to give us something, he may accept our request at the time. But he will then deliberate over the matter, and if he sees that it is not in the devotee's interest, he will withdraw it immediately. He will know that it is not going to benefit him, so he will take it back at once. The Satguru is always with the disciple, but only if he gives himself resolutely to the Satguru: "Surrendering the self, he merges in the Guru" (Nanak aap chhod gur maahi samaavai).[11]

Bibi's Radha Soami to you, her dear brother, and to Chanan Singh, Basant Singh, Babu Mohan Singh, and Babu Hari Ram. May grace and mercy be upon all of you. You should all do your bhajan and simran every day. Please convey my Radha Soami greetings to everybody; Radha Soami from Bibi to everyone. Radha Soami from all the satsangis and sadhus at the Dera to everyone there and to Babu Ji. So far no one has come to apply coal tar to the durbar hall. Its roof needs to be tarred. When you are free, remember to pick up some coal tar. I am pleased with you, my son. Do your work, happy in his will. All work done in the will of the Guru is spiritual in nature.

28 March [1898]

~ 35 ~

Radha Soami. Radha Soami Ji is the Comforter.

Radha Soami greetings from Jaimal Singh to my obedient son, Babu Sawan Singh. Dear son, your letter arrived, giving me all your news. I am happy that you reached your place of work safe and sound. Both volumes of the Tenth Guru's *Granth* have arrived by parcel; they were received on 25 March, and your letter on the 28th. Regarding your salary, perhaps the Lord intends to increase it later on since he has decreased it a little now. Please don't worry, and carry on your government duties cheerfully. I read the Tenth Guru's *Granth* in a couple of places; it contains some discrepancies and is not entirely accurate.

Please put in an application to acquire land and definitely try to get five squares. Make the effort, my son—for the rest, the Lord will do what is best. The present situation of the durbar hall is that its roof has been completed, and in four or five days the parapets will also be built. However, the frames and doors will be fitted only after the inside has been plastered, at which time the wall of the platform will be built as well. Two short pieces and four 6-foot lengths of deodar have been purchased for 45½ rupees. We have been able to manage for the rest. Three masons and two carpenters are working on the building, but the two men engaged to saw the wood have been discharged.

Pritam Singh came here and left after staying for a day or two. Do get some employment for Bachint Singh. You can have him enlisted in the cavalry at Rawalpindi Cantonment.

Do your bhajan and simran daily whenever you are free. Your bhajan, when you are doing government work, is my responsibility. When you sit for bhajan, please start with simran and drive out all worldly ideas from your mind, and contemplate fully on the Satguru's form. Then, slowly and gently listen to the inner Dhun for four or five minutes and, holding fast to that Sound, fix your mind and soul in it. While listening to the Dhun, no other thought should enter the mind. Then so long as your attention remains fixed in the Dhun, you will profoundly enjoy its bliss. Later, when you begin your official work you can mentally recall and remember all that you have to do, but at the time of meditation, do as I have written above.

Please tell Babu Hari Ram, Babu Mohan Singh, Chanan Singh, and Kaka Ram to do their meditation every day, and give them my Radha Soami greetings. May the grace and mercy of Hazur be upon them all. You are all my true sons and will certainly reach Sach Khand with me. The compassionate Lord will definitely take you to Sach Khand one day. Bibi's Radha Soami to you, her dear brother, and to all the other satsangi brothers. Radha Soami also from everyone at the Dera to you, Babu Ji. May grace and mercy be upon Basant Singh. Write and give my love to him, and tell him to study well and wholeheartedly.

29 March [1898]

~ 36 ~

Radha Soami. Radha Soami Ji is the Comforter.

Radha Soami greetings from Jaimal Singh to my obedient son, Babu Sawan Singh. Dear son, Nabi Bakhsh has been here since

1 May to do the painting and has now started doing it. He said that he could not come earlier because of the death of his nephew. Your letter written in Gurmukhi was received and I was extremely happy to read it. This postcard is in reply to that letter. You must do your meditation daily—even if you do it for a short time, yet it must be done daily. Love for the Shabd-dhun develops gradually, it does not come quickly. The Satguru himself will ferry you across.

Please convey Radha Soami greetings to Babu Mohan Singh, Babu Hari Ram, Chanan Singh, and Basant Singh. May the grace and mercy of the compassionate Anami Lord always bless them all. The construction of the parapet of the well has now been started.

Radha Soami from Bibi to you, her dear brother, and to all the others. Radha Soami to everyone from Bibi and from the satsangis at the Dera. I have received today, 2 May, 100 rupees by money order through the Sathiala post office. It will be used for the parapet, my son.

2 May 1898

~ 37 ~

Radha Soami. Radha Soami Ji is the Comforter.

Radha Soami greetings and Wahiguru Ji ki Fateh from Jaimal Singh to my obedient son, Babu Sawan Singh. Dear son, your letter has been inordinately late in arriving. You should write a letter every fortnight so that I am kept informed of your welfare. The construction of the durbar hall is now over; everything was finished by the 26th of Vaisakh. All the doors have been painted and a lot of paint was left over. It appears that only a half or a third was used; the rest has been stored here. Regarding the freight charges for the paint, I wrote two letters to you but received no reply. The station master told me that while the invoice indicated that the freight had been paid, the receipt denoted that it had not been paid, so he has charged me 1 rupee and 13 annas for it. You have not replied whether or not this is correct, or whether we have been charged twice. The account of the expenditure on the durbar hall will be drawn up and sent to you later; 200 rupees had to be borrowed to construct a platform outside. You may send 100 rupees now. The walls of the platform have been plastered with lime and whitewashed on the outside and top, but the platform has not yet been levelled by filling it with earth. That work will cost about 10 rupees and I will write to you when it is finished. Whatever work you do, I should definitely be informed about it every fifteen days. The rest is up to you; you may write at your pleasure.

You should read verses from the scriptures whenever you are free, because then if you become perturbed at work they will remind you of your Satguru. When the Satguru is remembered with love, all spiritual and worldly work becomes pleasing and the mind does not feel any distress. Then even worldly activities yield spiritual fruit. So the well you have put in and the durbar hall you have built have borne spiritual fruit for you. Thus, the bad karmas in your destiny that were to yield bad consequences have all been eliminated. My son, he who has found the perfect Shabd-form Satguru has had two types of karmas, the stored and the action karmas, cancelled that very day. Only the fate karmas of that individual are then left to be accounted for. Thus all actions become spiritual for the disciple whose inner mind has developed firm faith and deep love for the Satguru.

Listen to the Shabd-dhun every day, even if only for a little while. When doing simran, repeat the names[*] at each stage with a detached mind and full attention; afterwards sit in bhajan.

---

[*] Simran: *see* Glossary.

Your attention will then stay inside. Do not have any worry, you will reach Sach Khand one day—you are not coming back to this world. Do not get attached mentally to material things and activities of this world. Perform your duties faithfully, even eagerly, but like a guest who inwardly knows that the house does not belong to him. The whole world and all its affairs and possessions are false. So attend to them with that in mind. The mind and soul are to be kept at the Satguru's Holy Feet.

Please convey Radha Soami greetings to Babu Mohan Singh, Babu Hari Ram, Chanan Singh, Basant Singh, and Kaka Ram. May the grace and mercy of the compassionate Lord always be upon them all. The construction work on the durbar hall has all been finished; nothing more remains to be done.

Please give Bibi's Radha Soami to all her satsangi brothers. The account of the money has been given above. Radha Soami greetings from all the satsangis. Always be prompt with your replies.

This ink has gone bad; it smudges the hand. Please write of some remedy for it. My son, relinquish the self and consider everything you do to be the Satguru's work, that nothing is your own, and stay happy in his will. These are the marks of a gurmukh.

8 May [1898]

Radha Soami. Radha Soami Ji is the Comforter.

Radha Soami greetings from Jaimal Singh to my obedient son, Babu Sawan Singh. May the compassionate Lord bless you with his grace and mercy all the time. A letter was received earlier from you, and now a second letter has also arrived. I was very happy to read them both and learn of your well-being. Regarding the letter from home about purchasing land, if it is available please go ahead and buy it. Take leave for ten days and definitely go home. I have heard at Beas that the doctors are detaining people from Jalandhar and Hoshiarpur districts for eight days before allowing them to proceed. No one else is being detained. That is what we've heard; I have not personally seen it.

You write that your mind keeps hankering after the outer form because you have not been able to have darshan of the inner Shabd form. That is right; it will remain so until the outer form has become fully imprinted and the Anami Lord and Creator has taken a permanent abode in the inner self. Understand this fully and absolutely, my son, that when the mind is not attached to any external tasks or material forms in the world, when in hardship or happiness the mind does not waver, then is the command for attachment to the inner form given. There is no difference between this and the outer form. It is like seeing your face in a mirror: the face cannot be seen so long as the mirror is not clean. It is a mystery kept hidden by the Anami Lord: when the attention moves from the Shabd form to the physical, the Shabd form becomes invisible. I shall explain all this when you come here. As the disciple develops more understanding, the Satguru keeps on imparting more knowledge to him. And as he becomes more purified, the Satguru increasingly attaches him to the Shabd-dhun within. One day the Satguru will definitely guide you to Sach Khand, the final destination.

Bibi's Radha Soami to you, her dear brother. Radha Soami greetings to Babu Hari Ram, Babu Mohan Singh, Kaka Ram, Chanan Singh, Basant Singh, and to all the other satsangis. Bibi's Radha Soami to everyone; also Radha Soami from the other satsangis here. Your letter was received on the night of 30 May. I have written and mailed this reply on the 31st. Do please let me know when you leave and I will send someone to the railway station to receive you.

You also write that you are nothing. If you are nothing, then the Satguru is everything. Whatever work is done through his will is well done, so consider yourself a servant doing the work. He will carry out the work himself.

Please bring with you a quire or two of small-size writing paper, if available. At present we have no paper at the Dera for writing letters.

31 May [1898]

~ 39 ~

Radha Soami. Radha Soami Ji is the Comforter.

Radha Soami greetings from Jaimal Singh to my obedient son, Babu Sawan Singh. This to let you know that I received your 100 rupees on 27 June. They were used to pay the arrears of the durbar hall. You were expected here, but did not come—please let me know the reason. I had packed some parshad for sending to you by parcel, when Nabi Bakhsh the painter arrived here on 21 June. He said that Babu Sawan Singh would be coming to Waraich on 22 June, so I did not send it. The parshad was from the main bhandara at Agra and also some from the bhandara here. Now I will send it under your name or under the name of Babu Hari Ram. Please write when you are coming on leave and bring with you one or two quires of letter-size writing paper. Do remember this, because now I have no paper to write letters with. The painter, Nabi Bakhsh, stayed for four days to do the painting, and then left for his place, Sri Hargobindpur. He has not taken any payment from me. You must write to me about yourself. Even if you are very busy with work, you should all the same keep me informed about your activities. We still owe 150 rupees for the durbar hall; this can be paid later. Whenever you are free for a few hours at night, take half an hour right away to write to me. I do not know the date of Pritam Singh's wedding, so please let me know.

Do your bhajan and simran every day; even if only a little is possible, it must be done. Listen daily to the Shabd-dhun while doing your government work—whether awake or asleep, walking or sitting, at all times, never forget the Shabd-dhun. All work, temporal or spiritual, is done by the Shabd-dhun, but the mind takes undue credit for it, which is false. In fact, the Shabd-dhun does it all. So you should make your home in the Shabd. May the grace and mercy of the compassionate Anami Lord always be upon you. I am very pleased with you, my son. You will most certainly go to Sach Khand with me.

Radha Soami from Bibi to you, her dear brother. Please convey Radha Soami greetings to Chanan Singh and Basant Singh; Radha Soami also to all the others. May grace and mercy be upon you all the time. Please reply soon.

2 July 1898

$\sim$ 40 $\sim$

Radha Soami. Radha Soami Ji is the Comforter.

From Jaimal Singh to my obedient son, Babu Sawan Singh, and to Basant Singh, Chanan Singh, Babu Gulab Singh, Babu Gajja Singh, Narain Singh, Diwan Singh, Babu Hari Ram, Malik Thakar Das, the elder Bibi Ji and the younger Bibi Ji, and young Gursharan: Radha Soami greetings to all and everyone. May the grace and mercy of the compassionate Hazur, and of the Anami Lord, Radha Soami, always be upon all of you. His call is resounding within everyone's body; he is summoning everyone to his palace, Sach Khand. All the time, day and night, the Shabd-dhun is calling continuously—this, my son, is the cosmic law of the true Lord, Sat Purush. So please listen to the

Shabd-dhun every day and find out the source from where it is coming.

I was very happy to read your letter that arrived here on 2 August and to learn that you are all well. Please write to your Baba Ji; include also a reply on my behalf regarding the note he sent to me about your not listening to him. You should definitely send him 40 rupees every year. Please write about this to him.

A postcard has come from Babu Hari Ram about Gursharan's well-being. I am happy to read it. Please keep doing bhajan and simran every day. The grace and mercy of the compassionate Lord is upon you. This is the reply to your postcard; no other reply will be sent.

The younger Bibi is strongly advised not to eat hot pepper and other such spices. Give Basant Singh some tonic daily to sharpen his brain. I am very pleased with him; his labour will bear fruit. All of you should do your bhajan and simran every day. When free, do not waste time uselessly, because our breaths, morsels of food, walking, working, sleeping and waking, are all taken into account. This human body may not be given again. The major task in assuming the human form is to listen to Namdhun by attaching the soul to it, to keep the higher mind always firmly attached to the Shabd-dhun, and to wean the mind away from worldly desires. Only that which is written on our foreheads will be given to us, nothing else will come our way. Why then hanker after worldly ambitions and desires? Be content, and keep doing your official work. Whenever you are free, do your bhajan and simran. Our true work is bhajan and simran; doing even a little will add up to a lot. I am very pleased with you, my son.

Please set aside 10 rupees every two months to be sent here. This money from your salary will be used specifically for the Dera expenses. Always remember that we have to leave this world. We will have to suffer the consequences of whatever we do under the sway of the mind. Impress upon the mind to always live in the Satguru's will. Then everything is achieved.

Bibi's Radha Soami to you, her brother, and to all the satsangis. Radha Soami to everyone from all the sadhus at the Dera and from all the satsangis.

5 August 1898

~ 41 ~

Radha Soami. Radha Soami Ji is the Comforter.

Radha Soami greetings from Jaimal Singh to my obedient son, Babu Sawan Singh. May the grace and mercy of the compassionate Anami Lord always be upon you. I have received your letter and am very glad to read that you are well and happy. The letter included news of all the satsangis and I was very happy to read that too. Please do not worry about anything; whatever was to happen had already happened. Continue to do your official work with goodwill in mind. Whenever an officer visits your area, keep me informed about his remarks and observations about you. I should be getting three letters from you each month. If that is not possible, at least two a month must come.

You write that you still feel somewhat weak. Eat well, do your bhajan and simran, and also do your official work with diligence—you will then become strong. When you find that some senior officer is obstructing your work, you should use your judgement and ask for a transfer if it is not possible to get along with him. If he transfers you himself, do not take it ill, because whatever has to happen has already happened—nothing new is going to happen now, my son. So remain fearless: whatever He does can only be for your benefit. Wherever you go, keep your attention in the Satguru, then he himself is the doer. Do your bhajan and simran every day. Even if you are free for only ten minutes, it should still be done regularly.

Please convey my Radha Soami to Chanan Singh and Basant Singh. May grace and mercy be upon them. Radha Soami greetings from Bibi to you, her dear brother. Bibi has also sent a *rakhi* for you. I have given her a rupee and a quarter for it on your behalf, so there is no need now for you to send any money. We'll see to it when you come on leave. Please attach yourself firmly to the Shabd-dhun within. Even if you are unable to sit regularly, nurture love for it in your mind all the time. While walking, working, sitting or sleeping, keep the higher mind in love with the Dhun, and listen to it whenever you are free.

Radha Soami greetings from Jaimal Singh to my obedient sons, Babu Hari Ram, Babu Mohan Singh and the other sat-sangis who are there. May the grace and mercy of the compassionate Anami Lord always be upon you. I have received your letter and was happy to learn about your well-being. Whatever you wrote, all your supplications have been accepted in Hazur's court. Slowly, gently, you will receive everything. Keep doing your bhajan and simran every day and consider the Shabd-dhun especially to be your true friend and comforter. It is always with you; it looks after you with every breath. Please have no worry about work; everything will be done by the Lord himself.

Radha Soami greetings to the elder Bibi Ji and the younger Bibi Ji. May the grace and mercy of the compassionate Hazur always be upon them. Bibi's Radha Soami to the two Bibi Jis and to all the others. You all write that I should come there and give darshan. I will let you know later on, but at present I am not free. The worker who painted the door panels daubed very thick paint on them, with the result that the doors do not shut properly. The paint has run and settled heavily in the nooks and crannies. The doors do not close even when I try to shut them by force. Rather, good-size slivers of wood rip off the doors when anyone tries to shut them. The Muslim craftsman who came later applied too much paint. And—

> Always and ever my Guru's beside me.
>   *Guru mere sang sadaa hai naale.*[12]

He further says:

> Satguru is the Shabd form that dwells in the inner sky;
> You as well are surat's form, listen to the call within.
>   *Satguru shabd swaroop hain, rahen arsh manjhaar;*
>   *Too bhee surat swaroop hai....sun gagan pukaar.*[13]

Thus the Shabd-dhun calls you all the time to come home to Sach Khand. So place your love in it. I am very happy and pleased with you. The rope that you sent for the awning has been used for the punkahs in the durbar hall. It has been utilized in seva.

15 August 1898

[Note by Maharaj Sawan Singh:] After the broken leg had healed, I went back to my area. Col. Bruce, who was very kind to me, had been transferred. The new officer who replaced him was against Col. Bruce. For this reason, he made things difficult for me. Perplexed, I sent a plea to Hazur [Baba Ji], the response to which was this letter. After its arrival, the officer became all right.

~ 42 ~

Radha Soami. Radha Soami Ji is the Comforter.

Radha Soami greetings from Jaimal Singh to my obedient son, Babu Sawan Singh. May the grace and mercy of the compassionate Lord always be upon you, dear son. Your letter has arrived

informing me of your condition. I am glad to know that you are
well and happy. I have also understood the situation at home.
What you have done there is right: the outer guest-house *(haveli)*
should not be bought without a free transfer. This did not happen as there was some ambivalence in his mind.

You write of your deep anguish at not having had darshan
again. Do not worry, my son, you are always with me. The work
of the wedding could not have been discharged without your
presence. That's why Hazur sent you there. I will explain everything you want to know when you come to visit me. You are always by my side, my son, and Satguru's true form, Shabd, is
always with you. I am extremely pleased with you.

You write that you are requesting a transfer because of the
strictness of the officer-in-charge. Lots of officers will come, my
son, and lots of officers will go. Are you working for the state or
for this officer? What is there to be afraid of? If you thus fear
your superiors, how will you carry out your duties properly? If,
however, he regards your work as worthless, then of course opt
for a transfer. But do not ask for it of your own accord. If it is
within his authority, he will transfer you himself. At that time you
may agree to a transfer; but do not ask for it yourself. A servant
has no say, my son. Do your work wherever you are ordered to
do so, and leave when you are so ordered. Whatever had to be
done has already been done; that is not going to be changed.
The Lord carries out all activities in the manner in which he
himself has ordained. Ever and always he is by our side—we
should not have any fear. Kings and emperors are all his creation. Whoever commits an iniquity will have to bear the consequences. Whatever is to be done has already been done, and that
is what will happen—man does not do anything by himself. Believe implicitly, my son, the Satguru has told us that man does
nothing—only the means for doing appears to come through

him. Remain dauntless and do your duty. Whatever is to happen has already happened. For the rest, you may do as seems proper to you, but please do keep me informed. The Satguru will be with you wherever you go. Since I am not familiar with worldly work or with the diplomacy of the situation, you should do as seems appropriate. Every day, whenever you are free, do your bhajan and simran. You have my permission to go wherever you feel comfortable. Just keep me informed from wherever you are posted. You are my dearly beloved child; you will go to Sach Khand in my company.

Please convey my Radha Soami greetings to Babu Hari Ram and inform him that his 5 rupees were received and credited to the expense of the bhandara of Sunday, 31 July. This bhandara was yours.

Radha Soami greetings to Babu Mohan Singh. May grace and mercy be upon him. Grace and mercy upon Chanan Singh and Basant Singh as well. Also Radha Soami greetings to Kaka Ram and to the elder Bibi Ji and the younger Bibi Ji. May grace and mercy be upon them all the time. All are urged to do their bhajan and simran every day, whenever they are free.

Bibi's Radha Soami to you, her dear brother, and to the rest of the family. Also, Radha Soami from Bibi to the elder and the younger Bibis. Radha Soami to all the satsangis.

You should write to me sooner and also let me know whether or not Pritam Singh has arrived at your place. May grace and mercy be upon all of you. One day you will reach Sach Khand through the support of Shabd-dhun. Listen to the Shabd-dhun daily, attach yourself to it, make your home in it, meld the mind into the Dhun, then you will relish its bliss. What more is there to say? The soul will drink that elixir and experience the sweetness for itself.

29 August [1898]

∼ 43 ∼

Radha Soami. Radha Soami Ji is the Comforter.

Radha Soami greetings from Jaimal Singh to my obedient son, Babu Sawan Singh. May the grace and mercy of the compassionate Anami Lord always be upon you. Your letter has been received, giving me your news. I am extremely pleased to see that you are doing well. Whatever the merciful Hazur does will be good. My son, there is no way that I can come at this time. The reason is the doors of the durbar hall: they cannot be shut because the panels have been coated with too much paint. The last painter put too much paint in the crannies of the doors, so that due to humidity most of it has run and, consequently, the doors do not close. When they are shut by force, large pieces splinter off. The recent painting was done very badly. The first person who came to do the work applied varnish over the paint, which kept the paint from sticking to the other door panels. If the second painter had also put varnish over the paint, there would have been no damage. But now all the panels and also the frames that hold them have become warped and their wood has started to splinter. For this reason it is now absolutely impossible for me to come. But if by Kartik the doors dry out and begin to close properly, I will come to visit you then. Now you should send the money through Moti Ram, who is coming to your place and will personally explain the whole situation. Write to me about Basant Singh: how did he get hurt on the forehead?

Continue with your bhajan and simran every day. I have not written much because I am in a hurry. Please convey my Radha Soami greetings with lots of grace and mercy to Babu Hari Ram, Babu Mohan Singh, Chanan Singh, the elder Bibi Ji and the younger Bibi Ji.

You have asked me to catch hold of your mind. The mind will be captured by the Shabd-dhun. Listen every day to the Shabd-dhun with love and affection and keep the image of Satguru's form in the mind (dhyan). Then the mind will not wander anywhere. One day, merging in the Sound, it will reach Daswan Dwar and stay there. Then, with Satguru's grace and mercy, the soul will separate from the mind to merge into the pure Sound and so reach Sach Khand. There is no uncertainty about this; it will definitely reach there.

Bibi's Radha Soami to you, her dear brother, and to all the satsangis; Bibi's Radha Soami also to both the Bibi Jis. And Radha Soami from the satsangis at the Dera to you and to all the other satsangis there. May grace and mercy be upon all of you. My son, none of your worldly work will be obstructed; all will be done by Hazur, our Lord, himself. Listen to the Shabd-dhun every day.

7 September 1898

∼ 44 ∼

Radha Soami. Radha Soami Ji is the Comforter.

Radha Soami greetings from Jaimal Singh to my obedient son, Babu Sawan Singh. May the grace and mercy of the compassionate Anami Lord always be upon you, my son. Your letter has been received and I am very happy to read of your well-being. You write that the little boy is under his mother's control. That is all right, my son. In fact, Satguru is his father and mother; he is his true guardian.

To subjugate the mind the technique is: first, to receive the Satguru's instructions; second, to hear the Shabd-dhun; third, to love the Dhun; and fourth, to experience its bliss. Only then does the Satguru's form settle in the mind. The form of the Satguru's face will then be seen in the mind as clearly as we see our own face in a mirror. When day by day the mind's faculty of focused attention, which is an aspect of the soul, becomes pure through continuous practice, and all worldly desires have left the mind, the mind will never follow any external attractions, but stay only with the Satguru's form. Then the Satguru will look upon the disciple with his glance of mercy; and as the Satguru's compassionate glance keeps falling upon the disciple, all the gross and evil tendencies of the mind will go away, and the mind will love the soul. The flow of consciousness will then love the Shabd's current, and the celestial Sound, taking measure of that soul's worth, will blend it within itself, giving it a little taste of the spiritual bliss. Thereupon the mind's subtle (suksham) defects will also disappear. The Shabd-dhun will then keep the mind tightly in tow—tugging at it like a goat or an animal tied to a rope. Pulling the mind thus little by little, the Dhun blends it with itself and leaves it in Trikuti. When the consciousness again descends from Trikuti to the lower Dhun, it brings along the mind, but the mind then stays with the consciousness and does not indulge in any temptations. This, my son, is the technique by which the mind is subjugated.

There is another way, which involves firm faith and love for the Satguru; nothing else should come into the mind except "I am nothing." But this will be tested by the Satguru himself: that in pain or pleasure, in good or bad, in honour and pride, at no time does any thought of the self intrude into the mind. Then the Shabd-dhun itself is the Satguru, and very gently it takes hold of the mind.

When you sit in bhajan, begin by attaching the mind and attention to the sound that you hear first—which is like that of a grain handmill, or a steam locomotive, or an oven going full blast—and keep the faculty of inner seeing and hearing directed upward to focus on where the sound is coming from. Then attach the mind

and attention to the sound of the bell, and next to that of the
conch. The soul will then gently savour the bliss, and one day it
will surely reach Sach Khand. Please do not be in a hurry. When
the soul becomes steadfast in its love for the Sound, a bond is then
forged with the Shabd-dhun. Thus step by step, slowly, slowly,
the mind is tamed. One day you will certainly reach Sach Khand.

For the rest, my son, remain happy wherever your work takes
you; the Master will always be there by your side. You are not to
worry—just stay within his will. Bibi has prepared some glacéd
pumpkin sweets for you. We will send them by parcel within two
or three days. Bibi also intends to send you some spiced bean
dumplings *(warian)*. You have done very well in holding a bhandara at your village, Mehmansinghwala. I am very pleased with
you, my son. Moti Ram has sent four cotton durries, which fit
the durbar hall quite well. They are rolled out for use on Sundays. I would like you to have four mats made and sent to the
Dera, but they should reach here within two weeks. They should
be sixteen feet long by eight feet wide when finished, and should
not shrink afterwards. All four will be used in the durbar hall.
Also send two more of the same size and design, for a total of six
mats. However, they should all reach here very soon as the whole
sangat feels the need for matting. We have found eight printed
copies of Tulsi Sahib's *Granth*, which have been purchased and
brought here by me. It contains excellent material.

Radha Soami greetings to Chanan Singh, Basant Singh,
and Babu Mohan Singh. The gracious and merciful Hazur will
bless Basant Singh with a good education, provided he studies
with all his heart. Radha Soami greetings from Bibi and from all
the satsangis at the Dera to everyone and to you, Babu Ji. Bibi's
Radha Soami to you, her dear brother. May Chacha Ji's grace
and mercy be upon you. Do write as to how soon the above can
be arranged and the date on which you leave for Khairagali.

8 February [1899]

～ 45 ～

Radha Soami. Radha Soami Ji is the Comforter.

Sri Wahiguru Ji ki Fateh and Radha Soami greetings from Jaimal Singh to my obedient son, Babu Sawan Singh Ji. May the grace and mercy of the compassionate immortal Anami Lord always be upon you. A parcel of six floor mats has arrived here from Beas railway station. No freight was charged for them. Four of them have been laid out in the durbar hall where they fit in place perfectly, and the remaining two are used for sitting during the satsang. All six of them are very nice and useful. I am very pleased to have them.

You wrote a second letter that reached me on 2 March. I was very happy to read it. The compassionate Hazur in his Shabd form is always with you, my son. He is doing whatever is his pleasure. The disciple should not do what his mind dictates, but should remain within the will of the Master. Worldly duties have to be carried out, because when the fruit is ripe, it drops automatically from the tree. Then neither the fruit nor the tree experiences any pain and the ripe fruit is also good for use. But if the unripe fruit is forcibly plucked, the fruit begins to wither and the break in the branch of the tree or vine bleeds. That fruit is of no use. If after being born in a human body one meets a perfect Satguru, then everything is accomplished. This is the fruit. To stay within the will of the Satguru is the ripening of the fruit; to attend daily to meditation to the best of one's ability is watering the tree; and to merge in the Shabd-dhun is the ripening and the falling of the fruit. Then no one feels any pain.

So long as the soul has not merged into the Shabd-dhun, and the individual, due to laziness or mental speculations, does neither worldly nor spiritual work but instead abandons hearth and home, puts on the garb of a sadhu, begs from house to house to fill his belly, and also talks of renunciation in order to do bhajan and simran, he will never gain anything. Such thinking is of no use. The material world and one's kith and kin—sons, daughters, mother, father, wife, wealth, house, land, shops, mansions, riches, worldly honours—all make up the tree. The mind and the soul are intrinsically attached to them like the fruit to the tree. When the mind stays within the Satguru's will and obeys his instructions, then the soul, by loving the Shabd-dhun, takes on the form of the Dhun, and the mind, detaching itself from maya, merges into Kal at Trikuti. Thus the ripened fruit drops by itself and no one feels any pain. Please do not worry about anything. All your work has now been done. Listen daily to the Shabd-dhun—listen as much as possible. One day you will reach Sach Khand.

Bibi asks whether or not you have eaten the parshad of sugared flour-balls *(pinnian)*. Write if it was any good. Bibi's Radha Soami greetings to her brother. Also please convey Bibi's Radha Soami to everybody. Radha Soami from all the satsangis at the Dera to Babu Ji. Radha Soami to Basant Singh, Chanan Singh, and Babu Mohan Singh. Do your bhajan and simran every day; may his grace and mercy always be upon all of you.

Dear son, please write about yourself when you go to Khairagali. Babu Hari Ram stayed at the Dera for four days.

Fix your mind into the first sound that comes before the sound of the bell; then slowly, gently, focus the attention upwards and attach the mind to the sound of the bell. Remember, however, to do your simran beforehand. Do your bhajan and simran every day; please do as much as you can, but it must be done.

3 March [1899]

~ 46 ~

Radha Soami. Radha Soami Ji is the Comforter.

Radha Soami greetings from Jaimal Singh to my obedient son, Babu Sawan Singh, and to Basant Singh, Babu Gajja Singh, Chanan Singh, Diwan Singh, and any other satsangi whose name I might have missed, to Babu Hari Ram, Malik Thakar Das Ji, the elder Bibi and the younger Bibi Ji, to Maya Devi, and all the satsangis and satsangi sisters. May the grace and mercy of the compassionate Anami Lord, Radha Soami, always be upon all of you. My son, I received three letters in Urdu, including a letter from Bachint Singh, informing me about everyone's well-being. I have also written a postcard to you about this.

The news of the brick-kiln: one lakh (100,000) large-sized bricks, and twelve hundred of the small size for the roof of the durbar hall, were baked first. So the bricks are all done, but the entire kiln has not been opened yet because it is still hot. It was fired on the evening of 8 May. Two bricks were pulled out as samples; they were well baked—so the firing has been satisfactory. The expense of the kiln has come to 290 rupees, and there has been an additional expense of 10 to 15 rupees. So it all has turned out well: whatever has happened by the compassionate Hazur's will is good. An urgent issue: why has the painter, Nabi Bakhsh, not received the money for his work? It is imperative that honest labour be used for the durbar hall. I asked Nabi Bakhsh whether or not he had received his wages. Even upon asking him three times, he would not give me an answer. Then he said that the money was as good as received by him; but then he added that he won't take it and wished to leave it as seva. He is a very poor man, so the next time he comes to you, please definitely give him the money.

You already know about Agra. Do come if you get leave, but it is very hot these days. If you do not get leave, send money to Agra. I intend to go—the rest will happen as is the will of Hazur Maharaj. The money, however, should reach Agra by the 25th or 26th of Jeth. Please make arrangements accordingly. I cannot think of anything else—that which pleases the compassionate Hazur is going to happen. We only need the refuge (sharan) of his Lotus Feet all the time.

I have had absolutely no spare time to write a letter. Only now, during the last two days, have I been free. If you know someone in Multan, please ask him to send me 5 rupees' worth of crystallized sugar from there by parcel. Be sure to remember it. Crystallized sugar made in a clay pitcher is of three kinds. What I would like to receive is good, top-quality crystallized sugar, even if only a small amount is available. The parcel should be made out like this: Railway Station Beas, Recipient: Jaimal Singh Sant. After dispatching the parcel, the invoice should be put in an envelope and addressed: District and Tehsil Amritsar, Post Office Sathiala, Village Waraich, Dera Santan, Jaimal Singh Sant. Be absolutely sure to write this address. After buying the crystallized sugar—worth 5 rupees—it should be wrapped in a gunny sack, then packed in a box worth five or six annas, and sent here very soon, because I have now no Multani sugar left. Better still, send this person 6 rupees, or let me know about it.

In my heart I feel sorry at what Kishen Singh has done, but then I realized that he was destined to seek revenge from a previous birth, and he did his job. What does it matter that he called himself a brother? So why worry, though I am sorry that it happened—it is good that this debt is now paid off.

The day the individual being (jeevaatmaa), that is, the soul, separated from Sach Khand and the Shabd-dhun, that very day its trust in the True Lord (Sat Purush) and the Shabd-dhun was also severed. The Shabd-dhun looks after it all the time, but it does not realize this because its love and loyalties are deeply entrenched in mind and maya, and in maya's objects and the senses that deceive. But what kind of a love is this that has made it unable to understand its own loss? That loss it considers to be a gain. It is dizzy in the love of the mind, and the mind is dizzy in the pleasures of the senses. Maya has spread such a veil over it that it may never regain awareness. It does not have the slightest regret for the twenty-four thousand breaths that go to waste every day, that not a single breath can be bought at any price. From this it is evident that the being definitely has no consciousness of its self. For a few paltry pennies of maya it kneels before each and every insignificant man, with the result that when the soul parts from the human body, the highest form of all, the being goes wandering into the hell of eighty-four. So have full faith in the words of the Satguru, my son. These words are specifically of the Lord himself. The Satguru, attaching the disciple again to the same Shabd-dhun, will guide him back to Sach Khand. So the disciple's trust that remained broken in life after life has been restored by the Satguru.

On this point, there is a line in *Sri Guru Granth Sahib*: "The sundered of countless births He knots" *(Janam janam kaa tootaa gaadai)*.[14] I have written only a little as I did not have time to write more. Please understand it carefully. Do not think, "This thing should be given to me", or "This man was junior to me. Just see, now that he has been promoted, he hasn't even come to see me!", or "Why has the Lord not given it to me?" Such fretful thoughts and false desires should never be allowed into the mind. Rather, you should think: "For myself, I want only love and faith for the Lotus Feet of the Satguru. I should stay within his will. Let me look upon it this way: everyone is burning in the fire of maya; all are roasting in it day and night. Then why do I also beg for that?" The Satguru, my son, is the saviour who pulls us safely from the fire of mind and maya. We should have unshakeable love for him. We are never to go outside his words. "Only that which is written on my forehead will be given to me"—nothing more is to be desired. Whatever worldly work the Satguru considers appropriate, he will do it well. Do not worry about it at all. You must realize that with each and every breath he is always by our side.

Five rupees of Babu Hari Ram have been received and credited to the bhandara. Radha Soami greetings to everybody. May grace and mercy be upon the whole family of Babu Hari Ram. Blessings of grace and mercy upon all the satsangis. Radha Soami from Bibi to you, her dear brother. Please also convey Bibi's Radha Soami to all the satsangis. Also, Radha Soami greetings from all the sadhus at the Dera to all of you. Listen daily to the Shabd-dhun, my son, and do your bhajan and simran every day.

15 May 1899

Radha Soami. Radha Soami Ji is the Comforter.

Radha Soami greetings with grace and mercy in abundance from Jaimal Singh to my obedient son, Babu Sawan Singh, Pritam Singh, and to all the other satsangis in Murree Hills. I am well in every respect, and always pray to the compassionate Hazur for your well-being. Your letter has been received and I am very happy and gratified to read the request you made in it. Your request, my son, has been accepted at the Lotus Feet of the compassionate Hazur.

As the bhandara is definitely going to be held here at the Dera on the 15th of Asarh, I will not be coming now. I will come after the bhandara and will send you a letter five days before I come. I will come first to Sunny Bank and then let you know further. The money has been sent to Agra. All the satsangis are of the opinion that a bhandara must be held here. So I will go to Agra in Kartik—I cannot ignore the satsangis' unanimous view. The rest I will write and let you know how it all turns out.

There was a delay in writing this letter because I was not at the Dera, and then for four or five days I could not find the time to write. Please do keep an eye out for a job for Meya Singh and let me know whenever an opening comes up.

You wrote that "One day my work will finish, but when will that day arrive?" You should see what *Sri Guru Granth Sahib* says in this respect. It says that when the perfect Satguru has been found, and with it the whole secret of the saints' path, then nothing further remains to be done. The task was finished right then and there. So no other path is left to be trodden, because no other task remains to be done. Only that as long as any worldly affairs—taking from some or giving to others—are still to be finished, the inner attention will catch the Shabd-dhun infrequently. The barrier of karma will not be broken until the account with the world is settled. That is why the Sant Satguru takes the soul across the barrier of karma only after completing the account right here, so that it may not be born again. If any debit or credit is left out, the account of past karmas will have to be cleared by taking birth again. From the day the disciple meets the perfect Satguru, all work takes place with the Satguru's permission—he is not going to give another birth. From that day forth the disciple understands that "I am nothing. All that exists belongs to the Satguru—body, mind and wealth, all belong to the Satguru. I am nothing but an instrument." That is why work performed with the body, mind and wealth will not do him any harm. So, my son, you are already in Sach Khand. The Satguru can take a soul immediately to the place that he has pronounced, if the individual's transactions with his worldly relations have been discharged. In every way I am very pleased with you. Please continue doing your bhajan and simran whenever you have time.

Please accept Bibi's warm Radha Soami greetings. My son, you are not separate from my form. This is an amazing play that cannot be understood without the perfect Satguru—merely in order to transact the affairs of the world he appears as a separate body. Radha Soami greetings from all the satsangis.

11 June 1899

~ 48 ~

Radha Soami. Radha Soami Ji is the Comforter.

Radha Soami greetings and Wahiguru Ji ki Fateh from Jaimal Singh to my obedient son, Babu Sawan Singh. May the grace and mercy of the compassionate Anami Lord always be upon you. Some parshad from Hazur's bhandara has been sent to you by parcel. It is for distribution to all the satsangis. Let me know by postcard when you receive it. The freight charges for the parcel have been paid here.

My son, please do not be cross or resentful with Chanan Singh. Advise him gently. If you see him do anything wrong intentionally, by all means replace him with someone else, but if he has not done so wilfully, then it does not matter. Have patience, because whatever has to go wrong will certainly go wrong. He will do better the next time. Anyway, handle it as you deem proper since he is a satsangi. It is not right to get angry with him from the heart. Other than for important work, it is not advisable to disturb him when he is sitting in meditation. But if there is such work, then do not hesitate to call him. I will be coming for a visit by 13 July. If I do not come by that date, then I won't be coming at all.

5 July 1899

~ ~

Radha Soami. Radha Soami Ji is the Comforter.

Radha Soami greetings from Jaimal Singh to my obedient son, Babu Sawan Singh, and to Babu Hari Ram, Babu Mohan Singh, Malik Thakar Das, Babu Gajja Singh, Basant Singh, Narain Singh, Amar Singh, and the younger Bibi Ji. May his grace and mercy be upon all of you. I was very happy to receive your letter and know about your well-being.

Without the Satguru's refuge, the being (*jeev*) can achieve nothing. Whatever spiritual goal is to be attained will be through the grace and mercy of the Satguru. But the being is exceedingly impure, so all the time, every single day, he has to live within the Satguru's refuge and his will.

Chanan Singh is still at the Dera. He will leave for home on Monday, 2 October, and return to Khairagali, he says, in a month. You have subscribed to the *Khalsa Akhbar* for me. How much did you pay for it? I returned the single issue that arrived here in the name of Jawala Singh Sant—I would have kept it, had it been in my name. Since then there has been no word from them. I will accept it for the period for which you have subscribed, provided they send it under my name. Please write to them that since the correct name is Jaimal Singh, why was it sent to Jawala Singh?

The situation of the brick-kiln: water is not available because it has not rained here at all. Even the maize crop had to be planted by irrigating from the well. The well is working day and night, and still there is not enough water. We were told that we can use the well after the ploughed fields have been irrigated and the wheat crop sown. It is a matter of two or three months; the work on the kiln will start as soon as we get water.

Ghee is indeed very expensive here, but Bibi was determined to send you fresh ghee. How can we place a price on that? We, too, eat it here. I sent it to you because I look upon you as my own son. A value cannot be placed on that, just as bread and water belong to the Satguru but are beyond price. However, if you insist, send whatever you think appropriate, but only up to, or less than, 20 rupees, no more than that.

I am very pleased with you, my son. This separation is for a short while. Have no doubt: it will happen just as you have written, that your soul should never part from the real form, the Shabd-dhun. There are some debits and credits still to be settled, that's why there is a delay. I am very pleased that you hold satsang on Sundays, and also that you sit in bhajan for two or three hours. Advise your mind that its actions are not within the instructions of the Satguru. Whatever is done according to the instructions of the Satguru is the Satguru's work and is spiritual in nature. However little it may be, it will account for a lot. Here is an illustration for you to understand: if a field is sown with seed after timely ploughing and watering, each grain of that seed multiplies into a handful. Some wheat stalks even sprout sixty or seventy clusters, that is, ears of wheat, from a single grain. Sometimes a single grain grows into a kilogram of grain. However, if similar grains of seed are sown in barren soil, even the seed itself is lost. So whatever the mind does—the doubts it raises, the arguments it advances, the evil deeds it perpetrates, and the sensual pleasures it indulges in—is like sowing seed in barren soil. One should never desire such worldly things, my son. Rather one should always stay within the will of the Satguru. Whatever the Lord is to give a human being has already been given before his birth. To indulge now in low desires and thinking, or in false fruitless actions, is aimlessly wasting time. Nothing comes of such desires and reflections. If one were to put them all

aside to follow the Guru's teaching and keep oneself attached to
the Shabd-dhun, one would become entirely spiritual. The lines
from *"Ratan Mala," Sri Guru Granth Sahib,* are:

> Rare is the person who has realized the Lord;
> As also the one who retains Him in the mind.
> *Kot kotantar tat kaa baitaa;*
> *Gagan mandal me raakhe chaitaa.*[15]

We call *baitaa* the soul that after reaching Sach Khand comes
back with His command. The fruit that that soul received upon
reaching Sach Khand through the practice of the Shabd-dhun is
the same which in this age is received by the individual whose attention is absorbed in the inner universe. Then you, too, my son,
should keep the Lord in the inner mind, and consider it your
great good fortune that your human body has borne fruit.

Radha Soami from Bibi and all the satsangis at the Dera.
Radha Soami from Chanan Singh. Bibi's Radha Soami to you,
her dear brother. I am out of writing paper, my son. Listen to the
Shabd-dhun every day and give it true love and affection. Basant
Singh of your village came here; he went back after getting another
person initiated. This, my son, is in reply to your last two letters.

2 October 1899

∼ 50 ∼

[Dictated]

Radha Soami. Radha Soami Ji is the Comforter.

From Jaimal Singh: Radha Soami greetings to my obedient son
Babu Sawan Singh. I received your letter and was happy, indeed
delighted, to read it. Your money order of 20 rupees has also
been received—please have no worry. Keep doing your bhajan

and simran; grace and mercy will be upon you. Please convey Radha Soami greetings to Chanan Singh, Basant Singh, Narain Singh, Gajja Singh, and Sunder Singh. You need not have taken so much trouble in sending the 20 rupees so quickly. The money was not that badly needed and could have awaited your visit here.

You write that I should bring the books when I come. My coming is no longer possible; I will explain the situation personally when you come here. Continue with your bhajan and simran and keep the Lord in mind. I am very sure that I cannot come to Murree Hills. I can find no way to do it. Whenever I make up my mind to leave, some new command intervenes, which is impossible to explain. So you should now come yourself, and give darshan as well as receive darshan! I repeat: if it is Hazur's will that I come to Murree Hills, I will do so at once; otherwise I am helpless in this matter.

Please accept Radha Soami from Bibi to you, her true and dear brother; Radha Soami also from everyone else at the Dera. Continue doing bhajan and simran all the time. Whenever the mind thinks of inner darshan, the Shabd-dhun is at your service. Just attach your attention to it and you will receive the benefit of darshan—you will receive its fruit to the extent that your heart yearns for it.

[no date] 1899

~ 51 ~

[Dictated]

Radha Soami. Radha Soami Ji is the Comforter.

From Jaimal Singh: Radha Soami greetings to my obedient son, Babu Sawan Singh. This is to let you know that Chanan Singh arrived at the Dera from his home on 14 October 1899. There is some work for him, so he will stay here for ten days and reach your place on 24 or 25 October. Please carry on as best as you can in his absence. He has some urgent work to do here, that's why he has been asked to stay. Another point: the Gurmukhi *Khalsa Akhbar* people were asking me for 3 rupees and 14 annas. You wrote that you had paid the amount. If you have already paid, why are they asking me for money? Bibi's Radha Soami to you, her dear brother.

16 October 1899

∼ 52 ∼

Radha Soami. Radha Soami Ji is the Comforter.

Radha Soami greetings from Jaimal Singh to my obedient son, Babu Sawan Singh, and to Babu Hari Ram, Gajja Singh, Basant Singh, Narain Singh, Amar Singh, Malik Thakar Das Ji, and to all others. I received your 20 rupees on 30 October. Chanan Singh is with me at the Dera. Because of the heavy rush for Diwali, it has not been possible for him to catch a train to Amritsar. A seat will be available on 5 or 6 November, and he will reach your place without delay. Chanan Singh is not at fault; getting a seat on a train is not possible at this time. Please try to manage the best you can, my son. I will send a reply to your letter through Chanan Singh; in this letter I am being brief. Your last letter was very good; it was a pleasure to read it.

You wrote that if bhajan were to yield its bliss, the path would begin to open up. That is the entreaty I make to my Satguru day and night, that the path may please be opened up, but so far no reply has come. Have firm faith that one day you will reach Sach Khand. Please accept Radha Soami from Bibi to you, her dear brother.

30 October 1899

Radha Soami. Radha Soami Ji is the Comforter.

Radha Soami greetings from Jaimal Singh to my obedient son, Babu Sawan Singh, and to Babu Hari Ram, Babu Gajja Singh, Basant Singh, Malik Thakar Das Ji, Amar Singh, and the younger Bibi Ji. May the grace and mercy of the Anami Lord, Radha Soami, always be upon all of you. I have received your two letters and am very happy to read them and know their contents. Of course I am always ready to go to Agra. Whenever he wills it, I am ready. We will definitely go there, my son, but when it is his will.

About the brick-kiln, I wrote to you earlier that water is not yet available. We will get water in Phagun, at which time the kiln will be stacked. If it rains earlier, we will start making bricks right away. There is no other delay. Chanan Singh left here on 7 November. He had asked to be allowed to stay at the Dera for two or three months to do seva (he has done very good seva here) and I was agreeable to that, but you also could not do without him, so he should now stay with you—that is doing my seva. Whenever he requests permission to come to the Dera, you should give it; he can have darshan and then return. Handle this whichever way he remains happy. By all means let him do spiritual work if he so desires. You are to attend to your meditation every day. When you persevere in this practice, His grace will surely descend upon you one day. Keep lying before His door, my son; you may be called anytime. Hasty work is Satan's work.

Moreover, the Shabd-dhun is the very essence of the Anami Lord, and it is resounding within you all the time. When it pleases him to merge the soul within himself, he will do so in an instant. When the soul is as pure as the Shabd-dhun, there won't

be even a moment's delay. Ever since the material world was created the mind and soul have been gathering dirt. Never for a
spell of ten or twenty years has the soul been fixed in the Shabd-
dhun for seven or eight hours. How can it then find a place in
the Dhun so soon? Until the soul has intense longing for the
Dhun night and day, how can it merge into the Dhun? Submit
yourself and practise daily the technique imparted to you, because the Shabd-dhun Guru is anxious to purify your soul and
mind without delay. He showers such grace and mercy that not
even for a moment does he forget the time when the soul that he
has awakened through the Shabd-dhun will become pure so that
by merging it within his Shabd-dhun form he can take it to Sach
Khand. So ask for the Guru's refuge, and love his Lotus Feet.
Whenever you beg for something, my son, beg for the Holy Feet
of the Satguru. When the higher mind and the soul forge an inner union with the Satguru's Holy Feet, the Shabd-dhun merges
them both within itself. Surely one day you will join me, my son.
The Satguru's Holy Feet are in Sach Khand; you will definitely
reach there. Do not be afraid—there are no more births now.

[7 November 1899]

54

[Dictated]

Radha Soami. Radha Soami Ji is the Comforter.

From Jaimal Singh: Radha Soami greetings to Babu Sawan
Singh. I received your letter and was happy to read it and know
of your well-being. Your letter to the village land assessor
(*patwari*) was also received and passed on to him. My reply to
you has been delayed because I was absent from the Dera. This
letter is not being written in Gurmukhi because I have been down

with catarrh, but now I am all right, so do not worry. You have written that "I made a slip; please forgive me." Forgiveness will be given when you come here. Do not have any worry; his grace and mercy is upon you every single day. The money order for 5 rupees has been received. Every day keep the inner faculties of surat and nirat alert and continue to observe the guidance that comes from within. Grace and mercy is reaching you all the time. Make the attentive faculties of the soul a receptacle to receive the radiance of the grace and mercy that is coming from the Shabd-dhun. Then everything will become clear by itself. Keep the ideal of a perfect disciple always before you.

Radha Soami greetings from Bibi Ji and myself to Babu Hari Ram, Chanan Singh, Malik Thakar Das, Babu Gajja Singh, Basant Singh, Amar Singh, the younger Bibi, and Narain Singh. Also Radha Soami greetings from Bhai Jiwan Singh. A man named Harchand Singh arrived at the Dera from Quetta on 27 November. It was learnt from him that Pritam Singh would be arriving here on 28 November 1899, but so far he has not shown up. Let's see if he comes tomorrow. Please accept Radha Soami from Bibi Ji—but Bibi is somewhat displeased.

27 November 1899

~ 55 ~

Radha Soami. Radha Soami Ji is the Comforter.

Radha Soami greetings from Jaimal Singh to my obedient son, Babu Sawan Singh. I have received two of your letters: one in Gurmukhi, and another in Urdu to be forwarded to Milkhi Ram. This has been done. In your letter to me you have requested to be forgiven for the lapse—the compassionate Hazur

has forgiven you. May his grace and mercy always be upon you.
I am very pleased with you, my son. I feel that ten days' leave
will be enough: two days at Agra, and two or three days at home,
and everything will be done. This will also enable you to have
darshan. Is Ma Ji coming along for darshan? Please let me know
immediately. It would be good if Chanan Singh also were to
come, but only if your household work could be carried on in his
absence. If some other responsible person is there to look after
the goods in your residence, then Chanan Singh can also come—
the day you get leave, proceed directly to Agra at once—but if
no responsible person like Chanan Singh is available, ask him to
stay behind to look after the household and the horse. He can
then be taken to the bhandara in the month of Asarh. But first of
all let me know, now that you have come to Rawalpindi, which
department will you be working in? And also, under some officer
or independently? I have understood what is going on back
home, that your son is ill. This is his will, my son. Pain and pleasure come and go; he will be merciful.

Do your bhajan and simran every day. It would be extremely
beneficial to first listen to the very subtle, barely audible sound of
the bell, and partly also of the conch, at the point behind the
eyes. Directing both the inner hearing and seeing faculties, listen
gently and infix this sound of the Shabd-dhun—just as we listen
to a distant sound by concentrating on it. Listen! but do not be
in a hurry. Listen every day. His grace and mercy will always be
upon you. Please consider this brief note in its full import. You
have done very well to have acquired the books.

Please convey Radha Soami greetings to Chanan Singh,
Babu Gajja Singh, Basant Singh, Malik Thakar Das, Babu
Hari Ram, and to the younger Bibi Ji. Bibi's Radha Soami to
you, her dear brother, and to all the satsangis. Pritam Singh
brought Kishen Singh to my residence at night and, leaving him

here, himself stole away at eight o'clock the same night. Kishen Singh has been initiated, he is now a satsangi. He was telling me that the names of both of them have been struck off the service roll. I told him that he should be able to find work elsewhere. He was saying that he has to go to Murree Hills to visit you. Has he come there or not? I repeat: try as far as possible to bring Chanan Singh with you; but if other arrangements are not possible, Chanan Singh should stay behind. However, if some other responsible person is at hand, then definitely bring him along. If not, then it can't be helped—Chanan Singh will have to stay at your residence to take care of your things. Nihal Singh has arrived at the Dera from your place.

7 December [1899]

~ 56 ~

[Dictated]

Radha Soami. Radha Soami Ji is the Comforter.

From Jaimal Singh: Radha Soami greetings and blessings of grace and mercy to Babu Sawan Singh, and to Babu Gajja Singh, Chanan Singh, Basant Singh, Babu Hari Ram, and the younger Bibi Ji. Your postcard was received and I was happy to read it. Grace and mercy be upon you. When the army personnel come, please give them some of the parshad for the sevadars.

When you sit in meditation, continually give love and devotion to the Satguru's real form, the Shabd, with both the inner faculties of the soul, surat and nirat. Do not ask for anything. Remain present at his Holy Feet, and the moment he considers you fit, he will bless you with grace and mercy. Radha Soami from Bibi Ji and from all the satsangis.

14 January 1900

~ 57 ~

Radha Soami. Radha Soami Ji is the Comforter.

Radha Soami greetings from Jaimal Singh to my obedient son, Babu Sawan Singh, and to Basant Singh, Babu Gajja Singh, Chanan Singh, Babu Gulab Singh, Babu Hari Ram, and the younger Bibi Ji. May the grace and mercy of the compassionate Hazur always be upon you all. I received your letter; it was well written and I was happy to read it. It was indeed a very good letter. I have already sent a letter addressed to Babu Hari Ram with all the news from here, so please read it. Someone has come here from Quetta to be initiated. He belongs to the South and is a Subedar in the army. He will stay at the Dera for a month. If possible, I will come to visit you after he leaves. I definitely plan to visit and will write to you later on. Please continue daily with your bhajan and simran. Radha Soami greetings from Bibi and everyone else here. I do plan to come even if that person does not leave. Please help Babu Mohan Singh with some words of comfort. I am writing a postcard to you because I have so little spare time.

5 February 1900

~ 58 ~

Radha Soami. Radha Soami Ji is the Comforter.

Radha Soami greetings from Jaimal Singh to my obedient son, Babu Sawan Singh. Dear son, I am leaving here by the mail train on 12 February at eleven o'clock at night, and will arrive at Rawalpindi on the 13th at eleven o'clock in the morning. Someone should be at the railway station to receive me. Alternatively, I will leave here on 13 February by the 1 p.m. mail train. Then someone should be there at three o'clock at night. I shall stay for seven days, returning to the Dera on 21 February. Radha Soami to Basant Singh, Babu Gajja Singh Ji, Chanan Singh Ji, Babu Hari Ram, and the younger Bibi Ji from myself, Bibi, and the sadhus at the Dera. May Hazur's grace and mercy always be upon you. Please remember to send someone to the railway station.

12 February 1900

~ 59 ~

[Dictated]

Radha Soami. Radha Soami Ji is the Comforter.

From Jaimal Singh: Radha Soami greetings to my obedient son, Babu Sawan Singh, and to Babu Hari Ram, Babu Gajja Singh, Chanan Singh, and Basant Singh. May the grace and mercy of the compassionate Hazur be upon everyone. I received your postcard and was very happy to read it. The invoice for the tarpaulins was received, and all six have been collected from the railway station. The brick contractor was given an advance. That was twelve days ago, but he has not yet shown up. I hear that his men are making bricks elsewhere and that they will be here in eight days.

Please keep doing bhajan and simran every day for whatever time the mind remains attached to the Shabd-dhun and the soul hears and enjoys its bliss. Then even a minute or two, or five, are sufficient, and the task is done. Have firm faith; the worldly obligations you are fulfilling are all essentially spiritual. Do not allow the self to intrude; everything is the Satguru's work. Radha Soami from Bibi to you, her dear brother. Please convey Radha Soami greetings from Bibi Ji to everyone else at your place, and also from the Subedar and all others at the Dera. This letter was written in Urdu because of lack of time.

22 March 1900

Radha Soami. Radha Soami Ji is the Comforter.

Radha Soami greetings from Jaimal Singh to my obedient son,
Babu Sawan Singh, and to Babu Hari Ram, Babu Gajja
Singh, Chanan Singh, Basant Singh, Babu Gulab Singh, and
the younger Bibi Ji. May his grace and mercy always be upon
everyone. This is to let you know, my son, that we have now
started making the bricks: ten to twelve brickmakers are employed in moulding them, and 10,000 bricks have already been
made.

Do your bhajan and simran every day, my son. Two instalments of 50 rupees each should be sent here within a week because we need to buy firewood and dried cow-dung fuel very
soon. I am unable to write much at this time. Do write about
yourself.

The blessing in this age of Kaliyug is that with a longing
born of an unshakeable trust in the Satguru as the Anami Lord,
if the mind attaches the inner hearing and seeing faculties to the
Shabd-dhun for an hour, a half-hour, a quarter-hour, or for ten,
five, or even one minute, even then you will reach Sach Khand.
So do your bhajan and simran every day—they are not to be
omitted. Whether or not the mind is there, the daily routine is not
to be interrupted unless you are utterly helpless. I am very
pleased with you. Perform your official duties diligently; there is
plenty of time for bhajan and simran. As far as possible, imbibe
the spirit of devotion to the Guru. Surrender everything to the
Shabd. Inside and outside, all is He. The reality inside is the
Nam of Sach Khand, and all that is below Sach Khand,
whether gross or subtle, lustrous or earthly, Brahmand or Anda,
is perishable. Shabd-dhun is both in Sach Khand and outside it.
Shabd-surat alone is the doer of all deeds, but by descending

into the illusory creation, maya, the soul has separated from the Shabd. Since the beginning of time, layers of illusion have come to envelope it. To return to our home, my son, there is no means other than listening to the Sound.

Radha Soami from Bibi to you, her dear brother. Please also convey Radha Soami from Bibi and the sadhus at the Dera to all the satsangis there with you.

I have no time to compose a letter properly. May, his grace and mercy always be upon everyone. Subedar has left but he will go via Agra, stopping there for darshan. He sent Radha Soami greetings to all of you.

You have become worthy of Sach Khand. Stay firm in your devotion and true love for the Satguru; never lose faith in him. This, my son, is the real work—to stay always within his will.

30 March [1900]

∼ 61 ∼

Radha Soami. Radha Soami Ji is the Comforter.

Radha Soami greetings from Jaimal Singh to my obedient son, Babu Sawan Singh. May the grace and mercy of the compassionate immortal Lord, Anami Radha Soami, always be upon you. Your letter in Urdu arrived with the news that Basant Singh's son had passed away. This is his will, my son; it had to happen like this. He will be merciful.

I was pleased to hear the rest of the news, and did not reply earlier as I was waiting for the money order. Your letter has now been received along with two money orders of 50 rupees each, for a total of 100 rupees. I was very happy to read the letter. You ask if any inconvenience was caused by the late dispatch of the money. The money, my son, was received in good time; there was no delay. I am very pleased indeed. Babu Hari Ram's money order of 5 rupees has also been received, so please let Babu Hari Ram know.

The news of the brick-kiln is that 60,000 bricks have been moulded and stacked inside it. The kiln will take 50,000 more. The brickmakers mould 5,000 to 6,000 bricks every day. The kiln will use fuel—dried cow-dung and firewood—worth 150 rupees. You wrote that had you not left Kalabagh, you could have gone to Murree Hills to send the money. No, you should never feel such remorse. The government work is to be done first. What has happened had to happen. Never again feel such remorse.

Do your bhajan and simran every day and do not get perturbed when the workload becomes excessive. At such a time, fix your attention in the Satguru's Holy Feet and start your simran. Be patient. Then since the doer of every deed is the Lord himself, he will do the work as he wishes.

I was very happy to read your letter. Please convey Radha Soami greetings to Babu Gajja Singh Ji, Chanan Singh, Basant Singh, Narain Singh, Diwan Singh and Babu Hari Ram. Bibi's Radha Soami to you, her dear brother, and also to the other satsangis. Radha Soami from all the sadhus at the Dera to you and all the other satsangis.

Please note, my son, that I would like you to send an additional 100 rupees here by 8 May. My intention is to buy 25 or 30 rupees' worth of wheat for the Dera from your earnings. The rest will go to the expense of the brick-kiln. After that no more money need be sent here as there are no other expenses. I have to leave on 17 April to draw my pension, which is why this letter has been written early.

As you sit in meditation, my son, at that time along with repetition and concentration of the inner hearing and seeing faculties, bring the Satguru's form to the mind. Then slowly and gently listen to the Sound with rapt attention, binding the soul through an intense love for the Shabd-dhun—tie the mind and the attention tightly into the melody, and listen to it. This will yield inner bliss.

Please convey Bhag Singh's Radha Soami to all and everyone. He has come on two months' leave and is now at the Dera. Do not have any worry, my son; everything will work out well.

18 April [1900]

~ 62 ~

Radha Soami. Radha Soami Ji is the Comforter.

Radha Soami greetings from Jaimal Singh to my obedient son, Babu Sawan Singh, and to Basant Singh, Babu Gajja Singh, Chanan Singh, Diwan Singh, Babu Hari Ram, and all the other satsangis. May the grace and mercy of the compassionate Anami Lord be upon everyone. Dear son, I have received a money order for 10 rupees, which will be credited to the expense of the brick-kiln. A postcard and 5 rupees from Babu Hari Ram have also been received. I will give a name to the boy later, in two months' time. I am extremely busy these days, and so am unable to write much. The brick-kiln keeps me very busy.

Please do your bhajan and simran every day. Discarding all worldly desires, with love and devotion keep only the desire for the Satguru's Holy Feet in your mind and listen to the Shabd-dhun. No worldly desire should remain in the mind while the inner faculties of surat and nirat are fixed in the Shabd-dhun. Bibi's Radha Soami to you, her dear brother. Radha Soami also from Bibi and all the sadhus at the Dera to all the satsangis at your place. It continues to be very cloudy and wet these days.

20 April 1900

≈ 63 ≈

Radha Soami. Radha Soami Ji is the Comforter.

Radha Soami greetings from Jaimal Singh to my obedient son, Babu Sawan Singh, and to all the other satsangis. May the grace and mercy of the immortal Anami Lord always be upon everyone. This is to let you know that as of 10 May I have received two instalments of 50 rupees each, and that they have been spent on the brick-kiln. The overall expenditure on the kiln has come to 285 rupees; additionally, 5 or 6 rupees more will be needed. The brick-kiln was fired on 8 May; I will write later about how the bricks have turned out.

I received your letter, and also a letter from Babu Hari Ram and another from Bachint Singh, as well as news in person from the painter, Nabi Bakhsh. I was very happy to read the letters. It is good that you have sent money to Bachint Singh; he should now come home. The postcard received from Agra has been forwarded to you. Chacha Ji has commanded that we come to Agra. For the rest, we are happy in the will of Hazur in this. There are said to be checkposts at railway stations on the way. Please apply for leave: if you get it, we'll go; if not, we will send money—this is for your information.

You have written that you should be forgiven. Lord Radha Soami Ji, by forgiving all your sins, will most certainly take you to Sach Khand by the path of Shabd-dhun. Keep doing your bhajan and simran every day. When you sit in bhajan, do not keep any worldly business in the mind, nor should you ever worry about anything during that time. Radha Soami from Bibi and the sadhus at the Dera. Let me know if Babu Hari Ram has arrived from Rawalpindi. This postcard is brief as I could not write a full account and just wanted to give you the news. Please convey my Radha Soami to both the Bibi Jis.

10 May 1900

~ 64 ~

Radha Soami. Radha Soami Ji is the Comforter.

From Jaimal Singh: Radha Soami greetings to my obedient son, Babu Sawan Singh, and to all the other satsangis and their families. May the grace and mercy of the compassionate Hazur always be upon all of you. Your letter has been received and I was happy to read its contents. A letter has been received from Bachint Singh, as also one from Basant Singh's in-laws. I was happy to read all three letters. His will is like this, my son. I have noted your thoughts on going to the bhandara, and also about the post-wedding ceremony (*muklaavaa*) of Basant Singh. First, about Basant Singh's ceremony: by all means agree to it and send Basant Singh to his in-laws....

You should also arrange leave for the bhandara, which is on Thursday, 14 June, the 1st of Asarh. You must accompany us. So please arrange leave for four days before the bhandara and for three days afterwards. Any extra days will be for your stay at your village. Anyway, think it over and act as you think proper. Please take leave as we must go to Agra. And do not send the 200 rupees to Agra, because I have already sent your 100 rupees which were left in my care. I have also sent there an additional 30 rupees and about 455 kilograms of wheat by parcel for the bhandara. A total of 200 rupees has to be given. Therefore, bring with you a 100-rupee note; the 100 rupees already sent to Agra was also your money. The total contribution of 200 rupees may fall short by 40 or 50 rupees; it will be made up when we reach Agra. The money may be sent here or brought along when you come. Please see that your leave does not expire before the bhandara—keep this in mind. Send a wire or letter to Bachint Singh at his exact address so that he may receive the money and return home. I will go to the bhandara only if you come. For the rest, my son, we should remain happy in the will of Hazur. In case you have no leave time left to come to the bhandara, take the leave in the month of Kartik....Is it possible to arrange some other date before or after Nimani, say, a day or two before or after it? In my view, if the post-wedding ceremony cannot be arranged for 8, 9, or 10 June, then it should be postponed so that it does not conflict with our visit to the bhandara. Please keep in mind that we have to attend the bhandara.

It was thoughtless of Bachint Singh to give the whole island of Singapore as his address, instead of sending a proper address. A letter or money order could only reach him if he were to give his exact address. The Lord himself is doing what he wishes to be done; it is all for the good. Please continue doing your bhajan and simran every day.

Please convey my Radha Soami greetings to Basant Singh, Chanan Singh, Babu Gajja Singh, Narain Singh, Diwan Singh, Sher Singh, Babu Hari Ram, Malik Thakar Das, the elder and younger Bibi Ji, to Gursharan and all the others. Radha Soami from Bibi to you, her dear brother. You must come for the bhandara—we have to go. Convey Bibi's Radha Soami to all the satsangis. Pali's Radha Soami with folded hands to everyone. Radha Soami from all the sadhus at the Dera to Babu Ji and to all the satsangis. May his grace and mercy always be upon everyone.

What more is there to write, my son? Whatever Hazur does will be for our good. Remember to do your bhajan; reply soon. Whichsoever way the compassionate Radha Soami Ji wishes it, is all for our good. It is a request from all of us that you come for the bhandara. However, if the date of the post-wedding ceremony has to be changed, then please do so with the consent of the other family. At present they are in very straitened circumstances; we should do what pleases them.

27 May [1900]

~ 65 ~

Radha Soami. Radha Soami Ji is the Comforter.

Radha Soami greetings from Jaimal Singh to my obedient son, Babu Sawan Singh. Dear son, I received your letter of 12 June, redirected from Agra, and was very happy to read it, but it says nothing about Bachint Singh. You should have written about him, my son. You are thinking of coming on leave. It is very hot in Panjab, and also, in Asuj or Kartik, you will need to take leave for Basant Singh's post-wedding ceremony. So apply for leave at this time only if you can get it for both occasions. The bhandara at the Dera is going to be held on Thursday, the 29th of Asarh, the full-moon day. So come if you can get leave. I understand that Gursharan drinks too much milk and then, unable to digest it all, throws it up. Try to give him some other, more agreeable milk.

Radha Soami greetings to all the satsangis, including both the Bibi Jis. All should do their bhajan and simran every day. Radha Soami greetings from Bibi and all the sadhus here.

30 June 1900

~ 66 ~

Radha Soami. Radha Soami Ji is the Comforter.

Radha Soami greetings from Jaimal Singh to my obedient son, Babu Sawan Singh. May the grace and mercy of the compassionate Hazur always be upon you. I have received your letter and am very happy to read it and learn of your well-being. I will give you the reply when I come to your place. I will take the twelve o'clock or one o'clock train on Tuesday, 25 July, so please send horses to Ghoragali on the 26th. They should reach there by two or three o'clock. We could then reach Khairagali by nightfall. I will also send a telegram at the time of departure. Bibi and I both will be coming. We won't stay for more than eight days. Please convey my Radha Soami greetings to Babu Hari Ram, Babu Mohan Singh, Chanan Singh, Basant Singh, and the elder Bibi Ji and younger Bibi Ji. It is up to you if you wish to send a tonga to pick me up, but that will be very expensive. We will reach there at three or four o'clock at night, the scheduled time of the train's arrival. For the rest, it will happen according to Hazur's will. Radha Soami from Bibi and all the sadhus at the Dera.

23 July 1900

～ 67 ～

Radha Soami. Radha Soami Ji is the Comforter.

Radha Soami from Jaimal Singh to my obedient son, Babu Sawan Singh, and to Basant Singh, Babu Gajja Singh Ji, Babu Gulab Singh, Narain Singh, Chanan Singh Ji, Diwan Singh, Babu Hari Ram, Malik Thakar Das Ji, the elder Bibi Ji and the younger Bibi Ji, and to all the other satsangis. May the grace and mercy of the compassionate Anami, Hazur Radha Soami, always be upon everyone. My dear son, I have received the money order for 5 rupees as well as a letter, which I am very happy to have read. I am not going to write much, since you mention that you will be coming here on ten days' leave on 6 September. We have the limestone ready for the construction, which will start soon, in the beginning of the month of Asuj.

It would be all right if you have to go to Attock. You could then take leave next year, and also oversee the construction of the outer guest-house yourself. Let me know soon. When you receive this letter, write a postcard immediately about the date on which you will take the train. I will then send someone to the railway station—that's the reason for this letter. Also, the location of the buildings has been changed: the four small rooms and the veranda will be constructed in a field opposite the one where you had asked for the meditation cell to be built.* But you should personally come and select the site to your liking. If you get leave, then please do come.

I have not written much in anticipation of your visit. All the requests that you made in your letter have been accepted in the court of Hazur. One day you will definitely reach your home, Sach Khand, Alakh, Agam, Anami, the true residence of Radha Soami. Bhajan and simran are to be done daily, my son. This is a command for all of you, because you mark your presence in the court of the Lord when you listen to the Shabd-dhun every day. The sound of the Shabd-dhun is the spiritual cord of the Anami Being. It is doing everything through its presence within the body of each individual. He who has met with a perfect Master and has been handed the cord of Shabd-dhun—his daily effort is registered in Sach Khand every day. Your firm faith in the Shabd-dhun will take you home one day. Have absolute faith in the Satguru's words that he will take you there one day—but please keep doing your bhajan and simran.

Bibi's Radha Soami to you, her dear brother. Radha Soami also to all the other satsangis from Bibi. Please accept Radha Soami from all the sadhus at the Dera. Please send a postcard immediately if you are coming on leave.

28 August [1900]

---

* Meditation cell: *see* Glossary.

Radha Soami. Radha Soami Ji is the Comforter.

Radha Soami from Jaimal Singh to my obedient son, Babu Sawan Singh, and to Basant Singh, Chanan Singh, Babu Gajja Singh Ji, Babu Gulab Singh, Narain Singh, Diwan Singh, Babu Hari Ram, Malik Thakar Das Ji, the elder Bibi Ji, the younger Bibi Ji, and the boy, Gursharan. May the grace and mercy of the compassionate Hazur always be upon all of you. You are all urged to do your bhajan and simran every day whenever you are free. Dear son, your letter has arrived and I am happy to have read it. Please send the money now so that the building can be constructed. Two hundred rupees are needed soon to purchase the timber and also to pay the wages of the masons and labourers. If you like, you may send 50 rupees in four instalments, but the money should arrive here soon. To receive 100 rupees I have to go to the post office, while 50 rupees can be delivered at Dera—for this reason send 50 rupees each time. We will construct five small rooms, eight feet long by eight feet wide. The veranda will be eight feet wide as well. For the rest, the construction will be done as you wish. We are now stacking the bricks at the Dera, that is to say, we are carting them in from the kiln. The limestone for making quicklime is ready to be fired in the furnace, and the construction of the building will start soon. For the roof, nine-foot beams will be split into two in order to cover the whole room. The doors we instal will be of Panjabi design. They won't be painted; no red paint is to be used.

Please do your bhajan and simran every day, my son, and always keep in mind that we have nothing here that will help us at our last moment. Nothing is going to help the individual except the Satguru, the Shabd-dhun, and his grace and mercy. So do your worldly work with the body, and the work of your real home with the mind and the inner hearing and seeing faculties of surat and nirat. Do the Satguru's real work, bhajan and simran, and do not let the pride of anything enter the mind that it is yours. No! Even if you become the king of the universe, you must realize that "I have no share in it. I am merely a labourer. Whatever is there, belongs to my Master. I am nothing." The Master's words should stay uppermost in the mind all the time: "I am nothing. I am nothing. I am nothing." Simran should continue in the mind all the time, and when at work, the Satguru's form also should always remain engraved in the mind. This business of the world has been given to you as to a servant; it is like a dream. It is your great good fortune that you have found the way to reach Sach Khand. The Satguru will one day take you there. So, leaving the self aside, make your refuge firm in him. Every day, whenever you are free, try to listen to the sound of the Shabd-dhun and do so with love and devotion.

Radha Soami from Bibi to you, her dear brother; Bibi's Radha Soami also to all the other satsangis. Radha Soami from all the sadhus at the Dera and from all the other satsangis to you, Babu Ji, and to all the other satsangis there. I have not written much as I have no free time.

7 September [1900]

~ 69 ~

Radha Soami. Radha Soami Ji is the Comforter.

Radha Soami greetings to my obedient son, Babu Sawan Singh, and to Basant Singh, Chanan Singh, Gajja Singh Ji, Babu Gulab Singh, Narain Singh, Diwan Singh, Babu Hari Ram, Malik Thakar Das Ji, and the elder Bibi Ji and the younger Bibi Ji. Love to little Gursharan. Dear son, I received the letter you sent me and was delighted to read it. We are going to build five small rooms that will be nine feet wide and ten feet long—a single large room is not conducive to bhajan, as too many people together would indulge in idle talk. At your request, I have extended each small room by one foot in width and two in length. We are building them for meditation, and not for accommodating lots of people. After this letter I will write again when all the money has been received. Long logs cannot be found, whereas ten- to twelve-foot logs are abundantly available. Also, a small roof tends to be strong. Anyway, we will do as you wish. Write soon because the construction will start presently. I have borrowed 200 rupees and started the project. Over and above this amount, send some additional money so that the building may be finished by Kartik or Maghar, but send it only in instalments of 50, and never more than that. I have purchased 30 logs for 50 rupees and 6 annas for the six-foot door frames and panels; 5 twelve-foot logs for the ceiling under the roof for 22 rupees and 8 annas; and for the roof of both the five rooms and the veranda, 60 ten-foot logs for 157 rupees and 8 annas. Thus all the wood has been purchased. You may calculate the price per log by dividing the whole amount: the total for this deodar timber has come to 230 rupees and 6 annas. Four masons and eight labourers are working on the job, and they say that the building will be ready by Kartik. Three carpenters are also working on it. One hundred rupees, in two instalments of 50 each, have been received here. More is needed soon—probably you have already sent it. I should be getting two instalments of 50 each. The rest you can understand: an additional 200 rupees are urgently required.

Radha Soami to Babu Hari Ram; also Radha Soami to Malik Thakar Das Ji, to Gursharan, and to the elder Bibi Ji and the younger Bibi Ji. A letter from Babu Hari Ram was received and I was very happy to read it. All the entreaties he made in his letter will be fulfilled, but slowly and gradually. Whatever is requested will be received from the court of the compassionate Hazur. Please do your bhajan and simran. This is the full reply to Babu Hari Ram's letter; more cannot be written.

A letter was also received from Ram Piara; I was happy to read that too. Radha Soami greetings to Ram Piara. Stay happy in whatever circumstances you are placed, my son, and keep doing bhajan and simran every day. Everything that happens only happens through his command and his will. So wait and see, do not ask for anything, and do your meditation. When it pleases him, he will call you in order to give. This is the complete answer to your letter.

And now a brief response to Babu Sawan Singh's letter. What you ask for, my son, will all be given to you, and indeed has already been allotted, but is being held in reserve by the Satguru. You alone are to be given it. A father, for instance, has a treasure in store for his son but does not give it to him prematurely. It is the son's, of course, but the father gives it only after testing him, because if it were given right away, he would squander it. The father first observes the son's loyalty and obedience. That treasure is unreal, but still it is given only after testing the son's heart. This treasure, however, is real—it will never be depleted. The whole universe may use it to achieve salvation, and still it will not run out. It abides only where the vessel is that of a perfect disciple. Therefore become such a person.

Earthly wealth has already been given to you, my son. Now turn out all worldly desires from the mind and keep the Satguru's instructions within it, and then see how everything becomes his grace and mercy. Place everything that is yours—body, mind, wealth, and the attentive faculties of surat and nirat—everything, before the Satguru. Do not claim even a tiny bit as your own. Remain watchful for his command; keep in mind the Guru's words and act accordingly. He may order you to cut grass—for you that is the highest honour. Welcome it wholeheartedly as sweetness itself. Test your mind in this manner; only then is the work complete. Sach Khand is just behind this veil, my son, it is not far away. So why get perturbed? Rest assured, you will go home. You write that you will leave both home and service in order to do bhajan. What is yours in your home, my son, and what is yours in your service, and what is yours in your wealth? Just think a little. In all these, what is there to let go of, and what is there to hang onto? This is merely a juggler's trick. The world, my son, is a dream. You write that you haven't talked with anyone about money so that you may not become proud. What is there to be proud of, my son?

[September] 1900

Radha Soami. Radha Soami Ji is the Comforter.

Radha Soami from Jaimal Singh to my obedient son, Babu Sawan Singh. May the grace and mercy of the compassionate Anami Lord, Radha Soami, always be upon you, dear son. I have received 100 rupees in two instalments of 50 each. A plan of the rooms was also received; I have gone through it and have tried to understand it as much as I could. The stairs have been built in the veranda, alongside the wall of the small room that is towards the meditation cell. For the rest, your plan is quite good and was well prepared. The construction work is underway. The rains have been heavy. It rained for three days and three nights, so the work was interrupted for two days, but has now begun again. We have bought one hundred logs at an auction for 2 rupees, 10 annas per log. The total came to 262 rupees and 8 annas. They are ten feet long each. Another thirty logs, each six feet long, have cost us 50 rupees and 6 annas. The grand total for the wood is 312 rupees and 14 annas. We have overbought, because ordinarily a ten-foot log costs 3¼ rupees, while these have been bought at the cheap rate of 2 rupees and 10 annas each. If some are left over, we will sell them. I have paid for them by borrowing 200 rupees from Parmanand. So please send a draft of 200 rupees to Parmanand at this address: Parmanand Bajaj and Durga Das, Village Kahne Dhilwan, District Jalandhar, Kapurthala State, Post Office Kahne Dhilwan—the sub-district is also Kahne Dhilwan in that state. You may send it in both their names, or only to Parmanand Bajaj. Actually it should be sent in Parmanand's name. Please send it very soon, because he was in great need of money and I had him delay a transaction in order to loan it to me.

My love to Basant Singh, Chanan Singh, Babu Gajja Singh Ji, Babu Gulab Singh Ji, Narain Singh, Diwan Singh, Babu Hari Ram, the elder Bibi Ji, the younger Bibi Ji, and the boy, Gursharan, and also my Radha Soami to them all. They are urged to do their meditation every day. Radha Soami from Bibi to you, her dear brother; Bibi's Radha Soami also to all the others. Radha Soami also from the sadhus at the Dera. At present I have no free time, so I have not been able to write about other matters. Please send some thin coal tar which can be applied to all surfaces—we still have the coal tar which you sent earlier. For the rest, it will be done as you write.

Please do your bhajan and simran every day. Listen to the Shabd-dhun every day, whenever you are free. It is a fact, my son, that except for the Shabd-dhun nothing is our own. Believe firmly: "I am nothing; my Satguru is everything. I am a servant of the Satguru." When you sit in meditation, first put your attention in the Satguru's form, then start simran, and with intense love and devotion, slowly, gently, direct your inner hearing and seeing faculties, surat and nirat, and the higher mind *(nij man)* towards the Sound and fix them in it. Next, listen to the sound of the Dhun inside and nurture love for it. Your attention may remain focused for no more than a minute or two, or five or ten, or it may barely hear the Sound, but even then the news of your effort will reach right into Sach Khand, that you are offering a prayer. I am very happy and pleased with you, my son. Grace and mercy are always descending upon you. Never are you to keep a longing for the world within you, my son; keep the Holy Feet of the Satguru in your mind all the time. One day with that love you will reach Sach Khand. Chacha Ji sends you Radha Soami and his grace and mercy.

25 September [1900]

～ 71 ～

Radha Soami. Radha Soami Ji is the Comforter.

Radha Soami greetings from Jaimal Singh to my obedient son, Babu Sawan Singh. Your money order of 400 rupees has been received. I did not acknowledge each instalment separately because of shortage of paper. A total of 400 has been received up to 1 October. The work on the building is now in full swing, and money is being duly spent on it. The wages of the masons and carpenters, however, have not yet been paid. Three hundred and twenty rupees were spent on the timber. It is expected that, in addition to these 400 rupees, 200 more will see the whole construction through. I shall write to you later about the progress of the building. At present I do not have much time to write. This was simply to let you know that the money has been received.

Please do as much bhajan and simran daily as you can. It all goes to your credit. Convey Radha Soami greetings to all the satsangis. Bibi's Radha Soami greetings to you, her dear brother; Bibi's Radha Soami also to all the satsangis. A two-foot wide cupboard has been built in each of the five small rooms. Reply soon with full details. You will go home, my son.

1 October 1900

∼ 72 ∼

[Dictated]

Radha Soami. Radha Soami Ji is the Comforter.

From Jaimal Singh: Radha Soami greetings to my obedient son, Babu Sawan Singh. May the grace and mercy of the compassionate Hazur always be upon you. This is to let you know that some parshad from Janam Ashtami* is being sent to you through Hari Ram. Please mix it with more and distribute it among all the satsangis in the Murree region. Here, construction is going ahead and the buildings are coming along well. Hari Ram will personally give you a detailed account. Timber worth 320 rupees has been purchased. The labourers, carpenters, masons, etc., are all busy, and the work is continuing with the gracious mercy of the compassionate Hazur.

You are to keep doing bhajan and simran every day. Other than bhajan, do not regard anything as yours. Hold on to the Satguru's refuge all the time and keep doing your work and meeting your worldly obligations—keep the cord of love tied to his Holy Feet. Because ... and the mind then will never waver upon watching this worldly drama.

Please accept Radha Soami greetings from Bibi Ji and also from all the others at the Dera.

4 October 1900

---

* Soami Ji's birthday.

~ 73 ~

Radha Soami. Radha Soami Ji is the Comforter.

Radha Soami greetings from Jaimal Singh to my obedient son, Babu Sawan Singh. May the grace and mercy of the compassionate Anami Hazur Radha Soami, the Merciful, always be upon you. Your letter was received and I was very happy to read it. The five small rooms have now been built up to shoulder height; six masons are working on them. You were in danger of fever at this time. The command was for a serious illness, but the gracious, compassionate Hazur has been merciful to my pleading at his Lotus Feet to please end your suffering soon. So with his grace and mercy you have been forgiven. To avoid sending money frequently, you may please send 200 rupees upon receiving this postcard. Everyone's wages remain to be paid. I will write later and give the full details—this has been written in a hurry. Later on I shall reply to your entire letter. Do your bhajan and simran every day, my son, and send your letters promptly, even if you write very little. Please convey Radha Soami greetings to Babu Hari Ram, to both Bibi Jis, to Gursharan, Babu Gulab Singh, Chanan Singh, Narain Singh, and Diwan Singh. Radha Soami greetings from Bibi to you, her dear brother; also Radha Soami to everyone else. Whatever you said will be done. I am very happy and pleased with you, my son.

20 October 1900

~ 74 ~

[Dictated]

Radha Soami. Radha Soami Ji is the Comforter.

From Jaimal Singh: Radha Soami greetings to my obedient son, Babu Sawan Singh. I received your letter and was glad to read that you are well, and was extremely happy to learn about the promotion. May Soami Ji bless you with more promotions. Please accept our congratulations upon congratulations and still more congratulations! All that Hazur Maharaj is doing is good.

At this place, the small rooms will be ready for roofing in about a week; the bolts will no doubt arrive by that time. This is also a reminder to please send the coal tar. The work on the roof can be finished only when both those items have arrived. You are to continue doing your bhajan and simran. Do your worldly work with the body and the spiritual work with the mind and soul— both will continue to be done with the grace of Hazur Maharaj. Look upon money as the dirt of your hands. I will write to you in Gurmukhi as well. Please accept Radha Soami from Bibi Ji.

26 November 1900

∽ 75 ∽

Radha Soami. Radha Soami Ji is the Comforter.

Radha Soami from Jaimal Singh to my obedient son, Babu Sawan Singh. May the grace and mercy of the compassionate Anami Lord Radha Soami always be upon you. Dear son, your letter has been received and I am very happy to know of your well-being. Whatever he has given to you has come from his gracious mercy. Always keep repeating the name of the Satguru inside, and also do whatever work he gives you. Consider it all to be the Satguru's work. One should remember: "I am merely a labourer; nothing is mine." Bhajan and simran should be done regularly.

When the going becomes very difficult while you do your official work, immediately concentrate the inner seeing faculty (*nirat*) on the shabd stages within and continue with your simran, while casually attending to the work as well. It will give you a bliss just like meditation, and the official work also will keep getting done. In simran at least there is no problem, my son, so keep doing it. Simran's current links up with the Dhun, and the current of the Dhun links one with the Shabd—and Shabd is the very essence of the Anami Lord himself. For this reason, if simran is done with love and devotion steeped in the soul's seeing faculty, it brings great joy and bliss. Grace and mercy then descend in full measure. The mind and soul get intensely dyed in the hue of the Shabd-dhun, and every day the prayer and supplication reach Sach Khand. I am indeed very pleased with you, my son.

The situation here is that the walls of the small rooms have been constructed up to the roof level, and the beams have been placed on them. The roof will be finished with planks and ties in eight days. We have received the bolts; Dhanpat sent them from Khairagali. He sent thirty surplus washers, which have been of no use to us. We ordered ten plates from Amritsar—these have been fastened, two to each beam. A canister of coal tar is now urgently needed, because even though we have an extra half canister of coal tar, lots of it is going to be used. It is needed promptly. The beams and ties of the roof were placed ten feet high, that is, the height of the roof was set at ten feet. I think it is good; but now, good or bad, it is going to remain as it is. The bricks may suffice, or some may be left over; it will be as Hazur wills it. A postcard was sent to you earlier. It has probably reached you, or will reach you soon. Also, provisions worth 100 rupees have now been purchased for the masons and carpenters: 60 rupees' worth of wheat, 30 of ghee, and 10 of sugar—but ghee worth 40 rupees has already been consumed. Let's see if all the work can be done in fifteen or twenty days. This letter has been written on the 21st of Maghar.

You must write how much has been lost, and how it was lost. A letter in Gurmukhi will be read only by me. You should not worry. This much, however, is clear: that whatever we owe to others should be given. This taking from some and giving to others is a great snare of Kal. All beings of the entire creation—from gods and goddesses to the subtle beings or the gross—all have been caught in this net from the very dawn of time. The individual who, instead of his own rightful earnings, considers it better to fraudulently live off another's just labour has not realized that what the Lord has given is specific to his needs, that from it he should use nine parts for himself, as the tenth part is not his: it belongs to the Lord who created him. It was his promise to the Lord that from his earnings he would give the tenth share to Him—this he does not understand. As he acquires name and fame, he increasingly uses force or fraud in order to usurp the rights of those lesser or lower than him, while hoarding his own wealth, or spending it uselessly, or doing other bad deeds. Such a being subsequently has to pay those from whom he has taken, and pays it by taking birth repeatedly—by becoming an animal, cow, or donkey, again and again. So understand, my son, that, apart from your rightful earnings, you are never to use what belongs to others. This is the first step on the spiritual ladder. Even if you are the king of the whole world, you are still to eat only the rightful fruit of your own labour. So do your government service and earn your rightful remuneration. Use it for yourself and as far as possible share it with others, give it to your family, and to the sangat as well—and do your bhajan and simran every day.

Radha Soami to Chanan Singh. Bhajan and simran is to be done every day, my son. Bibi's Radha Soami to you, her true brother, and to all the others. And Radha Soami from all the sadhus at the Dera to you, and to all the others.

2 December [1900]

76

Radha Soami. Radha Soami Ji is the Comforter.

Radha Soami greetings from Jaimal Singh to my obedient son, Babu Sawan Singh. May the grace and mercy of the compassionate Hazur always be upon you. Your two letters were received and I was very happy to read them both. Upon receiving the first letter I sent you a postcard, which has probably reached you by now. This letter is in reply to both the letters. Please continue to keep me informed when you move to Khairagali. Always believe implicitly, my son, that all work is the Guru's work. "Nothing is mine; I am fit for nothing. All is the greatness of my Guru." Please do your bhajan and simran regularly every day, as much as you can. And realize with your mind and the attentive faculties of surat and nirat that you are to take refuge at the Satguru's Holy Feet. While working or moving around, keep the attentive faculties focused on the Shabd-dhun all the time. Then the mind, as if in bhajan day and night, remains deflated and becomes purified, and this message also reaches Sach Khand through the Dhun. So do it like this every day.

The news from the Dera: I have received two drums of coal tar. The roofing of the buildings has been finished; the parapets have been made with brick aggregate. What remains is whitewashing the buildings and bricking the floors inside. The inside floors must be bricked, my son. Some bricks have been left over. After you come, you can decide where to use them, but only a few are surplus. The expense was heavy, but the buildings have been well constructed. The wages of all the masons and carpenters remain to be paid. They are to be paid 150 rupees up to 27 December. If possible, please send the money soon so that all the wages can be paid. I do not have enough time to write a letter, so please consider this reply as substantial.

Bibi's Radha Soami to you, her dear brother, and to all the satsangis. Radha Soami from all the sadhus at the Dera to you and also to all the other satsangis. Please also convey Radha Soami greetings to Chanan Singh and Narain Singh. All are urged to do their bhajan and simran every day. This is because our real work is: bhajan and simran; a true love and faith in the Satguru; leading our mind within his will; looking upon everything as the Satguru's and nothing as our own. "Everything belongs to the Satguru; I do not exist." Knowing this, my son, keep your attention day and night in the Satguru's Holy Feet, and do your worldly work by looking on it as unreal. Consider the Shabd-form Satguru to be always by your side. Do not read this letter aloud, but understand its depth. You are very dear to me, my son; the day is coming when you will merge into me.

21 December 1900

∼ 77 ∼

Radha Soami. Radha Soami Ji is the Comforter.

Radha Soami greetings from Jaimal Singh to my obedient son, Babu Sawan Singh, and to Chanan Singh and Narain Singh. May the grace and mercy of the compassionate Anami Lord, Radha Soami, always be upon you. My dear son, your letter written in Urdu was received and I was delighted to read it. One hundred and fifty rupees were also received—100 at one time, and then 50—by 3 January. They have been spent on the construction of the buildings. The masons have now finished their work. Five men are still working on the roof, so all the work, including that on the doors and windows, will be finished in eight to ten days. A total of 12,000 unused bricks, as well as about 2,000 pieces of brick aggregate, are left over. So what should we construct now? There could be an upper-storey room, 10½ feet long by 9 feet wide, with the roof at a height of 8 feet—better make that 9 feet. Please calculate how many bricks will be needed for such a room. There will be a 6-foot high door on one side, and two windows, 3 feet high and 2¼ feet wide, on either side—the windows of the small rooms already built underneath are 2½ feet high and 2 feet, less 4 inches, wide. Calculate with these measurements, and let me know the total number of bricks that will be needed. Each brick measures 2 inches thick, 9 inches long, and 4½ inches wide. So please let me know. Write the letter in Gurmukhi. We will start the work only after your letter comes. The carpenters will now stop working after constructing the panels. The floors of the rooms and the veranda are to be finished with bricks or crushed brick aggregate. So let me know when you come, or write beforehand how you would like the floors to be done.

You have written that a brick meditation cell must be built. So calculate, my son, and let me know the height, length, and width for this room. Large-size government bricks are available at the railway station. Well-made bricks cost 10 rupees per thousand, plus 2¼ rupees for cartage. They are available in plenty. If the room is built with three thousand large bricks, their cost will come to 36½ rupees. But I also feel that both the meditation cell and the upper-storey room can be constructed with all these bricks. Please calculate and let me know, only then will we start the work. In the meantime, we will collect the brick aggregate. The floors of the veranda and the small rooms will be finished only after you come and inform us. Bibi wants to know whether you have eaten the tonic preparation she made for you. Please write. We rushed the construction of the buildings in anticipation of the satsangis coming at Christmas time, but no one came. Only Babu Kahan Singh came by himself and stayed for three days. Had we not expected the arrival of satsangis at

Christmas time, we would not have hurried and would have done the work slowly. Many of them wrote that they would come with their families, but then no one showed up. Because of the hurry, many details of the construction were not properly done. The parapets of the roof have been plastered with crushed brick aggregate and whitewashed.

Do let me know the day on which Basant Singh takes his examination. And always, day and night, at all hours, and at all times, keep your mind, through the attentive faculties of surat and nirat, in the Shabd-dhun. While moving around, sitting or sleeping, keep your attention in the sound of the Shabd-dhun and realize that "I am nothing. Whatever there is, everything is the eternal Shabd-dhun, and that is the Satguru's real form." The very Godhead, Anami Lord, Radha Soami—who projects himself as the Shabd, the Dhun, through his attributes of essence and being, the surat and the nirat—came into the regions Agam, Alakh, and Sach Khand, from where after separation he created Kal through his power in Sach Khand. Then from his fundamental form he sent out currents of Shabd-dhun to take the beings away from the nine doors to their real home.

So this Shabd-dhun, which is heard every day as the sound of the bell and the conch, is specifically the essence of the Anami Lord. Listen to it every day, my son, and give it your love and devotion. This sound is calling you, and calling us, all the time. If you say that you do not have time because of your official work, that is no excuse since work is done with the body, and occasionally with the mind too, although only for a short while, say, for ten or fifteen minutes, or a half or whole hour, in order to calculate or understand something. At such a time the mind and surat and nirat, all three, are oblivious of the melody. This is the way of ordinary workers. In Kaliyug, my son, only he reaches the real home who, receiving the path from a perfect Satguru, with his grace and mercy performs both tasks, worldly as well as spiritual. So stay within the command; the Satguru himself will take you to his real home.

Bibi's Radha Soami to you, her dear brother. Radha Soami from all the sadhus at the Dera to you and to all others. Bibi's Radha Soami to Chanan Singh.

[3 or 4 January 1901]

～ 78 ～

Radha Soami. Radha Soami Ji is the Comforter.

Radha Soami from Jaimal Singh to my obedient son, Babu Sawan Singh. May the grace and mercy of the compassionate Anami Lord always be upon you. Both Chanan Singh and Basant Singh arrived at the Dera on 5 February and left for your place on the 12th by the two o'clock train. They have been doing seva at the Dera. The roof of the upper-storey room will be ready in a week, but because of heavy rains the work on the meditation cell has not been started yet. Because of the wet ground, a bullock cart cannot be driven. We will begin the work when the ground dries up. My son, please do your bhajan and simran every day, whenever you are free. Whether walking around, sitting, sleeping, or doing your work, keep the love and devotion of the inner faculties of surat and nirat and the higher mind fixed in the Shabd-dhun. Whenever you find time to sit, do so to listen to the Shabd-dhun—your heart should remain attached to it all the time.

Radha Soami from Bibi to you, her dear brother. Also, Radha Soami from all the sadhus at the Dera and from each and every satsangi to you, Babu Ji.

Radha Soami to Babu Gajja Singh. Your letter has arrived

and I was very happy to read it. I have understood the whole situation. Certainly, the mind is just like you have written. However, keep doing simran all the time, and slowly, gently, place your attention in the sound of the Shabd. By doing this every day, the mind will slowly settle down.

Please give Radha Soami from Bibi, all the sadhus, and from myself to Babu Gulab Singh, Narain Singh, and all the other satsangis. You must continue with bhajan and simran every day; I would be pleased if you did it daily. A letter from your Baba Ji [grandfather] is enclosed in this letter, my son. You should read and answer it. Your letter has been received—it included an invoice—and I was happy to read it. You have written that you have sent ten pieces of clothing. Someone will collect the parcel from the railway station. I am glad that you sent the clothes because I was about to get some made. However, while only one piece of each item was needed, you have sent two of each. They have been received.

Keep your mind continuously in contemplation and fear of the Lord, and do your official work well. Keep alive within yourself the longing of the inner attentive faculties and the higher mind—this is as good as bhajan. Write to me when Chanan Singh and Basant Singh arrive there. Please have Basant Singh educated with love and encouragement. He will find employment if he studies for two years. It is said that Bachint Singh also is now doing well. Your grandfather's letter is enclosed in this letter; please take a look at it.

Radha Soami from Bibi and all others to you. We will start working on the meditation cell soon. Everyone is urged to do bhajan and simran every day. You should all attach your souls to the sound of Shabd-dhun and savour its bliss by listening to it every day. Repeatedly listening to it will cleanse you. Day in and day out stop the mind from indulging in base thoughts because we will bear the consequences of whatever we do. This is the reply to your last letter, which arrived on 12 February. It was in Urdu and was well written.

12 February [1901]

~ 79 ~

Radha Soami. Radha Soami Ji is the Comforter.

Radha Soami greetings from Jaimal Singh to my obedient son, Babu Sawan Singh, and to Basant Singh, Chanan Singh, Babu Gajja Singh, Babu Gulab Singh, and Narain Singh. May the grace and mercy of the compassionate Anami Lord always be upon you. Your postcard was received and I was very happy to read it. It does not matter if the container of pickles was lost. Whosoever eats will benefit from it. More will be given to you when you come here again—the lost one was not destined for you.

It has rained here again. The road from the brick-kiln has become muddy, so the bricks for the meditation cell will be brought here after the ground is dry. Nothing is possible at present because of the rains. The upper-storey room is now ready, and from tomorrow we will start crushing the bricks for aggregate in the small rooms. We will send the pickles when your letter comes.

Do your bhajan and simran every day: this is for everybody. With love and devotion, keep the mind and the attentive faculties of the soul, surat and nirat, attached to the Shabd-dhun. During work, never let the ego or arrogance of any kind enter your heart that you are the one doing something. No! Rather, it should be, "I am nothing. You alone are everything, O Lord." Bibi's Radha Soami to you, her dear brother. Radha Soami from the sadhus at the Dera to everyone. Please also convey Bibi's Radha Soami greetings, my son.

20 February 1901

∼ 80 ∼

Radha Soami. Radha Soami Ji is the Comforter.

Radha Soami greetings from Jaimal Singh to my obedient son, Babu Sawan Singh. This is to let you know that the wicker stools were received on 6 April. I wrote a postcard to you in Urdu that we had not received the chairs, but you are not to worry about them now as they have arrived. Let me know when you receive the postcard. Please give Radha Soami greetings to Basant Singh, Chanan Singh, Narain Singh, Babu Gulab Singh, and Babu Gajja Singh. Basant Singh is reminded to study hard day and night. Everyone else is reminded to do his bhajan and simran every day.

Keep the higher mind *(nij man)* and the attentive faculties of surat and nirat attached to the Shabd-dhun with deep love and devotion within. Leaving the self aside, do your worldly work, but keep your love and devotion in the Satguru's words. The Shabd-dhun is always with you, my son; it is protecting you at every step.

Bibi sends Radha Soami to you, her dear brother. Radha Soami to everyone from the sadhus at the Dera and from Bibi.

6 April 1901

∼ ∼

Radha Soami. Radha Soami Ji is the Comforter.

Radha Soami greetings from Jaimal Singh to my obedient son, Babu Sawan Singh. May the grace and mercy of the compassionate Anami Lord always be upon you. I was very happy to receive your letter and read it. In fact, I was hoping to hear about your safe arrival at Khairagali, which, happily, you have now confirmed, as also that Basant Singh's tutor has arrived. Basant Singh should now make it a point to study with full attention.

Please convey my Radha Soami greetings to Basant Singh, Chanan Singh, Babu Gajja Singh, Narain Singh, and Babu Gulab Singh. My son, whenever you are free from work during the day, always do your bhajan and simran immediately, so that no time is wasted. When an individual is free from work, he starts recalling and regretting old incidents, saying to himself, "Had I known, I would have done like this." This is all false, because every event takes its predestined course. Nothing is gained by feeling sorry later on. Similarly, time is wasted in gossiping about people's joys and sorrows, or in criticizing or praising them, which gives neither spiritual nor material benefit. Every breath we take and every morsel we eat is apportioned. Time is not to be wasted in pursuits that further neither worldly aims nor spiritual goals. Bhajan and simran are not to be neglected even while doing worldly work. Nor are you ever to become lazy. Keep the attentive faculties of surat and nirat, and the mind's inherent sense of longing, alert to the Shabd-dhun. If day and night the longing to hear the Shabd-dhun is there, then even during work the mind will remain unsoiled. Then whenever you are free, the thought of meditation alone will arise in the mind. Whether through sheer determination or with love, you must listen to the Shabd-dhun every day. This time will never come again. So do your meditation daily—not a day is to be missed. And please keep me informed about yourself.

My son, I would like to know if you can ask someone in Multan to send me crystallized sugar from there. Please send me his address, and I will mail him a money order for the expenses. The crystallized sugar should be clean and white. If you write to him directly, give Beas railway station as my address, and also let me know so that I do not ask anyone else to send it. If you are not free, inform me so by a postcard. Nihal Singh says that the doors should now be painted. Please write about how you would like to see them done.

Bibi sends Radha Soami greetings to you, her dear brother. Radha Soami to everyone from Bibi and all the sadhus at the Dera. When you are free, first start simran in your mind and keep the attention towards the Shabd-dhun—be alert, and gently, slowly, listen to the Sound for ten or fifteen minutes. Then sit in bhajan and, while doing it, do not think at all about worldly affairs. The mind will then become absorbed. Counsel the mind thus: "When you go to sleep, you forget all worldly activities. What do you then lose? If nothing goes wrong for you then, why during bhajan and simran do you indulge in worldly thoughts? What will go wrong if you do not recall worldly affairs during meditation?" Be firm, and admonish the mind severely in this manner. The grace and mercy of the Shabd-dhun is reaching you with every moment, my son. Please get Chanan Singh treated for dysentery.

18 April [1901]

~ 82 ~

Radha Soami. Radha Soami Ji is the Comforter.

Radha Soami greetings from Jaimal Singh to my obedient son, Babu Sawan Singh. May the grace and mercy of the compassionate Anami Lord always be upon you, dear son. I have received three letters from you, one written in Gurmukhi and two in Urdu, and am glad to read that you are well and happy. Your 200 rupees were received, out of which 100 were sent immediately to Agra. We have also sent there utensils worth 60 rupees for the bhandara kitchen. Here at the Dera, paint costing about 40 rupees will be needed for the doors—23 rupees worth has been purchased already, the rest will be bought later. Also, the ceiling of the upper-storey room has been painted once, but may need two more coats.

You must send money to Baba Ji [grandfather] as well. He should never remain in want in any way. From his letter it appears that he would like to accept the matrimonial offer that he first mentioned. The match that he mentions is good and should be accepted, so that he doesn't get offended. As he is the eldest in the family, we should accept what he says. For the rest, it is one's individual destiny: what is written on the forehead will definitely happen. Apart from this, you may do as seems right to you. Bachint Singh was destined to become sick this year, but he will be forgiven through having boils on his body. You shouldn't worry on this account.

Regarding bhajan and simran, you write that your mind gives you a lot of trouble, that it does not let you do bhajan and simran, and aimlessly creates waves and ripples. This is the mind's job, my son, because it is the creator of all gross and subtle evil tendencies. The thoughtless sins, the whole creation in its gross and subtle aspects, and the gross energy *(shakti)* whose power is unlimited, are all born in the mind like little sparks that fly off a burning fire. The sparks fly off, but the fire is unaware of it. So this is how the mind works. Those who have accepted the Guru's teaching and have steered the mind within his will, receive praise and honour both in this world and in Sach Khand. To stay within the directives of the perfect Guru is the real work, my son. So relinquish the self, surrender your mind, body and wealth to the Satguru, and do not claim anything as yours. Then the mind will never stray anywhere, because once something is given away, you cease to have any claim on it. You, however, ignore the Guru's will and bring your self in between, and this allows the mind also to put forth its demands. That is why the mind gives trouble. Listen always to the Shabd-dhun and do your simran mentally. Put your own reasonings aside and direct your attention to the Shabd-dhun. The Shabd-dhun will then automatically capture the mind. Whatever official or worldly work you do, all is the Satguru's work. The Guru is ready to ferry you across the ocean of the universe. Why then should you feel perturbed? The Shabd-dhun, which is always resounding within your body, will never forsake you. Hold on to it. Have absolute faith that it will not rest until it has taken you to Sach Khand.

A letter from Chacha Ji at Agra informs me that the wicker stools have been received. He has asked me to convey to you his Radha Soami with grace and mercy. I would definitely like to go to Agra for Hazur Soami Ji's bhandara. You should also come along if you can get leave. A postcard from Agra, which came with Chacha Ji's directive, has been forwarded to you. The day and month of the bhandara are mentioned in it: Monday, 3 June, the 22nd of Jeth. For the rest, my son, it will happen as Hazur wills it; we can do nothing by ourselves. And please carry out all the domestic tasks that your Baba Ji has asked you to do. I am very pleased with you, my son.

Convey my Radha Soami greetings to Basant Singh, Chanan Singh, Babu Gajja Singh Ji, Babu Gulab Singh, Sher Singh, Diwan Singh, and Narain Singh. They are to do their bhajan and simran every day. Inform Narain Singh that I have received his postcard and am very happy to read about his well-being. The mind is certainly as he writes: it never allows anyone to escape across its boundary at Trikuti. To begin with, it does not even allow one to come near bhajan and simran. There is, however, a way to deal with the mind: listen to the Shabd-dhun every day and, putting aside the self, hold fast to the refuge of the Satguru.

Bibi wishes to convey her Radha Soami to you, her dear brother, and to all the other satsangis. Radha Soami from the sadhus and other satsangis at the Dera to you and all the other satsangis. It rained very hard on Sunday, 4 May, the 23rd of Vaisakh.

In your letters, my son, why is the full name, including "Singh," not written in the address? Twice it has been omitted. The true and real name, of course, is the Surat Shabd Dhun alone, but in this phenomenal world the given name of the body should be definitely written out in full. Your 100 rupees were received at the bhandara in Agra, and its receipt has arrived. The money reached there at a very good time. The balance of 100 rupees will be sent now, or I will take it with me when I go there. Your 200 rupees will be put specifically in Hazur's bhandara. Your income has borne fruit, my son. You are reminded to restrain your mind, do your bhajan daily, and give up the self. The Shabd-dhun will definitely take you to Sach Khand.

7 May 1901

∼ 83 ∼

Radha Soami. Radha Soami Ji is the Comforter.

From Jaimal Singh to my obedient son, Babu Sawan Singh, Sunder Singh the carpenter of the Fifth Unit, Basant Singh, Chanan Singh, Babu Gajja Singh, Narain Singh, Babu Gulab Singh, Diwan Singh, and Sher Singh: Radha Soami greetings to all of you. Babu Sawan Singh's postcard has been received, and I am very happy to read the news in it. Do write whether or not you can get leave at the time of the bhandara. Let me know this immediately, my son. Please do your bhajan and simran every day, and stay happy within his will and command. The Shabd-dhun is always within you. He does whatever he thinks is proper. So stay happy wherever he keeps you; do not let the Shabd-dhun leave your mind even for an instant. Inside and out, is the ever-vigilant protector. Keep the mind and soul fixed in the sound of the Shabd-dhun and also carry on with your worldly work. You are all to do your bhajan and simran every day.

There is a satsangi, Sunder Singh the carpenter, in the Fifth Unit. I received a postcard from him and was happy to read it. Please let him know that the reply to him is to do his bhajan and simran every day—a separate reply is not going to be sent. Convey this to Sunder Singh wherever he is located.

A postcard came from Bachint Singh. He wrote that he will come for darshan when he brings the wheat. Also, a message was received from Agra from Chacha Ji, in which he wished you Radha Soami with lots of grace and mercy. Bibi sends her Radha Soami to you, her dear brother; Radha Soami also to all the satsangis at your place from the sadhus at the Dera.

18 May 1901

Radha Soami. Radha Soami Ji is the Comforter.

Radha Soami greetings from Jaimal Singh to my obedient son, Babu Sawan Singh. May the compassionate Radha Soami in his grace and mercy always keep you with him; may he bestow upon you the Shabd-dhun, his eternal real form, and grant you love and devotion in surat, nirat and the higher mind, in all three. May his gracious mercy grant you the bliss within the Shabd-dhun. I received two postcards from you on the same day and was happy to read them. When you get leave with the compassionate Hazur's pleasure, please proceed directly to Agra. If you do not get leave, it is still his will and remain happy in that as well. He is always by your side and will do what he considers to be good. With love and devotion, keep the inner faculties and the higher mind always attached to the Shabd-dhun, and remain content at whichsoever place he keeps you. All work is his work; remain happy wherever he keeps you, and take on whatever work you do as the Satguru's work—do not keep your self in it. Instil it firmly in your mind—this idea should never leave the mind— that the body, mind, wealth, and the inner faculties, the eyes, mouth, nose, ears, hands, feet, all, everything, each and every article that exists in the world, belongs to the Satguru: "I do not exist." Look upon everything you do as the Satguru's work; do only that which is appropriate.

This advice, the directive I have written above, should never leave your mind at any time. Keep these words firmly in the mind while doing your work, and also during simran and while listening to the Shabd-dhun. You will then certainly receive the bliss of the Shabd-dhun. Always remember these three points: Do not feel elated even if you receive the kingship of fourteen realms, because it would be false and transitory—if you love false things, you will be deceived. If such a sovereignty is taken away, do not feel depressed, because he who gave it took it away. It belonged to him and it was unreal. However much respect or criticism someone may offer, neither be pleased with the respect and praise nor offended by the criticism. Always remain happy and content wherever the Lord is pleased to place you. When our attachments do not touch the mind, and the mind always remains in balance, then the boon of entering Sach Khand by way of the Shabd-dhun comes daily through the Satguru's Word. Grace and mercy especially are upon you all the time. Keep listening to the Shabd-dhun every day with the inner faculties of surat and nirat.

Please convey my Radha Soami to Basant Singh, Chanan Singh, Babu Gajja Singh Ji, Babu Gulab Singh Ji, Narain Singh, Diwan Singh, and Sher Singh of the army battery. All of them are urged to do their bhajan and simran every day. Sher

Singh wrote a postcard to me in which he asked for Hazur
Soami Ji's books. Please tell him that I will get them when I go
to Agra. Convey my Radha Soami to Sher Singh. This is the
reply to his postcard; no other reply will be sent.
The crystallized sugar—around 38 kilograms in weight—
has arrived here. It is of very good quality. Please let me know
the cost: how much was paid for it? It was received on 24 May;
the freight charges came to eight annas. We have also received a
nice-looking sedan chair, as well as three cotton cushions. They
arrived undamaged, except for a sizeable tear on one side and
the bottom, and a small one on the other side. No other damage
was done. We have not paid anything for the sedan chair. Both
articles were received at Beas railway station on 24 May. I will
leave for Agra on 29 or 30 May. If you get leave, bring money
for your own expenses; I have plenty of money for myself. There
are no other expenses, my son, you have already done enough
seva. I am very pleased and satisfied with you.

Radha Soami from Bibi to you, her true brother. She says:
"Dear brother, I am very pleased with the seva you have done by
sending the sedan chair. It is a very nice chair."

Pritam Singh sent me a postcard in which he wrote that, if
permitted, he would go to Khairagali to be with his "brother". I
told him that he should first write a letter to you and then go if he
is invited. I do not know what he will end up doing.

Radha Soami from Bibi and all the sadhus at the Dera to
you and the others. When you sit in meditation, do simran for a
quarter-hour, and also keep your attention towards the sound of
the Shabd-dhun. Then, slowly and gently, keep focusing the attention into the sound of the Dhun within. The inner faculties of
surat and nirat will not then allow the mind to stray outside.

24 May 1901

~ 85 ~

[Dictated]

Radha Soami. Radha Soami Ji is the Comforter.

Radha Soami greetings from Jaimal Singh to my obedient son, Babu Sawan Singh. A telegram was received here on 8 June, but the name in it was incorrect and could not be made out. Hence this reply. Write a brief note explaining to whom you would like the 85 rupees to be given. We are leaving here on the 10th of this month and will arrive at the Dera on the 11th. So now, whatever you write, address it to the Dera. A plan to construct two rooms at Soami Bagh has been proposed. The rooms will be 14 feet long and 8 feet wide—there will be an 8½ foot wide veranda as well. Its cost will be approximately 900 rupees. I have given Chacha Ji Sahib some money—50 rupees so far—from my pension. These two rooms will be constructed if you agree. Everyone is of the view that these rooms ought to be constructed. At present, an expenditure of 900 rupees has been proposed as an estimate, but the actual cost will probably be somewhat less.

Continue with your bhajan and simran every day. And please convey Radha Soami greetings to Basant Singh, Chanan Singh, and all the other satsangis. Radha Soami greetings from Bibi Ji and Chacha Ji. Radha Soami with folded hands from Moti Ram. We have found out that your cotton filling is also there; it is ready, and is of very good quality. We have obtained two copies of *Sant Sangreh* and one of Hazur Soami Ji's *Sar Bachan.*

9 June 1901

~ 86 ~

Radha Soami. Radha Soami Ji is the Comforter.

Radha Soami greetings from Jaimal Singh to my obedient son, Babu Sawan Singh. May the grace and mercy of the compassionate Hazur always be upon you, dear son. You sent a telegram to me, but the name inside it was not clearly written, and so I could not understand to whom 85 rupees was to be given. Write about this again. I am now back at the Dera, where I returned on 11 June. My mother is sick now, so tomorrow I will go to Ghuman and return on Sunday. Your Baba Ji has written to me that Babu Sawan Singh should give 50 rupees to him every year. His letter arrived the day I was to go to the bhandara. Please always look after him, my son. There is a proposal to build two rooms with a veranda in Soami Bagh at Agra. You have already borne very heavy expenses, so please write to me what you think about it.

Radha Soami to Sunder Singh the carpenter. Your postcard arrived, and I was very happy to read it. Do your bhajan and simran every day.

My son, please convey my Radha Soami to Basant Singh, Chanan Singh, Narain Singh, Babu Gajja Singh, and Babu Gulab Singh. Continue with your bhajan and simran every day. With love and devotion in your mind, keep the attention always alert to the melody of the Shabd. This postcard has been written in a hurry as I did not have much time. Radha Soami from Bibi to you, her dear brother, and to all the others.

14 June 1901

~ 87 ~

Radha Soami. Radha Soami Ji is the Comforter.

Radha Soami greetings from Jaimal Singh to my obedient son, Babu Sawan Singh and to all the other satsangis. Dear son, parshad from the bhandara has been sent by parcel to Rawalpindi railway station. Chanan Singh should go there and collect it. Please distribute it to all the satsangis; be sure to give it to every satsangi at Murree as well. If there is not enough, buy some four or eight annas' worth more and after mixing the two, distribute it among the satsangis. This blessing is from Hazur's bhandara. I have paid the freight charges.

You are all to do your bhajan and simran every day. Always keep the soul and higher mind alert to the sound of the Shabd-dhun. This should never be forgotten, because our time should never be devoid of bhajan and simran. While doing your official work, or walking around, or sitting, or sleeping, this thought should always remain in your mind.

Radha Soami from Bibi and all the other satsangis. Send a reply as soon as you receive this letter. The bhandara will be held here on the full-moon day in Asarh, the 18th of Asarh.

15 June 1901

~ 88 ~

[Partially dictated]

Radha Soami. Radha Soami Ji is the Comforter.

From Jaimal Singh: Radha Soami greetings to my obedient son, Babu Sawan Singh. Your letter and postcard were received, giving me your news. I was happy and gratified to read them. The reply to your telegram is that whenever you send money home, there is no need to ask me because you already have my permission.

You may send it as you like. Ma Ji has the gracious blessing of Hazur; she will get well when the karmic debt has been paid off. You have written that your [budgeted] work this year will amount to only ten or twelve thousand rupees, that this is not enough.* Don't worry—if there is not enough, do more bhajan and simran. Keep your mind turned towards the will of Hazur. You are all asking me to visit your place, but it is difficult for me to come now, because I am neither able to walk in the mountains, nor free to leave here. For the rest, it is up to the will of Hazur. I have no idea if I can come, but if he sends me, I will not hesitate. When a disciple's love is deep enough, He will send me even if I have no legs or hands. In any case, you are always with me.

A very large bhandara was held at Agra. The bhandara here will be held on the full-moon day, Monday, the 18th of Asarh, Samvat 1958, that is, 1 July 1901. Your telegram was received but no one could read the name of the person for whom the money had been sent—that's why you didn't receive a reply to it. Earlier also you were informed that parshad from the bhandara at Agra had been sent by parcel to Rawalpindi railway station; the freight charges were prepaid. Ghee is sold here for eight annas a kilogram. It will be purchased and dispatched to Rawalpindi railway station, so please send Chanan Singh there to collect it.

On behalf of Bibi Ji, Radha Soami with love and affection to you, her true brother. Radha Soami from all and everyone at the Dera. Please accept respectful greetings also from your obedient servant, Ganda Ram, postman of Sathiala.

Please convey Radha Soami greetings to Basant Singh, Chanan Singh, Narain Singh, Babu Gulab Singh, Diwan Singh, and Sunder Singh the carpenter. Regarding Basant

---

* The income of a military engineer in those days would have consisted of a basic salary supplemented by an annual allowance calculated in proportion to the budgeted work allotted to him to supervise during the year.

Singh, please make it a point to watch closely over his education. We are all very happy with you.

[In Gurmukhi script, Baba Ji's writing:] The letter above has been written in Urdu, my son. Radha Soami from Jaimal Singh to my obedient son, Babu Sawan Singh. The news from here has been given above in Urdu. Realize the importance of keeping this time always in mind, because now at every moment the Shabd-dhun is resounding in your body. This is the Sound which is the Creator of all. It has brought forth everything and by giving support has made all and everything exist. This Sound, the life and breath of all, the maker and prescriber of the order of each and everything—the regions Agam, Alakh, and Sach Khand, and the radiant and earthly creations below them—is calling you in the form of Shabd-dhun within your body. Keep your love and affection, the higher mind and the faculties of surat and nirat alert to the sound of the Dhun within. Lots of grace and mercy is being showered upon you, my son. My thoughts stay with you constantly, to know when you will attach your attention with love to the Dhun of the Shabd—because the Lord is now about to bless you with the bliss of the divine melody.

June 1901

∽ 89 ∽

Radha Soami. Radha Soami Ji is the Comforter.

Radha Soami greetings from Jaimal Singh to my obedient son, Babu Sawan Singh. The compassionate Anami Hazur Radha Soami is a wondrous Lord. Fathomless, nameless, and formless is he. The stream of divine knowledge is flowing; so the current of mercy is about to come, and is already coming, but a single veil still remains. Surrender your self, my son. All that exists— the inner faculties of surat and nirat, the gross mind, the higher mind, the vital energy, the physical body, the three bodies [gross, astral, causal], etc., that is to say, the states that manifest themselves in the cycle of twenty-four hours, the attributes of the three bodies, the worldly possessions of the physical body—do not let your mind desire any of these. Nor should you concern yourself with what will happen next, or how you will do it. Put aside all such anxieties. All your possessions were given to you in the beginning by the Satguru, so they should have been held in trust. They were never to be regarded as your own. Now the Satguru's will has to be engraved in your mind. Understand that "I am nothing. All is the Satguru's; I do not exist." Everything that exists, the soul, intellect, mind, and all the means for performing worldly activities, none of these belongs to you—they all belong to the Satguru. They should be completely removed from your mind.

The reality of life is the soul, my son. The mind and soul received every provision from Sach Khand to go about their duty in the land of Kal after receiving the Shabd from the Satguru. They were to merge into the current of the Shabd to enable the soul to return to Sach Khand. The soul and mind, however, have completely forgotten this command, and by intermingling with maya have fallen under its control and now consider everything to be their own. The soul and mind have both been imprisoned by maya, and Kal has pressed them down with the weight of karmas.

So long as the disciple does not take out the self by surrendering his all to the Satguru and removing himself from everything, he will not be liberated. So surrender your self and step aside, my son. Consider that each and every thing in the world—body, mind, and wealth—belongs to the Satguru, that you are nothing. Do all your work knowing it to be thus, and stay within the Satguru's instructions. He will then take you with him when he considers you fit. Engrave within your mind a deep love and devotion for his Lotus Feet and keep lying in their refuge. The Shabd-dhun is a blessing from the Satguru, my son, it is a gift

that will never disappear. One day the Dhun will take you to
Sach Khand. Love the Shabd-dhun with devotion every day,
and keep alive the inner longing for it.

The rest of the news is that I received your letter and was
happy to read it. A letter from Bachint Singh also came, saying
that your Baba Ji had been ill but was better now. At the Dera,
a bhandara was held on the full-moon day, the 18th of Asarh,
Monday, 1 July. Please write and let me know if my visit to your
place is for darshan or to initiate some people there. Write how
many seekers are there, and I will then let you know, but please
reply promptly. It would be good if you could get leave to go
home to visit Ma Ji and your Baba Ji. For the rest, we are to remain happy in the will of the compassionate Hazur.

Convey my Radha Soami greetings to Basant Singh, Chanan
Singh, Narain Singh, Babu Gajja Singh Ji, Diwan Singh, and
Babu Gulab Singh. All of them are urged to do their bhajan and
simran every day. You never write about Basant Singh's studies:
how is he doing in school? We still have a month to send money
to Agra. We will see to it later on; it has not yet been fully decided. A canister of fresh ghee has been packed and sent to you,
addressed to the railway office at Murree Hills. It has not been
weighed; you may weigh it, although there is no particular need:
a full canister of ghee weighs around nineteen kilograms. Let me
know when you receive it.

So, you have received less work this year. Stay pleased with
that, my son, and do your bhajan. The only thing that is ours is
Nam, the Shabd-dhun. With love and devotion, keep the inner
faculties of the soul, surat and nirat, fixed in that alone. With
your hands and feet and the help of the mind attend to your
worldly work, and keep the love and faith of the higher mind at
the Satguru's Holy Feet. Radha Soami from Bibi to you, her
dear brother. Radha Soami from Bibi and all the people at the
Dera to all of you. Your 10 rupees arrived here by money order

and have been credited to the expense of the bhandara. May grace and mercy be upon everyone.

Sher Singh of the army battery wrote to ask for both of Hazur Soami Ji's books. They are with me. From Agra, I brought two copies of Hazur's *Sar Bachan* in verse, two copies of the prose version, and two volumes of *Sant Sangreh*, Part I and Part II. I will send them as soon as you write, or you can take them with you when you come on leave.

All of you are asking me to come. The fare costs 50 rupees, which would be a sheer waste; and the discomfort of the journey that I would have to go through—well, who cares about that! But the expenditure of 50 rupees would not serve any meaningful purpose. For the rest, my son, I welcome whatever is the will of Hazur Soami Ji.

The parcel was booked from Beas railway station to Murree railway office. The invoice will indicate whether or not the freight has been paid. It was sent on 4 July 1901.

4 July 1901

∾ 90 ∾

[Dictated]

Radha Soami. Radha Soami Ji is the Comforter.

From Jaimal Singh to Babu Sawan Singh: Radha Soami greetings. Your letter was received and I was happy to read it. You have written that you will be coming on leave on 3 August 1901. If you are coming on leave, I will travel to Murree Hills with you as I would like to accompany you. I cannot come earlier because the servicemen who are returning from China have written that they will pass through Beas on 28, 29, or 30 July 1901. I think, however, that you should definitely take leave and visit your home even if only for two days. So do go there, I urge you.

You should do your bhajan and simran every day. Chacha Ji sends you lots of grace and mercy and Radha Soami greetings. Regarding the rooms, Chacha Ji has written that some bricks and lime, etc., have been purchased and work has started at Soami Bagh. He has further written that seven square slabs and three long slabs of stone have been purchased and stored. The foundation of the rooms will be dug in two or three days. Bricks worth 100 rupees and pine wood worth 125 have been purchased. And another kind of stone has also been purchased for making lime, as good lime is not available in the market. Regarding the money, I will send 200 rupees. I gave 50 rupees at the time of the bhandara. For the rest, as you would like, or as is the will of the compassionate Lord, Radha Soami. By 25 July 1901, 200 rupees will have been sent to Agra.

Basant Singh, Chanan Singh, Narain Singh, Babu Gulab Singh, Babu Gajja Singh, Diwan Singh, and Sunder Singh the carpenter: please convey my Radha Soami to them; they are to do their bhajan and simran every day. It is very strongly urged that they continue with their bhajan and simran. A postcard arrived from Basant Singh. This letter is a reply to his postcard as well. It was very well written. Also please let Chanan Singh know that I have been informed about his well-being. For him, too, the reply is the same, that he is to keep doing his bhajan and simran. And Basant Singh is also reminded to please continue doing his bhajan and simran and to keep up with his studies.

A letter also came from Sunder Singh the carpenter. It was very well written. I am very happy with him. For him, too, this letter is the reply. Continue to do bhajan and simran; without bhajan, no problems will be solved. Do not waste any time by being without bhajan. Keep in mind the Satguru's command; whether awake or asleep, you are not to forget it at any time.

Bibi Ji wishes her Radha Soami to be conveyed to you, her true and dear brother. Radha Soami to all the satsangis. Also please accept Radha Soami from all the satsangis. The mind, that is the heart, wavers when it strays from the Satguru's teachings. Make it a habit to keep your thoughts in the Satguru's words—remember this.

July 1901

~ 91 ~

[Dictated]

Radha Soami. Radha Soami Ji is the Comforter.

From Jaimal Singh: Radha Soami greetings to my obedient son, Babu Sawan Singh. Your letter arrived and I was happy to receive your news. With regard to your inquiry about how to send money to Agra: beloved son, do not worry, 200 rupees have already been sent there. If possible, bring some money with you, but do not bring too much, as you can send the rest upon your return. No acknowledgement has been received from Agra, but the money was sent. You have not written when you will be coming—you should have given the details of your arrival so that someone can meet you at Beas railway station. We need to know the scheduled date, and also who else will be coming with you, or if you are coming alone. Keep doing your bhajan and simran every day. The rest of the news will be given to you in person. A letter from Chacha Ji came in the same post as yours; he wished you Radha Soami. Radha Soami greetings to Basant Singh, Babu Gulab Singh, Chanan Singh, Diwan Singh, and Sunder Singh. Let Sunder Singh know that his letter has also been received here. The reply to him is to continue doing bhajan and simran. Grace and mercy will be upon him. Radha Soami from Bibi Ji and from all the residents of the Dera.

July [1901]

~ 92 ~

[Dictated]

Radha Soami. Radha Soami Ji is the Comforter.

Radha Soami from Jaimal Singh to my obedient son, Babu
Sawan Singh, and to Basant Singh, Chanan Singh, Narain
Singh, Diwan Singh, and Babu Gulab Singh. This is to let you
know that your letter arrived, informing me of your well-being.
You have written that you cannot come until 25 August 1901.
It does not matter; after all, work has to be done. I will write
about my visit in a subsequent letter. The Twenty-Fourth Battery passed through [Beas] on 29 July 1901 at 3 p.m. We went
there at 6 p.m., so we missed them—such was the will of Hazur.
Continue doing your bhajan and simran. Keep the inner attentive faculties of surat and nirat alert to the stream of Shabd-dhun
every day, and continue listening to it with love and devotion.
Remain inwardly attached to it; grace and mercy are always
upon you. Slowly and gradually the Lord will take you to his
home. Everyone is urged to continue doing bhajan and simran.
Along with your letter, a letter was also received from Chacha Ji
at Agra, in which he wrote that the 200 rupees had been received. I will write later about the money for Agra. The rains are
good here. Chacha Ji has sent you a piece of cloth for a coat as
parshad; it will be given to you when you come. Radha Soami
on behalf of Bibi Ji; please also accept Radha Soami from all
others at the Dera. Because of heavy work, this letter has been
dictated in Urdu.

July 1901

∾ 93 ∾

[Dictated]

Radha Soami. Radha Soami Ji is the Comforter.

From Jaimal Singh: Radha Soami greetings to my obedient son, Babu Sawan Singh, and to Basant Singh, Chanan Singh, Sunder Singh, and Babu Gajja Singh. In an earlier postcard I had written about my visit; that programme still stands even though I am unwell. When the previous letter was written to you, I was very seriously ill, but now I am somewhat better. Bibi Ji also was seriously ill with dysentery. When I feel better, by the grace of the compassionate Hazur, I will write and let you know. A letter from Chacha Ji came from Agra: the construction of the rooms is in progress; the workers are busy. If you feel like it, send 200 rupees by money order to Chacha Ji at this address in Agra: Seth Lala Pratap Singh Ji, Brother of Hazur Soami Ji Maharaj, Panna Gali, Agra City. Send the money order like this, and also include in it your name and a message, if any. Let me know by return post whether or not you have sent the money order. Everyone else is urged to continue with bhajan and simran every day, because without bhajan and simran the mind does not stay in its place. If the inner longing for bhajan is there every day, the mind remains unaffected by worldly attractions. Therefore, you are strongly reminded to do your bhajan and simran. This letter has been written in Urdu because I have been sick. Keep in mind that when you receive a letter in Urdu it means that I am ill.

Radha Soami from Bibi Ji to you, her true brother. Please accept Radha Soami greetings from all the residents of the Dera. Do not worry now about my illness as this is his will. I have discovered that whenever I think of going to Murree, I fall ill—I do

not know what is the will of Hazur Soami Ji in this respect. We
all remember you with every moment. You should not become
perturbed, but keep your mind inwardly engaged; the fruit of
darshan will come to you. The other platoon, the Twenty-
Fourth, has arrived at Jhelum after returning from China. All the
satsangi servicemen from your department have kept on sending
Radha Soami to you and to everyone else. Ever since they went
to China, in every letter that they wrote they wished Radha
Soami to all the satsangis living with you.

[August 1901]

∿ 94 ∿

Radha Soami. Radha Soami Ji is the Comforter.

Radha Soami from Jaimal Singh to my obedient son, Babu
Sawan Singh. Your letter was received and I was happy to read
it. A dictated reply in Urdu was sent, but it was not written
properly. Pandit Ganda Ram wrote it. You wrote that I should
let you know the date of my visit. My son, it is my firm command
that you are never to ask that I should come. Have the satsangis
taken a vow to have darshan, but by my going to them instead?
Well, if they were unable to come, I could visit if I had the time,
and if my body could stand the strain of travel. You do not consider, my son, whether or not I am able to come. I will be free
only in the month of August by the 28th or 29th. I hope that
then, with the grace of Hazur, I can come for ten days. As of
now, I definitely intend to come at that time. For the rest, whatever is the pleasure of Hazur Soami Ji will happen. Do your
bhajan and simran every day, my son. Please accept Radha
Soami from Bibi and all the others. The train to Rawalpindi is
always heavily crowded.

6 August 1901

~ 95 ~

[Dictated]

Radha Soami. Radha Soami Ji is the Comforter.

Radha Soami from Jaimal Singh to my obedient son, Babu Sawan Singh. I received your postcard and was happy to read it. Regarding your request that I come to Khairagali on 20 September, I am unable to come under any circumstances. Perhaps in the winter I may come to Rawalpindi. Please inquire and let me know when the troops will arrive there in October. Perhaps at that time I will let you know whether or not I can come.

Up to the 19th no letter has been received from Bachint Singh Ji at Mehmansinghwala. What could be the reason? Write to him immediately and tell him that he should come and return the shoes himself; I will give him the fare both ways. I had only one pair of shoes to wear, which Bachint Singh borrowed, so now I have no shoes for my feet. I do not have any shoes with me—impress this upon him. From Rawalpindi, Ram Chand the treasurer sent a postcard in which he wrote that you had been transferred to Rawalpindi. No date, etc., was given.

Anyway, keep doing your bhajan and simran every day whenever you are free. This is a must. At that time, focus the mind, surat and nirat, all three, with feeling and the longing of the higher mind, to listen to the Shabd-dhun and develop love and devotion for it. At all times, even while working, keep the mind's attachment in it. I shall write more fully after your letter arrives.

Chacha Ji sends his Radha Soami greetings to you; all of them wish that grace and mercy be upon you. He has also written that he has received 210 rupees and that the rooms are half-ready. He further writes that money should be sent only when he asks for it. Do not send it now. Radha Soami from Bibi Ji to you, her true brother. Also Radha Soami from the Dera residents. Radha Soami as well from Bhag Singh and all the servicemen, and from the satsangis of Wadala and the satsangis at the Dera. Please convey Radha Soami from Bhag Singh to all the satsangis who are at Khairagali.

19 September 1901

∽ 96 ∽

Radha Soami. Radha Soami Ji is the Comforter.

Radha Soami from Jaimal Singh to my obedient son, Babu Sawan Singh, and to Chanan Singh, Basant Singh, Narain Singh, and to all the other satsangis at Rawalpindi. My dear son, the money order for 10 rupees has arrived. You should now write to me about the total number of those who want to become satsangis. Let me know the address to which I should send a postcard or letter. A canister of ghee is packed and ready, and when you write I will send it immediately by parcel to Rawalpindi railway station. I will write about other matters after hearing from you. Do your bhajan and simran every day, my son. At work or while moving around, always keep listening to the Shabd-dhun. Listen to it with the surat and nirat, with an inner yearning and the love of the higher mind. Do not yearn for any worldly work. Do not allow the mind to waver, keep it within the will of the Satguru. Bibi sends her Radha Soami to you, Babu Ji, her true brother. Radha Soami from everyone.

11 November 1901

~ 97 ~

Radha Soami. Radha Soami Ji is the Comforter.

Radha Soami from Jaimal Singh to my obedient son, Babu Sawan Singh. May the grace and mercy of the compassionate Anami Lord always be upon you, dear son. Your letter was received and I was absolutely delighted to read its contents. I have sent a canister of ghee to you. Two satsangis of the Twenty-Second Battery, Sunder Singh and Surain Singh, both of Company No. 5, agreed to take it with them. They are both reporting to their station in Rawalpindi on 20 November 1901. They will get off the train at 8 or 10 a.m., so send Chanan Singh at 6 or 7 a.m. on the 20th. They will call out his name after getting down; Chanan Singh should respond and meet them, get the canister of ghee, and take it to your residence. If they do not show up on that particular train, he should stay there that whole day—20 November—but they will definitely come, because they have to report back to their battery that same day. They are in line nos. 22 and 24. Chanan Singh knows about this; send me a letter about it afterwards.

From your village, Mehmansinghwala, Bachint Singh has sent over 400 kilograms of flour by railway delivery. It has been ground very finely and with loving care, and is being used for the sangat. I am very pleased with Bachint Singh. My son, in your letter you have neither noted your locality, street, or house number, nor have you put a return address on the envelope. Many days have passed and you still have not sent your address. You mentioned that I have not written to you for a long time. That is because I was waiting to hear if you were permanently located in Rawalpindi. Since you will now stay there, so I have sent you a letter. You have not written about how Basant Singh is doing in his studies. Be sure to write about it. Also write and let me know whether you will receive the same allowance and extras at Rawalpindi that you were getting at Khairagali.

Bhajan and simran is to be done every day, my son. Keep it in mind that all that exists is the Satguru's. All occupations, material goods, every worldly thing, sons, daughters, relatives, the physical body, and the love and inner yearning of surat and nirat, and the higher mind, the Shabd-dhun, one's intelligence and intellect, and the hands, feet, tongue, nose, mouth and eyes, everything is the Satguru's: "I have handed over all to the Satguru and work only to serve him." The sound of the Shabd-dhun that comes from our original home, from the wondrous Anami Radha Soami, is the true form of the Satguru. All that is happening in the world emanates from within his command. Always listen to the Shabd-dhun with love and devotion. While continuing with your worldly duties, listen to it devotedly with the mind and the surat and nirat. Never let the mind become detached from it. Do not yearn for any worldly work. Nothing in the world is greater than the wealth of Nam. Why hanker after anything when you have already found the greatest home of all?

I will let you know about my visit when you write to let me know your address. The words in this letter were put down haphazardly, so please read them carefully.

Radha Soami greetings from Bibi to you, her true brother. Radha Soami to Chanan Singh, Basant Singh, and all the other satsangis who might be there. Radha Soami from Bibi, from the sadhus and all the Dera residents, and from Bhag Singh to everyone and to you. I had a fever when I started this letter, but it is gone now.

16 November 1901

∼ 98 ∼

Radha Soami. Radha Soami Ji is the Comforter.

Radha Soami from Jaimal Singh to my obedient son, Babu
Sawan Singh. Dear son, I will either take the mail train leaving
here on Tuesday, 26 November, the 12th of Maghar, at 1 p.m.
to reach Rawalpindi at 3 a.m. and shall need someone to meet
me at the railway station. Or if I do not catch that train, I will
take the one leaving Beas at 6 p.m., arriving at Rawalpindi
railway station at 10 a.m. on Wednesday, 27 November. The
day of departure will still be Tuesday, whether at 1 p.m. or 6
p.m. in the evening. That day, someone should be definitely at
the railway station. I shall come as the will of Hazur commands
it. He can do whatever pleases him.

Do your bhajan and simran every day, my son. Give my
Radha Soami to Basant Singh and Chanan Singh. Bibi sends
Radha Soami to you, her true brother. Radha Soami from Bibi
and everyone at the Dera.

23 November 1901

∼ 99 ∼

Radha Soami. Radha Soami Ji is the Comforter.

Radha Soami from Jaimal Singh to my obedient son, Babu
Sawan Singh. May the grace and mercy of the compassionate
Anami Lord always be upon you, dear son. Your letter has arrived and I am very happy to know of your well-being. You have
written that a few seekers did not get initiated. Please send me
their names with their districts, and also let me know how many
there are, and I will send you a reply. It is good that you are

holding satsang on Sundays. A letter from Chacha Ji stated that
a stone with your name engraved on it would be placed in the
rooms. I have made a request to him that this should not be
done, because no other room in Soami Bagh has any name engraved in it.

Babu Gajja Singh stayed here for seven days. Sub-Tehsildar
Sant Lal came on ten days' leave; he also stayed at the Dera.
They both left on the 30th—we had satsang every day. Whenever you are free from work, my son, immediately focus your attention in simran; then lovingly direct the inner seeing faculty,
nirat, and the mind's inner longing towards the higher mind, and
catch the sound of the Shabd-dhun, leaving behind all the desires of the mind for worldly activities and attractions. Nothing
but the Dhun should be heard; everything else should be ig-
nored. Gradually, little by little, distinguish the Dhun and control the mind's agitations. By doing this every day the soul will
develop such a love for the Shabd-dhun that it will only want the
rapture of the Shabd.

Please convey my Radha Soami to Basant Singh. He
should work wholeheartedly with love and perseverance. Radha
Soami to Chanan Singh, Narain Singh, Babu Amar Singh, and
Ram Chand the treasurer. You should do your bhajan and simran every day. Radha Soami to all the satsangis of the three batteries. All are urged to daily attend to their bhajan and simran,
and also to do their government work well and wholeheartedly.
My son, please write also about all those who still remain without Nam.

Bibi sends Radha Soami to you, her dear brother. Radha
Soami from Bibi and all the sadhus at the Dera. Live in the
town, my son, but remain unaffected as though you were living
all alone. I am very pleased with you.

31 December 1901

~ 100 ~

Radha Soami. Radha Soami Ji is the Comforter.

Radha Soami from Jaimal Singh to my obedient son, Babu
Sawan Singh. May the grace and mercy of the compassionate
Anami Lord, Radha Soami, always be upon you, dear son.
Please instruct the men from the batteries in the technique of
practising simran and sitting in bhajan. They should do it like
this: they should first do simran of the five names for a quarter-
hour and then contemplate on the form of the Satguru. After that
they should gradually attach the attention to the sound of the
Shabd. Then slowly and gently fix the inner hearing and seeing
faculties, surat and nirat—the inclination of the inner mind towards love is called *nirat*—into the sound of the Shabd-dhun.
Then the mind will never run hither and thither. Please explain
all this to these people, and you, too, should never miss your
daily bhajan and simran. Always keep your mind inclined in that
direction, and do not bring your self into any work you do.
Rather, realize all the time that you are nothing: "Body, mind,
wealth, all, everything belongs to the Satguru; I am not in them."
Realizing this, with love and devotion merge the surat, nirat, and
the mind into the Shabd-dhun. Then the mind will not go anywhere. When your self is absolutely uninvolved in anything, then
the sound of the fundamental form, Shabd-dhun, that is like the
sound of the vina, will descend immediately through grace from
the highest. And even now it is coming every day, but the mind,
surat and nirat have been filled with ego, leaving no space for
grace and mercy. Thus, through the sound of the Shabd-dhun
one reaches Sach Khand. It is a heavy and difficult task to part
company with the self and to realize that "I am nothing, everything is the Satguru's; nothing is mine." The ego within should

disappear completely. Then whatever work is performed is actually done by the Lord himself, who comes and does it all.

Do your bhajan and simran every day, my son. If you say that you are occupied with too much work, that is no excuse, because the mind, surat and nirat still continue to be unoccupied. The mind stays intoxicated with the world like a person drunk with alcohol: all inebriated, the mind does not engage in bhajan and simran, and offers excuses that there is no free time for meditation. This is all false; it is a deception of the mind. Our breaths, our eating, sitting, walking and sleeping are all accountable. Except for the Satguru, no one is going to get the individual liberated. Even now try to understand! Keep your attention in the Shabd-dhun, and think how much of your time has been wasted in idle talk. This time will never come again. Think! Remember your own death. We are not going to live here forever. Our days, time, hours, seconds, breaths, are all numbered. Pull your mind out of worldly desires and fix the attention in the Shabd.

Please give my Radha Soami to Chanan Singh, Narain Singh, and Basant Singh. Chanan Singh Ji, the cake of soap that you gave is not with me; it was left behind at your place. Please look for it. All are urged to do their bhajan and simran every day.

Radha Soami to Babu Amar Singh. I received your postcard; it was well written. Before sitting in meditation, do simran for a quarter-hour or more, and then slowly and gradually put your attention into the Shabd. The attention will become fixed in the Shabd-dhun by doing this every day. The mind will also become still through the daily practice. This is the reply to your postcard. Since the mind and soul are still soiled, they will become pure through practising meditation every day.

Please give my Radha Soami to Sunder Singh the carpenter, Bhai Sher Singh, the satsangis of the three batteries, Havildar

Ladha Singh of the Twenty-Second Battery, Sunder Singh, Surain Singh, Ram Chand the treasurer, Asa Ram, and the tailor satsangis of the army barracks. Everyone is urged to do his bhajan and simran every day. Bibi's Radha Soami to you, her true brother. Radha Soami to everyone from Bibi and all the sadhus at the Dera.

The enclosed names have been sent for your record. Please keep this paper with you. Instructions may be given to those who come to you, but you are not to seek them out. If you are free, hold satsang for an hour on Sunday. Those who come are to sit in bhajan for half an hour, but do not send for anyone who does not come. Bachint Singh has not arrived as yet. Probably he is busy.

2 January 1902

~ 101 ~

[Dictated]

Radha Soami. Radha Soami Ji is the Comforter.

Radha Soami greetings from Jaimal Singh to my obedient son, Babu Sawan Singh, and to Basant Singh, Chanan Singh, Narain Singh, Babu Amar Singh, and Diwan Singh. A letter was received from you, and I was very happy to read it and learn of your well-being. A letter also came from Babu Amar Singh, Sant Singh, Chanan Singh, and Narain Singh, with the news from all four of them in one letter. I was very happy to read it too. Whatever they all have requested will be granted slowly and gradually by Hazur Radha Soami. All four of them are to know that this is the sole reply to their letter. May grace and mercy be upon them.

A postcard came from Diwan Singh. I was very happy to read it. The reply to it is the same: I learnt about your situation from your postcard. All of you are urged to do your bhajan and simran daily and to listen to the Shabd-dhun with love and devotion.

Babu Ji, you are reminded to send a postcard two days before the day of your arrival so that someone can receive you at the railway station. Let us know about the train as well. Because of your expected arrival, the reply to your letter is being given in a postcard. Radha Soami on behalf of Bibi Ji to you, her dear brother. And Radha Soami to all the satsangis from all the other residents of the Dera.

29 January 1902

∼ 102 ∼

Radha Soami. Radha Soami Ji is the Comforter.

Radha Soami greetings from Jaimal Singh to my obedient son, Babu Sawan Singh. I have received your money order of 10 rupees which I will use for the sangat's expenses. Have you received the copy of *Anurag Sagar?* Please take good care of it. I have sent it through a satsangi, Ganga Singh, of the Third Battery; he was to join his battery on 20 February. Write to me immediately upon receiving the book. When you are ready to have it printed, assign someone to be at the printing press to go over the contents and remove all mistakes, or you may go over it yourself. Only then should it be printed. The pages of the book should be carefully examined before printing so that there are no mistakes. This book, *Anurag Sagar*, contains many additional pieces of writing by Kabir Sahib that are very good, so please have them all printed. They are absolutely first-rate. It also includes a section entitled "Pran Sangli," which is not to be printed. But whatever the cost, have all the other sections printed. I have not read these myself, but I have heard them. If I were to read and examine them myself before sending them, it would cause a long delay. So it does not matter; they are all good. You should go ahead and have them all printed.

Bachint Singh wrote a letter from home that he had reached there safely. Convey my Radha Soami to Chanan Singh, Narain Singh, Diwan Singh, and Babu Amar Singh. Please tell them all to do their bhajan and simran every day. And you too, my son, listen to the sound of the Shabd-dhun with love and devotion. Keep the inner faculties of surat and nirat, and the higher mind, all three, engaged in the subtle Sound and do not let any speculations about worldly work distract your attention. When you are engaged in work for the Satguru, the Lord of all, or doing bhajan, simran, or reading sacred texts, at those times no other thoughts should remain in the mind. Remember this well, my son.

Radha Soami to everyone from the sadhus at the Dera, and Radha Soami to the satsangis of the three batteries. Please tell them to sit in meditation every day. Ganga Singh of the Third Battery came here on 13 February. He left for his home on the 14th. I gave him the book, *Anurag Sagar*, and asked him to deliver it to you at your residence. So please get it from him. Bibi is not at the Dera now; she has gone on a visit. My son, I repeat: during bhajan or simran, keep no thoughts of worldly affairs in your mind, nor allow mental speculations of any kind to remain within. First do your simran for a quarter-hour, and then slowly and gently fix the attention in the Shabd-dhun. At that point give up simran; keep the mind and soul fixed in the sound of the Shabd-dhun—you will then taste its bliss. Grace and mercy from the highest will descend upon you.

24 February [1902]

∼ 103 ∼

Radha Soami. Radha Soami Ji is the Comforter.

Radha Soami from Jaimal Singh to my obedient son, Babu Sawan Singh, and to Chanan Singh, Narain Singh, Babu Amar Singh, and Ram Chand the treasurer. The news is that the canister of coal tar has arrived; some freight was charged for it. Both of the previous canisters of coal tar were used up in putting a protective layer under the walls of the veranda, the small rooms, and the durbar hall. Ismail Khan, brother of Nabi Bakhsh the painter, stayed for six or seven days and applied the coal tar. Your letter came and I was very happy to read and know about your well-being. Remain happy wherever the Lord places you, my son. Wherever he keeps you, consider it as his grace and mercy.

All of you should do your bhajan and simran every day. Always, with love and devotion keep the inner faculties of surat and nirat and the higher mind attached to the Shabd-dhun within, while doing your worldly work with the body. You are never to keep love for worldly work or material possessions in your mind. Instead, think like this: "It is not I in the body; the Satguru is all in all." The attention is definitely to be kept in the sound of the Shabd-dhun every day.

Please give Hazur Soami Ji's books to Sunder Singh the carpenter. I have received the information on its price. Have the books bound.

Bibi's Radha Soami to you, her true brother. Radha Soami from Bibi and all the sadhus at the Dera. Please also give Radha Soami to the satsangis of the three batteries.

26 February 1902

∼ 104 ∼

Radha Soami. Radha Soami Ji is the Comforter.

Radha Soami greetings from Jaimal Singh to my obedient son, Babu Sawan Singh. Dear son, two books, *Ghat Ramayan* and another that includes *Anurag Sagar, Ratan Sagar,* and some other sacred writings, have been sent to you. They are free from errors, and are printed in Gurmukhi. It would be good if they could be printed. If that is not possible, please send them back with Bachint Singh, and let me know whether or not the previous copy of *Anurag Sagar* has been printed. I promised the person from whom these books were borrowed to return them in a month, but it would be all right if they could be printed even in two months.

Please send 100 rupees in two money orders of 50 each, because to receive a single money order of 100 rupees I have to go personally to the post office.* My intention is to get 150,000 bricks ready—the dung fuel is very expensive. So far about 40,000 bricks have been made. Do remember to send the books back with Bachint Singh if they cannot be printed.

Please do your bhajan and simran every day. Do not keep the self in anything. Place your hope in Anami Radha Soami, the wondrous-form, fathomless Duvami. *Duvami* means that as far as the Anami Being, all is effulgence. A single ray reaches Agam, Alakh and Sach Khand (Sat Lok). Within Sach Khand and the fathomless wondrous form, all is He. The attentive faculties of the soul, surat and nirat, and the merciful glance of the Satguru reside in that home. Now fix your hope in that home, which is our own, while you perform your worldly duties with the Guru's grace, since all the material things of the world are perishable. Keep the inner faculties of surat and nirat, and the

---

* At Sathiala, quite a distance from the Dera.

higher mind, all three, attached to the sound of the Shabd every day.

Please convey my Radha Soami to Chanan Singh, Narain Singh, the treasurer, and the satsangi devotees of the three army batteries. Radha Soami from Bibi and the sadhus at the Dera. Karam Singh has been here for the last two days and will be leaving today.

10 March [1902]

~ 105 ~

Radha Soami. Radha Soami Ji is the Comforter.

Radha Soami greetings from Jaimal Singh to both my obedient sons, Chanan Singh and Narain Singh. I have received your letter and I was happy to read it. What you write about the mind— that it keeps thinking of bad deeds all the time—is very true. The mind is like that. But always remember the words of the Satguru, then the mind will calm down. Do your simran inwardly—while sitting, sleeping, walking, or doing any other work, continue with it in your mind. The approach of death can be heard overhead; remember it, and don't keep the self in anything. Consider the body, mind, and wealth to be the Satguru's. Tell the mind that since you have sold it to the Satguru, why is it working uselessly? And inwardly pray and appeal to the Satguru all the time that he may protect you. Do not put your hopes in worldly affairs. Whatever happens will happen with the will of the Satguru— consider that to be for your benefit. Listen to the sound of the Shabd-dhun every day. Decrease the night-time hours of sleep by a couple of hours. His grace and mercy will always be upon you.

Radha Soami greetings to Babu Sawan Singh, Basant Singh, Nikka, and all and every satsangi. The news is that all the parshad that was sent with Bachint Singh has arrived here.

The other things that were sent have also been received. Bachint Singh arrived by the twelve o'clock train and went home the same day by the night train. I have followed your information about the books. Please arrange to get 500 copies of *Anurag Sagar* printed—the rest is up to you. And *Ghat Ramayan* also must be printed regardless of the cost—of course it is again up to you whether to get it printed up to 500 copies or less. Fifty thousand bricks have already been made; we are now making them every day. Please do your bhajan and simran every day. Stay happy wherever the Lord wants you to work. Whatever he does will be for your good. I will write a detailed letter later on. The canister of ghee will be sent to you on 17 March by railway delivery; please collect it from the railway station. Radha Soami greetings from Bibi and all the others.

16 March 1902

∼ 106 ∼

Radha Soami. Radha Soami Ji is the Comforter.

Radha Soami greetings from Jaimal Singh to my obedient son, Babu Sawan Singh. Dear son, a canister of ghee has been sent to you by parcel. Please send someone to Rawalpindi railway station to pick it up and then inform me by letter. Your 100 rupees have been received (Bachint Singh left five notes of 20 each) and credited to the expense of the bricks.

Ghat Ramayan must be printed, my son—whatever it costs, the money spent for such spiritual ends is well spent—and get two hundred copies of *Anurag Sagar* printed as well. This will be a benevolent act on your part. We shall see to Hazur Soami Ji's books later on, in two years' time or whenever his will ordains it.

The brick-kiln has been stacked with 60,000 bricks. Please continue with your bhajan and simran every day, and give my

Radha Soami greetings to Basant Singh, Nikka, Chanan Singh, Narain Singh, Ram Chand Ji the treasurer, and to the satsangi brothers of the three army batteries. You and the other satsangis must remember to do your bhajan and simran every day. Detach yourselves from everything and love the Satguru from within. Keep the surat, nirat and the higher mind inwardly focused on the music of the Shabd-dhun, and with the Satguru's love examine the quality of that sound. Since the human body is unreal like a dream, always be apprehensive that we won't stay in the world forever. As the body itself is unreal, everything else in the world is unreal too. Nam-dhun alone is real, so hold fast to it. When every day you wholeheartedly attend to the Shabd, the mind will shed its evil tendencies, and worldly desires, which are the cause of birth and rebirth, will leave it. The mind will then love the Satguru. Always remain within the will of the Satguru.

Radha Soami from Bibi and the sadhus at the Dera to everyone. I am very pleased with you, my son. Do not be afraid. Hazur will do everything himself; you should detach yourself from it all.

18 March [1902]

∾ 107 ∾

Radha Soami. Radha Soami Ji is the Comforter.

Radha Soami from Jaimal Singh to my obedient sons, Chanan Singh, Narain Singh, Basant Singh, Babu Sawan Singh, the treasurer, and the satsangis of the three batteries. This is to let you know that your postcard was received and I was happy to read it. Do your bhajan and simran every day, my sons, and whether working, moving around, walking, sitting or sleeping, never forget to think of Shabd-dhun and simran. Grace and mercy are upon you all the time. It is Shabd-dhun which is our protector.

Babu Ji, you should know that there is no need to become perturbed in any work, because our real storehouse of wealth is the Shabd-dhun and that already has been bestowed upon you. All other baggage belongs to the world. So merge yourself in the sound of the Shabd-dhun and do your official work with the body. Keep the attention of the mind and surat and nirat in the Dhun. His gracious mercy is blessing you with every breath. I will write a detailed letter later on. Radha Soami from Bibi and all the sadhus. May grace and mercy be upon all the satsangis at Rawalpindi. My son, please convey my Radha Soami to Basant Singh and Ma Ji.

4 April 1902

∼ 108 ∼

Radha Soami. Radha Soami Ji is the Comforter.

Radha Soami from Jaimal Singh to my obedient son, Babu Sawan Singh. Your money order of 10 rupees arrived on 7 April. I meant to write a letter to you, but due to lack of time ended up writing this postcard instead. Please consider it substantial; a full letter will be written later on. The brick-kiln is now ready: one hundred and six thousand bricks have been stacked in it. It will be fired on 14 April, the 2nd of Vaisakh. After that, if I am free, I will come to Rawalpindi for six days. If I am not free, I won't come. Please have *Anurag Sagar* and *Ghat Ramayan* printed as quickly as possible. A lot of people want them as soon as they are ready.

Do your bhajan and simran every day. Day and night, the surat and nirat and the higher mind should keep yearning to hear the Shabd-dhun within. By all means carry on with your worldly work, my son, but your inner longing should always be for the Shabd-dhun. Keep a continuous watch over your mind so that it does not go out of the Satguru's will—Satguru's will is to be kept in mind all the time.

Please convey Radha Soami to Chanan Singh, Basant Singh, Narain Singh, and the satsangis of the three batteries. Everyone is urged to do his bhajan and simran every day because this time will not come again. Indeed, you must try to listen to the sound of Shabd-dhun, for only then will all your work be accomplished. Radha Soami from Bibi and all others. Please convey my Radha Soami to Ma Ji.

8 April 1902

∼ 109 ∼

Radha Soami. Radha Soami Ji is the Comforter.

Radha Soami greetings from Baba Jaimal Singh Ji to my obedient son, Babu Sawan Singh Ji. This is to let you know that on 14 April I will leave Beas by the night train to arrive at Rawalpindi at ten o'clock the next morning, so someone should be at Rawalpindi railway station on Tuesday at the time of the train's arrival. Bibi Ji will accompany me. After staying there from Tuesday to Friday, we will leave on Saturday morning—we will come for four days only. It is my firm command that at the time of departure no one should implore me by saying "Please do not go today, leave tomorrow."

Please continue with your bhajan and simran. Radha Soami from Bibi Ji. Radha Soami from all the Dera residents. And please inform all the disciples in the army batteries that they should make it a point to come. Your man should wait for the train from morning till evening.

10 April 1902

∾ 110 ∾

[Dictated]

Radha Soami. Radha Soami Ji is the Comforter.

From Jaimal Singh: Radha Soami greetings to my obedient son, Babu Sawan Singh, and to Basant Singh, Harbans Singh, Narain Singh, Babu Gulab Singh, Dr. Ishar Das, Babu Gajja Singh, and Aya Singh. Your letter arrived and I was happy to read it. It was very well written. You should continue doing your bhajan and simran. The compassionate Radha Soami Ji is always by your side; his grace and mercy will be upon you. Chanan Singh and Inder Singh came to the Dera, and left for home after staying here one night. Inder Singh asked for initiation, but I did not give it because I had no information about his character.

You have written that you would like to invite Ma Ji and also the young Bibi, Basant Singh's wife, to stay with you. You have my permission gladly to invite them both. Write to them immediately so that they can come. For the rest, do as it seems right to you. You have written about the education of ————'s son. Have him educated as you think best; that is a good thing to do. Do this as you please; I can only instruct you to handle such matters well so that you do not feel any hardship. If he studies, that's well and good, but he should not spoil the other boy. Anyway, you have my permission. But why inquire about such household matters from me? I can give advice if all the family members are gurmukhs, but here one person goes one way, and the others go some other. So among them all, how many will you turn back? That is why I have written to you that you should have the younger Bibi, Basant Singh's wife, and Ma Ji join you. Also read Hazur Soami Ji's book and keep doing bhajan and simran. The compassionate Radha Soami Ji is always by your side; his grace and mercy will be upon you. Once again I write that I cannot advise anything about ———'s boy, nor should you inquire about him from me: neither am I asking you to educate him, nor not to educate him. What do I have to do with all this—just think about it!

You and other satsangis are urged to keep doing your bhajan and simran. If there are mosquitoes around, that's good. At least you will get up at night to do your meditation! Otherwise you and the other satsangis may not remember Nam; this way at least you will do so. Chanan Singh also tells me that Ma Ji and the younger Bibi, wife of Basant Singh, will be coming there. Will you be coming here this Sunday? You must come. Do come if you get leave. Radha Soami from Bibi Ji to you, her dear brother. Radha Soami also from everyone else at the Dera.

Radha Soami. From Jaimal Singh: Radha Soami greetings to my obedient son, Diwan Singh. Your letter in Gurmukhi was received and I was very happy to read it. There is no need to worry about anything. Request Babu Sawan Singh to find employment for you. When everyone else has work, why should you remain without it? You too should have work. You will get it if there is a vacancy; when a vacancy is found, you will fill it. You should do your bhajan and simran, and not become perturbed. The worldly work will be done by the Lord himself. All the satsangis who live in one place should send only one letter, and not write separately. How can I write separate replies to everyone? I do not have that much time. You should go and see Babu Sawan Singh Ji and have him include your letter in his. Radha Soami on behalf of Bibi Ji. All of you should write to me in one letter. In future do not write so many separate letters.

April 1902

~ 111 ~

[Partially dictated]

Radha Soami. Radha Soami Ji is the Comforter.

Radha Soami greetings from Jaimal Singh to my obedient son, Babu Sawan Singh. This is to let you know that so far no answer has been received from Agra. We received one message, but there was no mention of the books. If you received a letter from there, please let me know. I now think that only 250 or 200 copies of *Ghat Ramayan* should be printed. However, the money thus saved, by reducing the number of copies of *Ghat Ramayan* to below 250, should be spent in printing up to 500 more copies of the prose edition of Hazur Soami Ji's *Sar Bachan*. The total amount spent would then remain the same, and 500 copies of Hazur's *Sar Bachan* in prose would be printed at the same time—otherwise they will have to be printed later. The cost of *Ghat Ramayan* will come at the most to 200 rupees, not more, and both jobs will get done—Soami Ji's prose *Sar Bachan* should cost about a third or half of *Ghat Ramayan*. Please ask the printer. It is in his interest, and also in our interest, as everything will be done simultaneously. But do ask him, because the cost of *Ghat Ramayan* won't be much, and there will be lots of people who will want to buy Hazur Soami Ji's book. If this can be arranged, well and good, but let me know even if the printers do not agree. Thus both the verse and prose editions of Hazur Soami Ji's books in Gurmukhi will be printed. Write your letter in Gurmukhi, and also let me know whether you have moved into the bungalow in the cantonment. Chanan Singh has done good work here, and I am very pleased with him. Radha Soami to all, and to Basant Singh, Chanan Singh, Narain Singh, Diwan Singh, the Bibi Jis, Ma Ji, the younger

Bibi Jis, and the boy, Narinder Singh. May grace and mercy be upon them all. Please convey Radha Soami to these men from the army platoon: Sunder Singh, Surain Singh, Subedar-Major's son Kharak Singh, and the treasurer. They are all urged to do their bhajan and simran every day. May grace and mercy be upon them all.

Do not be afraid of anything. And do not worry about the work at the kilns. It is government work, and government work will take care of itself. You remain ready to do your task; the compassionate Radha Soami will do all the work himself. Continue working with an honest heart—Radha Soami himself will help and bestow his grace and mercy upon you. If the previous officer was able to profit the government to the tune of thousands, that will happen during your tenure as well. Remove all apprehensions from your heart and work fearlessly. Know that you should be nervous only about doing your meditation. Do not waste time uselessly. Be concerned about time spent in vain, and regret why so many breaths were wasted, since they were utilized neither in worldly affairs nor in spiritual pursuit.

Do not mourn over the passing away of family members. Our material wealth and the three bodies—physical, astral, and causal—are all like leaves on a tree. Shabd is the tree on which all—from the transcendent, enlightened souls down to the householders—grow like leaves. The leaves do not last more than a year. Every year they all drop from the tree, but the tree does not feel the loss nor does it accompany any leaf that falls. Just see! How much understanding the tree displays! Our knowledge, however, is not even that of a tree; and yet the tree has no sense, and we humans are conscious beings. The tree cannot attain liberation like we can. You see, our pride of worldly things—of honour, praise, possessions, rank, wealth, money and dignity, sons, daughters, shops, mansions, wife—in fact of all material things, including that of kingship, is false. We do not have the understanding of even a senseless tree that does not mourn for its leaves. So regard the world as false; believe firmly that the world and its relationships are like a dream. Carry on with your worldly business knowing within your heart that it is unreal. Always keep simran in your mind, knowing that the true wealth is Shabd, and that all the rest is false. Only the Satguru's words are true, they are never false. Always keep them in your heart and continue to do your simran. With love and devotion attach your higher mind and soul to the Shabd-dhun and merge yourself into it. When attending to meditation and listening to the Shabd-dhun, put all your worries aside, because there is nothing higher than meditation. Increase the duration of your practice from day to day, never decrease it; always keep this in your mind. Whether awake or asleep, or moving about, keep the thought of Sach Khand, the Alakh, Agam, Anami Radha Soami's abode, in your heart. Remember that you are to go there—that is your home. Your love will thus remain detached from the world. The sound of that Shabd and the image of the abode of Anami Radha Soami should always remain imprinted on the mind. That is our real work. There is no higher work than this. Keep doing it every day; then all your endeavour will bear fruit.

Keep the Satguru and the Satguru's words in your mind, and take the self out. When the body, mind, wealth, everything belongs to the Satguru, then all things of the world and all relationships also belong to him—we are nothing. The Shabd-dhun also is the Satguru's, we are nothing—always remember these words. Radha Soami is always your protector. He will never let you feel the pain of the world. I am pleased with you. Drive out forever the love of the world from your heart and replace it with love for the Satguru. Eliminating the world from your mind, always study and deliberate over the sacred texts so that the mind and soul may enjoy the rapture of the stream of Shabd-dhun, which has already been bestowed upon you. Eliminate desire for the world, then all will be Shabd and nothing but Shabd. I am exceedingly, immensely pleased with you. Radha Soami is always showering mercy upon you, but make your mind worthy of that mercy. When the Lord, through his grace, sends pain or gives death, do not question why he has done so. Instead, give him thanks, and submit to his command—then you will become a gurmukh.

Have you received a letter from Mehmansinghwala? Please let me know this when you write to me. Radha Soami on behalf of Bibi Ji and from everyone else at the Dera, and also from all the satsangis of Wadala. Your grandfather brought your letter on 2 May at 1 p.m., and I was happy to read it. I have understood the whole situation. I did not mean that you should not live in the cantonment. I thought that there were restrictions in the cantonment, while life in the city would be more free. In the cantonment, live by yourself, like the officers. The lifestyle in the cantonments generally prohibits too many people lodging together, so now you should not allow too many people to visit you, as they used to do in the town. That's why I said it, but I am very pleased with the situation now. It is good to live in the forest, but in solitude. You shouldn't have unnecessary visitors; live like the Englishmen whose visitors come only by invitation. The atmosphere is good but one should not get attached to anyone. You should not let anyone but a satsangi stay there, nor should you encourage people to come for a visit. However, for a satsangi, there is no bar. Do not encourage anyone to know about your bungalow. I am very happy with you. Baba Ji will be at the Dera tomorrow, 4 May 1902, and will give the Sunday satsang. The army servicemen are near you but please do not enter into intellectual discussions with any of them. Remain meek and humble—I am pleased with that. Chanan Singh also likes outdoor living. So all this is good.

[In Gurmukhi script, Baba Ji's writing:] My son, I had this letter written in Urdu by someone else. The Dhun that comes from the right side comes from Sach Khand. Keep your mind, the higher mind, and surat and nirat attached to the Shabd-dhun so that they all may become the Shabd form. Then the mind will become pure.

3 May 1902

∼ 112 ∼

[Dictated]

Radha Soami. Radha Soami Ji is the Comforter.

From Jaimal Singh: Radha Soami greetings to my obedient son, Babu Sawan Singh, and to Basant Singh, Narain Singh, Surain Singh, Chanan Singh, Sunder Singh, Ma Ji, the younger Bibis, the little boy, and all the other satsangis at Rawalpindi. Your letter arrived and I was very happy to read it and know the contents. I have understood its import. Do not be perturbed about Basant Singh; continue educating him, and train him in draftsmanship as well. What does it matter if twice he has not passed his examination? He will pass later. Who has seen his destiny? You are feeling sorry that your boys do not study, when even the little ones of others do. Just think: have those other boys received Nam? When they die, they will go to the earthly hell, while yours will go home to Sach Khand. How can your family be compared with others? Why do you go downwards? Move upwards. For the rest, do as you think proper.

This book is also Hazur Soami Ji's text; use it for proofreading—it has been corrected here. Have the printing done from the first copy, that is, the original text that came from Agra. This one is a recent copy. Wherever it needed corrections, I have made them, so have the printing done according to it, but leave the first copy of Hazur Soami Ji's text as it is. I have sent Babu Gajja Singh to take care of the proofreading if you are not free because of your work. If you can do it, well and good; then send him back. Five hundred copies of the prose edition also should be printed. I will write to Chacha Ji about it and let you know his reply. I will request that we keep the book for two months; the rest will be according to his wishes. As for *Ghat Ramayan*, 200 copies should be enough. For the rest, do as you wish. Your grandfather came here; he complained that ———— drinks heavily. We should realize that if a drunkard and bad person stays in the house, your family will get a bad name as well. Tell him to stop, and if he does not do so, give up his company.

You are requested to please keep doing bhajan and simran every day. Fix your love in the Shabd-dhun and listen to it with love and devotion, for by listening repeatedly you will become pure. Worldly activities go on according to previous karmas: as the karmas become manifest, they work themselves out. So have no apprehension about them; sometimes they are good, sometimes bad. There should be no anxiety about them; your anxiety should be about meditation. Always keep in mind that everything is a dream. Do not fall in love with the activities of the world; keep the mind unattached, and remember the Satguru's instructions. The whole workshop of the world is unreal like a dream, and it will continue like that. Attach the mind and the faculties of surat and nirat, with love and devotion to the sound of Shabd-dhun. Let go of any anxiety about worldly work. When you engage in meditation, do it with an unattached mind, as in a dream when there is no awareness of any worldly business. Basant Singh, Ma Ji, the Bibi Jis, and Sher Singh are all urged to keep doing their bhajan and simran every day.

Radha Soami on behalf of Bibi Ji to you, her dear brother, and also Radha Soami from all the residents of the Dera. No one has written from Mehmansinghwala since your grandfather went back.

Radha Soami to Ram Chand the treasurer. This is to let you know that two brass kitchen pans were bought with your 15 rupees and sent to Agra. The freight was paid from here. Keep doing your bhajan and simran.

[May] 1902

∼ 113 ∼

Ik Onkaar Satgur Parsaad.[*]

"There is but one God. By the True Guru's Grace He is obtained."

Radha Soami. Radha Soami Ji is the Comforter.

Wahiguru Ji ki Fateh and Radha Soami greetings from Jaimal Singh to my obedient son, Babu Sawan Singh Ji. May the grace and mercy of the compassionate Hazur be upon you all the time. I am well and happy in every respect, dear son, and always beg for your health and well-being from the compassionate Hazur Maharaj. This is to inform you that the money order of 10 rupees that you sent on 11 May has been received. You had already done a lot of seva, so why did you take this trouble again? Your letter written in Urdu was also received. It was very well written and was read out to all the satsangis on the day of satsang.

I am immensely pleased with you, my son. You are the very breath of my life. Listen to the Shabd-dhun every day and also always keep simran in the mind for then the compassionate Hazur will do your official work himself. You are not to worry. To become purified and acquire the power to reach Sach

---

[*] Traditional Sikh invocation. *See also* footnote to letter 1.

Khand; to possess the energy to ascend to each stage; to obtain bliss by reaching the land of Alakh, Agam and Anami Radha Soami and merging into it; and to break loose from all attachments in order to become liberated—all will be attained through the munificence of the Satguru's real form, the Shabd-dhun, by listening repeatedly to it every day. The condition, however, is that this can be obtained only through love for the physical form of the Satguru—to begin with, it can be found only through this form. The individual who has not developed faith in it will receive nothing, because the Supreme Being, the absolute Lord, Anami Radha Soami, has incarnated himself in the form of a saint for the sake of living beings. Whosoever develops love and faith in him, and knows that he is all-in-all, will cross over the phenomenal ocean by holding fast to the Shabd-dhun.

The rest of the news is that I have sent a letter to Agra to inquire about the date of the main bhandara. If the bhandara is held during Nimani Kasti in Asarh, I will come and visit you for fifteen or twenty days. Please let me know if you can arrange a separate room for me at your place. I will come in the month of Jeth and return to the Dera on the 2nd or 3rd of Asarh, in order to leave for the bhandara on the 7th or 8th of Asarh. You should write your letters to me in Gurmukhi. If the bhandara is to be held now, then I will come in the month of Sawan, but I do not want to stay in Sadar Bazaar in Murree Hills. Write your letter soon, and give my Radha Soami to all the satsangis. Bibi sends her Radha Soami to you, her dear brother. Radha Soami to all the satsangis. Also, all the other satsangis send their Radha Soami to you.

16 May 1902

~ 114 ~

[Dictated]

Radha Soami. Radha Soami Ji is the Comforter.

Radha Soami greetings from Jaimal Singh to my obedient son, Babu Sawan Singh. We have received an envelope containing a letter and the proof-sheet. The fact of the matter is that the ink on the printed sample of Hazur Soami Ji's book is faint. Please tell the printer that he shouldn't use such ink. For this purpose they should use a good quality ink. The reason why it is faint is that they have used washable ink. The printing, however, is good. I have corrected the mistakes wherever they occur on the proof-sheet. Since you also have a copy of Hazur Soami Ji's book, in future you can correct the proof-sheets yourself. Please impress upon the printer that if the ink on even one line is faint, the whole page will be rejected. He should correct it, otherwise the whole page will need to be reprinted. The revised copy of Hazur's book was sent to you with Babu Gajja Singh, so use it to correct each proof-sheet. Now you have both copies of the book. A letter came from Chacha Ji in which he wished Radha Soami to everyone.

Have the printing done from Hazur Soami Ji's book that came from Agra, but check it with the copy that Gajja Singh brought with him. One or two proof-sheets must be sent to me every week so that I can check that the ink is not too light. It is to be stressed that these books will not be printed repeatedly, and for this reason, the ink, etc., everything, must be of the highest quality. Please examine the printing yourself and strongly impress upon the printer that the ink and typeface must be of the best quality. The typeface on the sheet you have sent is good but the printing is faint. Keep doing your bhajan and simran. Hari Ram sends you his respectful Radha Soami.

20 May 1902

~ 115 ~

Radha Soami. Radha Soami Ji is the Comforter.

Radha Soami from Jaimal Singh to my obedient son, Babu
Sawan Singh. May the grace and mercy of the compassionate
Anami Lord always be upon you, my son. This is to inform you that
I have received the money order of 200 rupees. Your letter was
also received; I was very pleased to read it. I have understood every-
thing. I will leave for Agra on 11 June by the four o'clock train.

Believe it firmly, my son, that the creator of all worldly activities, of statecraft and everything else, is Radha Soami Ji himself. Every single thing is within his will. The spiritual path
(parmarth) also is under his command. It does not matter if you
do not get leave. Since everything is under the will of Anami
Radha Soami, why even think about it? Wherever he places you,
that for you is the best place. You are never to come without
leave; you will receive grace and mercy right where you are. Both
the spiritual and material worlds are lost, my son, if we do what
pleases the mind. So become a gurmukh, accept his will as truth,
and be happy wherever he keeps you—then there never will be
any question of suffering, my son. Don't ever write such words
again, that you will come here just like that. Even ordinary holy
men say that man should never follow the dictates of his own
mind. It is my firm command that you should never come without getting leave. The work that you do at your place is also that
of Radha Soami Ji.

Radha Soami greetings and blessings of grace and mercy to
all the satsangis and to the elder Bibi Ji and the younger Bibi Ji.
Bibi wishes to convey her Radha Soami to you, her dear brother.
Radha Soami from Bibi to all the satsangis and the Bibi Jis. I
am very pleased with you, my son.

8 June 1902

∼ 116 ∼

[Dictated]

Radha Soami. Radha Soami Ji is the Comforter.

From Jaimal Singh: Radha Soami greetings to Gajja Singh, Chanan Singh, Babu Sawan Singh, Basant Singh, Narain Singh, Nami Ji, the elder Bibi Ji, and the younger Bibi Ji. Please convey Radha Soami also to Surain Singh and Sunder Singh of the Twenty-Second Battery. Your letter arrived, informing me about your well-being. The letter had all the information but nothing about the printing of Hazur Soami Ji's book. Well! I will find out from Babu Sawan Singh in person. I was worried to learn about your illness. It is Hazur's will; we should be content howsoever he keeps us—pain and pleasure are the body's lot. The illness will leave after the karmas have played themselves out. You did not write whether or not the Bibis will go home. We will leave for Agra on 15 June 1902 to be at Chacha Ji's service. Radha Soami to Aya Singh, Babu Gajja Singh, Babu Sawan Singh, and Chanan Singh. Radha Soami also from Bibi Ji. Also Radha Soami from all the residents of the Dera.

15 June 1902

∼ 117 ∼

Radha Soami. Radha Soami Ji is the Comforter.

Wahiguru Ji ki Fateh from Jaimal Singh to my obedient son, Babu Sawan Singh Ji. May the grace and mercy of the compassionate Radha Soami always be upon you. Dear son, your two letters were received, informing me of your well-being. You had written in the first letter that you would be coming here. That is why I did not write to you and was instead waiting for your visit.

I did not, however, send anyone to the railway station, because in my heart I was not sure that you would come. That is why no one was sent.

Only that which is Hazur Soami Ji's will is going to happen, my son. He is always with us, and he alone is doing everything, all our worldly activities and all our spiritual work. But he has hidden himself behind a veil. One form he created was that of man, and for the eighty-four lakh life species he created separate forms. Then assuming the Shabd-dhun form himself, he extended his Sound into everything, but did not let anyone know the One who is living in the temple of the body. Kal hoodwinked all and everyone by binding them tightly with the ropes of various faiths: the Vedas and scriptures, holy books and religious disputes, pride of caste and colour, images and pilgrimages, in reading of holy books, bowing before idols, and in the customs and rituals of the past. The whole universe, from all the kindred of one's family, mother, father, wife, and sons, to every other kith and kin, has been tied up by him in the ropes of attachment. None did he let go home to Sach Khand; instead, he put everyone on the path that leads away from that home. Then the Indestructible, the compassionate Radha Soami himself, through his gracious mercy assumed the saintly form of a Satguru and through the path of Shabd-dhun revealed the secret of the ultimate home, Sach Khand, Sat Lok, and of every other stage. So now that the whole secret of our home has been revealed, we should go there every day.

This Shabd-dhun is perfectly described in *Sri Guru Granth Sahib*. You are not to consider anything as yours, because everything belongs to the immortal Anami Radha Soami. Your body is his, your soul also is his. Sons, daughters, wife, mother, father, wealth, home, house, shop, mansion, everything that exists belongs to him and is to be entrusted to him. The self is not to be kept in anything, my son. When you have entrusted everything to the Lord, then all becomes he, and you also are he. Entrust everything to him and do all your worldly work, and also keep doing your bhajan and simran. But know in your heart that "I am not the doer. I do not exist at all." Accept hardship or happiness with goodwill, since both come with his command. Always think that the Satguru is everything: "I do not exist; you are all and everything."

I am immensely pleased with you, my son. Read Hazur Soami Ji's books every day because much is revealed by reading them. When the soul, by becoming pure, merges into the Shabddhun, everything will automatically become clear. When a letter from you arrives I become so full of joy and happiness that it cannot be described. May the longing for darshan stay with you all the time. That is as good as time spent in meditation. So you will receive darshan. Radha Soami from Bibi and Ganda Singh.

18 June 1902

∼ 118 ∼

[Dictated]

Radha Soami. Radha Soami Ji is the Comforter.

From Jaimal Singh: Radha Soami greetings to my obedient son, Babu Sawan Singh. Your letter arrived, and I was happy and delighted to receive all your news. Banta Singh left here today for your place, and a message, etc., for you has been sent with him. He is also bringing parshad of pickled berries of *kareer* and roasted chickpeas for you. I hope it reaches you all right. It is also for Chanan Singh, Narain Singh, and Basant Singh, for all three of them. Your letter arrived today, so I sent these things to you immediately. Your dear mother arrived here on the day of Guru Poornima, and the news of your well-being was given to her. I hear that both Bachint Singh and his wife are ill. Well, there is no need to worry; Maharaj Radha Soami Ji will be gracious and merciful. One point more: at the time of the bhandara, nothing—no flour, pulses, or jaggery [raw sugar], etc.—is to come from your village. It is not right. Nor is any clothing, etc., to come from there on the occasion of the bhandara. Do not look upon this as unfriendly advice, as if something bad has been said to you. You yourself are wise; you can find out about it.... For this reason it is not proper. Worldly people are not aware of such things—there may be only one gurmukh in the household. Ever since the day the flour, etc., for the bhandara came into the Dera through ———, every single satsangi has fallen sick. Do not ever be angry with them, just let them know. Let me say quite frankly that when everything, money and materials, is sent by you, why should they, too, feel the urge?

Radha Soami from Bibi Ji to you, her true brother. Do your bhajan and simran every day, and never let the surat, nirat and the higher mind wander free. Keep them attached to the sound of the Shabd-dhun. Regard Satguru, the Lord, as ever present. Narain Singh, Chanan Singh, and Basant Singh should make it a point to continue with their bhajan and simran. Please give Chanan Singh two days' leave if you can manage without him. However, do not give him leave if you cannot do without him, since you are at a new post. Radha Soami greetings from all the residents of the Dera.

July 1902

~ 119 ~

[Dictated]

Radha Soami. Radha Soami Ji is the Comforter.

Radha Soami greetings from Jaimal Singh to my obedient son, Babu Sawan Singh. In reply to your previous letter in which you had asked about the brick-kiln, it was opened on the 20th of Sawan. It was fairly well baked, but a few bricks came out underdone— that is, they were only half-baked—but only a few, some six to eight thousand. The rest of the kiln has come out well; there was very little waste. So, generally the bricks have come out very well. I did not write earlier because I had not seen the end-product.

Regarding the books, Gajja Singh has informed me that the printing has been stopped, and that it will resume when the new type arrives. The copy of *Ghat Ramayan* in Gurmukhi that we borrowed is being asked for; the owners of *Anurag Sagar* also would like to have it back. Letters requesting the return of both the Gurmukhi books have been received. The printer, Buta Mal, has done no work so far: none of the books, *Anurag Sagar*, *Ghat Ramayan*, or Hazur Soami Ji's book, have been printed. He has done absolutely no work. Write to him soon, that he should finish printing at least one book, either *Anurag Sagar* or one of the other two. The original copies of these books are being asked for, so they have to be returned—*Anurag Sagar*, however, is to be returned immediately. *Ghat Ramayan* also has to be given back, and Chacha Ji will be asking for Soami Ji's book as well, although he has not yet done so. Buta Mal, on the other hand, has not printed a single book so far, nor does there appear to be any sign of his doing so. Gajja Singh and Aya Singh are in Rawalpindi. Write to them and also to Moola Mal. Hazur Soami Ji's book, which has been printed up to the seventh hymn, is not correct, because the vowel marks have not been properly inserted.

A separate paper has come from Chacha Ji—I do not know what they call it—and I am passing it on to you. Please read it, try to understand its import, and then write to me. Return the paper also to me because I will never share ———'s point of view. Since ——— had not remembered Maharaj Soami Ji's way of meditation, the technique of sitting, the method of discourse, and Hazur Soami Ji's teachings, then how could ———

recall or know them? This is being written for your information—and personally, too, I will mention this to Chacha Ji, and
that person also knows about it. You know full well that Soami
Ji's technique is the real one, and that is what has been imparted
to you. You should keep this in mind.

All is well at the Dera. The bricks are being brought in from
the kiln and stacked at the Dera, but so far no work has been
started. For the rest, write how you would like to see things done.
Please continue with your bhajan and simran. Whenever you are
free, sit for bhajan and simran. Bhajan must be done every day.
Keep the mind yearning inwardly for the Shabd and remain firm
in simran. Place your love in the sound of the Shabd-dhun. And
with inward longing, keep the surat and nirat focused on that
Sound all the time, while you do your worldly work with the
body. Do write to me whenever you are free.

Radha Soami to Basant Singh, Chanan Singh, and Narain
Singh. Everyone is urged to do bhajan and simran every day.

Radha Soami to Babu Gulab Singh. Your postcard arrived
and I was happy to know of your well-being. It is good that you
have been transferred to this new place. Hazur Soami Ji's books
were sent to Khairagali through Budh Singh of the First Battery—perhaps he reported there after you had left. Write to him
and have him send them to you. This is the reply to your postcard. Keep doing bhajan and simran every day.

Radha Soami from Bibi Ji to you, her true brother. Also,
Radha Soami to all from Bibi Ji, from the sadhus at the Dera,
and from all the other ladies here. Read this letter carefully in
order to understand its contents. Engrave the image of Sach
Khand in your mind in line with the teachings of the Satguru.
Believe in this firmly.

12 August 1902

~ 120 ~

[Dictated]

Radha Soami. Radha Soami Ji is the Comforter.

Radha Soami greetings from Jaimal Singh to my obedient son, Babu Sawan Singh. This is to let you know that Chanan Singh has arrived at the Dera. He was ill but is better now. I have learnt from him that you are going home on the 1st. Do go home first, and then come to the Dera on your return. You must go on the 1st and inform me of the date you will arrive here, as well as the date you will leave. You have informed me neither about your arrival nor about Agra.

The climate at your place is very hot and also very humid, so every fourth or fifth day eat some food made with a piece of dried ginger, using a good amount of ghee. I have heard that you have stopped taking ghee, but ghee should definitely be taken—you will become weak if you do not eat ghee. Do not stop using it.

Keep doing your bhajan and simran every day, and daily continue to read Hazur Soami Ji's book, staying mindful that we are living in this world only for a few days. This time will not come again, so continue with bhajan and simran, and keep listening to the Shabd-dhun with the love and devotion of surat and nirat every day. This work comes first, and everything worldly comes afterwards.

Radha Soami to Basant Singh, Narain Singh, Babu Gulab Singh, and all the other satsangis. Radha Soami on behalf of Bibi Ji to you, her true brother. Radha Soami from all the residents of the Dera. It is urged upon all the satsangis that they must keep doing their bhajan and simran every day.

21 September 1902

～ 121 ～

[Dictated]

Radha Soami. Radha Soami Ji is the Comforter.

From Jaimal Singh: Radha Soami greetings to Babu Sawan Singh. Your letter arrived, and I was happy and gratified to read it. It was a good letter. You have written that you have caught the same infection as Chanan Singh because you allowed him to borrow your clothes. Well, do not worry, do your bhajan and simran, and you will get well. It had to be like this; it was not in your hands. Since you understand such things well, why do you not act more thoughtfully? You know about such matters and yet you become forgetful. In future, you should be careful. Grace and mercy will be upon you. The forgiveness that you have requested for mistakenly loaning your clothes is hereby given to you. It has been mentioned to you many times that you should use only what is purchased from your own earnings. I find that besides what your own labour provides, you have started to go astray, and have begun to accept gifts of food and drink from others. It is not at all proper to do this. Anyway, it is up to you. Do you or do you not compensate them sufficiently for it? If a non-satsangi brings something to distribute at the Dera, doing so creates problems. Satsangis, whether here or there, are all one, so you also would suffer from similar problems. This has cast a suspicion in my mind which should not be there. In any case, if someone brings you a gift, give it to a third person and compensate him adequately for the gift; that is, fulfil the request of the person who brings the gift but do not use the gift for yourself. Do not worry about the ailment; it has come through His command—grace and mercy will follow.

Regarding *Anurag Sagar*, inquire well and leave it where you think best. Do as you think appropriate. A letter from your grandfather has arrived from his village, Mehmansinghwala, and is being enclosed in this letter. He asks you to fulfil his wish: to brick the nine-yard side of his tank. He says: "Are you going to spend money on me only at my funeral, after my life is over? My wish is that you get the nine-yard side of my water tank bricked during my lifetime." So it should be constructed—it is a small matter. Keep doing bhajan and simran every day; grace and mercy will always be upon you.

Radha Soami on behalf of Bibi Ji. And Radha Soami to Babu Gulab Singh, Basant Singh, Narain Singh, and all the other satsangis there. All are reminded to continue doing their bhajan and simran every day. Bibi Ji wishes to inform you that Chanan Singh has given her the 5 rupees for the *rakhi*, and that she has passed these on to me. May grace and mercy be upon you. You have aggravated your illness by not using ghee for the past two months. You were advised to use three ounces. You did not listen and now must pay the price. When you obey the command, grace and mercy will be upon you.

For the upper-storey rooms, forty beams will cost 120 rupees, and seven large twelve-foot beams, 42 rupees. The freight charges will be 5 rupees, so the total cost of the wood will come to 167 rupees. Moreover, a kiln has been installed for making quicklime, and work will start in two or three days. You should always keep doing bhajan and simran. An additional expense of 23 rupees has been incurred for the kiln, the grinding mill, and the limestone. So the total has come to 192 rupees.

Today, two proof-sheets of the prose *Sar Bachan* were received. The print is good. The ink, however, is somewhat faint—not enough ink was used. Write to the printer about these pages and tell him to start printing. If we can settle with him better than elsewhere, we can get the printing job done by him. So even if he demands an extra 10 rupees, give the money to him and settle the matter, although he did not consult with us at all.

Then even if only the two books of Hazur Soami Ji, the verse and the prose editions, are printed, at least they will be well printed. For the rest, do as you think proper. Always keep doing your bhajan and simran.

Also let me know about your health: you have not written again about your weakness. Are you feeling any better now? It is all right to take care of one's body. Do not accept things from an outsider, but if you do, then duly compensate the giver. Do not make a false promise; rather, frankly refuse him. Suppose a suppliant came to your door and you made him a false promise. His hopes are going to depend on you. If he does not receive anything at your door, what will his heart say? I have said enough! Think about it—you are a man of integrity.

Radha Soami from Bibi Ji to you, her true brother, and also from Chanan Singh. He is better now. I have heard from Chanan Singh that you will be going home, but you did not write about it. Write whether you are going, and if so, when. If you wish to change your residence, you may do so. Radha Soami on behalf of Bibi Ji to you, her true brother. Radha Soami from all the residents of the Dera. Reply by return post, and please send 50 rupees at the earliest—it is urgent.

[September] 1902

∾ 122 ∾

Radha Soami. Radha Soami Ji is the Comforter.

Radha Soami to my obedient son Babu Sawan Singh, and to Basant Singh, Babu Gulab Singh, Narain Singh, Nanak Singh, Khushal Singh, and all the other satsangis there. Dear son, your letter was received, and I was very happy to read it and learn of your well-being. I have received 98 rupees, and they have been used to pay for the construction of the upper-storey rooms. The construction has been going on since the 7th of Asuj. The roof over one of the upper-storey rooms was laid today; two more are left to do. The roofing of all three will be finished shortly, and the masons will then move inside to do the plastering.

Twenty-seven hymns of Soami Ji's *Sar Bachan* have been printed. The rest will be finished in a few weeks. The printing is better than before, though here and there the print of some letters is faint—still it is better than before. The introduction to *Anurag Sagar* has been kept as you wrote it. I have also approved it. The printer has not yet quoted his price for printing the prose edition of Hazur Soami Ji's book. It could be printed soon if he were to let us know the cost. Earlier I sent you a postcard in Urdu; I trust you have received it. You have written for a reliable cook to be sent to you, but no such person is available here. Chanan Singh develops a mild temperature daily or every other day; he will be given a purgative this Sunday, and as soon as he is slightly better, he will be sent to you.

A letter from Chacha Ji at Agra has been received, in which he writes that the ten members have been appointed. He sends you Radha Soami greetings and has blessed you with grace and mercy.

Babu Gulab Singh Ji is to be informed that one should not get upset in illness. Pain and pleasure befall us due to the actions of our previous lives, and both will definitely happen. All those who are sick will receive his grace and mercy. So he should not worry but accept his will cheerfully. Also he should do his bhajan and simran every day, because during illness the mind does not run anywhere. Becoming dejected, the mind engages in meditation, and the inner attentive faculties, surat and nirat, become focused. So "look upon the hour of pain as a blessing" (*Dukh kee gharee ganeemat jaano*).[16] Why? Because the attention of the satsangi then stays fixed in meditation, which does not normally happen with other people. So whenever there is suffering, his will should definitely be accepted. The mind must be kept fully engaged in bhajan and simran. During suffering, the physical senses, the five elements *[tattva]*, and even the mind, feel pain, but in no case does the soul feel any pain. So focus the soul's attention on the Shabd-dhun. Then as long as the attention is lovingly fixed in the Shabd-dhun, pain will never be felt during that time—just as in deep sleep the soul, mind, and the vital energy become so absorbed in the navel centre (which is a 6 to 7 inch long tube) that there is no awareness of the body nor knowledge of any pain or pleasure. This place is in the navel, within the nine doors, but the place of the Shabd-dhun is far above the nine doors and the region of Maya. How then would the soul be affected by pain or pleasure? So:

> Pain is the medicine; pleasure, a disease.
> *Dukh daaru sukh rog bha-iaa.*[17]

Please remember well, my son, that whatever happens is by his command and is to be accepted cheerfully.

Now let me explain to you how to live. You yourself know, my son, that our every breath is numbered. It is to be spent either in spiritual pursuits or in specific worldly activities in order to earn a living or do good deeds and acts of devotion. Otherwise life is a waste. What sense or wisdom is there in chit-chatting uselessly and wasting time with people who have not met a perfect Master or do not have a desire to meet the Lord? Will these breaths or this human body ever be given again? Write the answer to this. Well, I might as well give the answer myself: "No, never." My son, this time will not be had again. Still you do not understand! After you have finished your official work, do not converse with others, and from six to eight o'clock in the evening sit in meditation for as long as you can, whether for a quarter-hour, a half-hour, an hour, or an hour and a half. After that,

simran is to be done with the attention kept at the Shabd stages.
Then from eight to ten o'clock participate in satsang activity,
after which you may sleep or chat with others. In the morning,
sit in meditation at 4:30; keep sitting till 5:30. Then throughout
the day do your official work and also talk and socialize with
others. But when you have finished your official duties, you are
not to indulge in small talk or waste time by socializing with non-
satsangis. Take your meals by yourself, sitting in the kitchen;
never are you to sit down to eat with non-satsangis or take your
meals sitting at a table. My son, you are to keep yourself hidden
from the world. You are never to have meals prepared in your
kitchen for one who is a non-satsangi and takes meat and alcohol. If you begin to socialize with such people, you too will acquire their habits. No. You are to work with people, but your
lifestyle should be different. If someone offers you anything free,
you are never to accept it. When will you be able to recompense
him for it? If you do not refrain from such acts, your spiritual
journey will never be completed. You will definitely have to compensate them; and so long as you do not compensate them, how
will the door of the Shabd-dhun open for you? These are the
points that struck me from within; that's why I have put them
down. One day, in a dream, I saw you behaving in this manner,
that's why I have written to you. My son, you are to live in the
world just like the waterfowl which floats on the water the whole
day but is absolutely dry when it flies off. This is how you are to
live in the world. It is my personal plea that grace and mercy be
upon you at this very moment.

Bibi's Radha Soami to you, her true and dear brother. Radha
Soami to the others from Bibi and from all the other satsangis.
With love and affection and the inner yearning of the higher
mind, attach the faculties of surat and nirat to the Shabd and
remain detached in the mind. Love the Shabd and have no desire for any activity of the world. Chanan Singh asks you to

please sow some mustard for making *saag*, and to sow gram between the rows of mustard. Bibi asks you to have six or seven
pounds of *chibbar* dried for her. Please have them dried for use
at the Dera.

Four copies of Hazur Soami Ji's book were received today
at the time of this letter's dispatch; 7 shabds from the 31st hymn
have been printed.

                                                    17 October 1902

~ 123 ~

[Dictated]

Radha Soami. Radha Soami Ji is the Comforter.

From Jaimal Singh: Radha Soami greetings to Babu Sawan
Singh, Basant Singh, and Narain Singh. Your letter was received
and a postcard was sent in reply; I hope it has reached you. Secondly, I would like to write to you in Gurmukhi, but what can I
do? I get so little free time because of the heavy work on the upper-
storey rooms. The work is going well. Three masons, three carpenters, and five labourers are engaged in the work. Timber
worth 195 rupees has been delivered, and the work is progressing
well. Earlier also I had written to you for 50 rupees, so please send
them. Do not send a money order for a larger amount, as then I
have to go to the post office. If you wish to send more, divide it
into two money orders, as up to 50 rupees is delivered here.

The other news is that three letters from Gajja Singh have
arrived from Rawalpindi, informing us that Buta Mal has
stopped work on the books for the past week. Our loss has been
eight copies. He is not printing because the payment he gets for
printing *Ghat Ramayan* is the same as for Hazur Soami Ji's *Sar
Bachan* in verse. So I have recalled *Ghat Ramayan*. More copies of it are not to be printed because he was printing them very

badly. The print was exactly like that of *Anurag Sagar*, but some words had been poorly inked, others had damaged lines, in some the vowel marks were not there, while still others had the diacritics missing. The ink was of very bad quality, too. For these reasons, the printing of *Ghat Ramayan* has been stopped—we will have it printed elsewhere by another printer. So I am writing to ask you to please go to Rawalpindi for a day or two, pay him for the printing already done, and stop the rest of the work.

Pay him for *Anurag Sagar* and for as much of Hazur Soami Ji's verse text as has been printed, and settle the matter. If he demands 10 rupees extra, give it to him. It does not matter. That Buta Mal is a very careless fellow. We'll have the books printed elsewhere—this is what I suggest. He is going to make a mess of the books. We will have both the verse and prose editions of Hazur's *Sar Bachan* printed at another press. You had better give him notice first that if he wants to print the books he should do so honestly, and that if he acts dishonestly, the wages of Gajja Singh and Aya Singh, the two people who are deputed there especially for these books, will be charged to him. Along with this, stipulate that if he can finish printing the three books in three months he should do so, otherwise he should frankly refuse the job. We will then make other arrangements. If he can do it, he should print the three books—Hazur's main text, the prose edition and *Ghat Ramayan*—within three months, and we will accept them if the printing is like the sample page of the first copy. If the lettering on a page is damaged or faint, that page will be rejected. Price the printing charges of the three books separately. If the charges for *Ghat Ramayan* and Soami Ji's verse text have already been decided, leave them as they are. But he won't print them. *Ghat Ramayan* in Gurmukhi script has arrived at the Dera. Just imagine! What good would it do to spend so much money if the letters start fading out in a year's time?

October 1902

~ 124 ~

[Partially dictated]

Radha Soami. Radha Soami Ji is the Comforter.

From Jaimal Singh: Radha Soami greetings to my obedient son, Babu Sawan Singh. This is to inform you that I had already sent a letter to Chaudhri Buta Mal asking him not to have the books bound—except for those already done—when a thought struck me that we should get them bound. So if you want to have them bound, by all means go ahead—I am agreeable—tell Chaudhri Buta Mal to get them bound. I am writing so that you may tell him to arrange the binding of 500 copies of the verse edition, and 500 of the prose. I am very well contented with Buta Mal; may Hazur Maharaj show him grace and mercy. However, he has made a serious error by mixing the introduction with the text. You should also write about how much you paid for the black stone, as well as for the four tins of paint that you sent here.

Your letter was received and I was very happy to read about your welfare. The reply is that you should continue doing bhajan and simran whenever you are free from your official work. This bhajan is for people who work, not for those who sit around or remain idle. Please convey Radha Soami to Ram Chand the treasurer, and tell him to continue doing bhajan and simran. Radha Soami from Bibi Ji to you, her true and dear brother, and also from all the other satsangis at the Dera. When you have time, visit the people in the batteries and counsel them; go to those in the Second and Third Batteries. You are reminded to go to Buta Mal also and tell him to have the books bound. This letter has been written now because you are visiting Rawalpindi.

[In Gurmukhi script, Baba Ji's writing:] My son, the letter above was written by one who knew little Urdu. Try to understand it well even if a word is missing here and there. Mangal

Singh reached the Dera at six o'clock on Thursday evening and brought everything with him. I have received 300 rupees, as well as the 20 rupees from Ram Chand the treasurer—he has taken a great deal of trouble. If you can come, my son, please do so for a day. Do your bhajan and simran every day. I will keep 5 rupees of Ram Chand the treasurer, and return the other 15 by draft to him—he has sent too much. Four tins of paint, along with the oil, have arrived here. For the rest, you should come personally and see for yourself. Keep bhajan and simran in your mind all the time. The binding should be done for all the copies of the verse and prose editions.

October 1902

~ 125 ~

[Dictated]

Radha Soami. Radha Soami Ji is the Comforter.

Radha Soami greetings from Jaimal Singh to my obedient son, Babu Sawan Singh, and to Basant Singh, Narain Singh, Babu Gulab Singh, and all the other satsangis at your place. May the grace and mercy of the compassionate Radha Soami always be upon you. I understand that you have now returned from your home and rejoined your duty. Your Radha Soami was received personally through Nihal Singh the baker. I sent a postcard to you earlier; you must have received it. Gajja Singh arrived here on Saturday, and was present at the Sunday satsang. He waited eagerly for you. He brought 100 printed copies of *Anurag Sagar*. I had called him here for three days, and since neither he nor Aya Singh had extra clothing, he took some clothes from here. Hazur Soami Ji's text has been printed up to the thirty-third hymn. Immediately send to Rawalpindi the introduction that Chacha Ji wrote at your request. Please make sure that it does not say that Hazur Soami Ji had no Guru. Whatever you think is good in the Devnagri edition may be put in the introduction, but do not add anything of your own. Send one copy to me and another to Gajja Singh in Rawalpindi. If, however, you do not have time, send the copy only to Gajja Singh. But there should be no delay. The printers are asking 200 rupees for the prose edition. They are now doing a better printing job than before.

The situation at the Dera is like this: all the three upper-storey rooms are ready. Only five days' additional work on the doors, etc., remains. An additional 560 rupees, approximately, will be spent. Furthermore, write if there are plans to build a satsang hall or any other building. The proposal for the satsang hall is that a sixty-foot long and thirty-foot wide building would need eleven beams. For this purpose, three twelve-foot planks would be spliced into one beam, that is, bonded together with nails, battens, grips, and wooden joints. If a beam is made from three pieces of timber, it will not sag. For the beams, we will need thirty-three (11 x 3 = 33) pieces of twelve-foot long timber. Counting everything, the joints, etc., a total of forty twelve-foot planks will be needed, and also 200 ten-foot long planks for making the doors and cross-ties. That is, the total for the wood will come to 1,000 rupees, with another 1,000 for labour. The expenses for pukka bricks and other materials will be about 500 rupees. That is to say, not counting some bricks already in the Dera, some 2,500 rupees will need to be spent. If it is to be done, please write soon, and send a plan. Please send a reply even if it is not to be done.

Furthermore, the introduction to *Anurag Sagar* has come out well. Also write about your home: if you went there, how was the visit? Were they all doing well? Please keep doing your bhajan and simran every day. Do not be affected by pain or pleasure; regard them both as his will. Whatever the compassionate Radha

Soami does, and will do, is all for our good. Day and night keep your inner longing, that is, your love, in the Shabd-dhun, and continue doing worldly work with your hands and feet. Accept whatever happens cheerfully. For the rest, whatever is the will of the compassionate Hazur Radha Soami will be for our good.

Chanan Singh's condition is such that he gets a temperature every day from ten to five o'clock. Next week, whether or not he is well, he will definitely be sent to you. A letter from Hazur Chacha Ji at Agra came, asking me to sign my acceptance of the ten members who were appointed. I submitted to Chacha Ji that I would not accept anyone except the compassionate Hazur Soami Ji, Chacha Ji himself, Maharaj Suchet Singh, Sudarshan Singh, and the other relatives of Soami Ji. I have not accepted in the past, and will not do so in the future. Chacha Ji sent a second message that this was how it should have been, that he was testing my love and devotion, and had done so. He was very happy. Grace and mercy upon you and all the other satsangis from Hazur Chacha Ji.

Always remember: you are never to feel perturbed that you were happy there and are unhappy here. Consider it all as his will. Every satsangi should do his bhajan and simran. Once again, it is urged: do not become perturbed by any situation, painful or pleasant. Remain within the teachings of the Satguru. On behalf of Bibi Ji, Radha Soami to you, her true brother.

[Postscript:] Chanan Singh will board the train from here on Wednesday, 5 November 1902, at eleven o'clock at night. On Thursday, from eight or ten o'clock till 4 p.m., your man should wait for him with a horse at Malikwal railway station, so that from there he may come to your residence on horseback.

[October] 1902

～ 126 ～

[Dictated]

Radha Soami. Radha Soami Ji is the Comforter.

From Jaimal Singh: Radha Soami greetings to Babu Sawan Singh, Babu Gulab Singh, Basant Singh, Narain Singh, and to all the other satsangis. Your letter arrived and informed me of the news there. You have written about Babu Gulab Singh's serious illness. Pain and pleasure are the lot of this body; he will get well after going through the illness. Do not be perturbed—there was some suffering destined for him at this time. It would be right and proper to give him something which has a cooling effect. He will get well when the karmic penalty has been paid off. It is not right to become agitated during illness; an illness becomes aggravated if one gets perturbed during its course. He will get well in time.

A telegram arrived here in your name, care of myself; it was returned because it had nothing to do with me. Today both the Bibis will leave for Mehmansinghwala accompanied by Chanan Singh. The drawing of the buildings that you made and left with me has been misplaced. It would be good if you could make another and send it to me. Please send it promptly. Babu Gulab Singh should keep doing bhajan and simran; he will get well. In my opinion you should not send the iron beams because they are very expensive, and we will make do with the wooden beams by trussing them up. But whatever you desire is acceptable: we will use the iron or wooden beams as you advise. Work was started today; the foundation has been dug. Please keep doing your bhajan and simran, and write soon. Babu Gulab Singh is in my thoughts day and night. Rest assured, he will get well. Please make the drawing right away and send it to me; the work can then be started.

Radha Soami on behalf of Bibi Ji to you, her true brother. Also Radha Soami from all the residents of the Dera. Heartfelt Radha Soami on behalf of Chanan Singh, who says: "I am better than before. I will return after leaving the Bibis at home."

As long as the building plan does not arrive, the doors, etc., cannot be made. Please draw it and send it soon—this is important.

10 November 1902

∼ 127 ∼

[Dictated]

Radha Soami. Radha Soami Ji is the Comforter.

From Jaimal Singh: Radha Soami greetings to Babu Sawan Singh Ji. This is to let you know that the letter you wrote to your grandfather has been sent on to me. You should not write such letters to your home or to him. Even now, please write to him by return post that you are sorry, as he is in great anguish. You should treat him with care because he is of advanced age.

The building work is progressing well. The arches of one veranda have been fitted and one side has been completed up to ten feet. About the rest you have already been informed. You have not written any letters. A letter has come from Narain Singh and Chanan Singh in which they write that Babu Sahib is well. Please remember that you must take ghee without fail. The reply to Chanan Singh and Narain Singh is that they should continue doing bhajan and simran; they will receive his grace and mercy. Remember to take ghee daily. Also, send one canister of coal tar—this is urgent. Radha Soami greetings from Bibi Ji to you, her true brother. Radha Soami from everyone at the Dera.

The introduction has been written incorrectly, showing my name first. The first name should have been that of Chacha Ji

Pratap Singh. He writes that the book has been printed according to Jaimal Singh.

[November 1902]

～ 128 ～

[Dictated]

Radha Soami. Radha Soami Ji is the Comforter.

From Jaimal Singh: Radha Soami greetings to my obedient son,
Babu Sawan Singh. Your letter was received, informing me of
your well-being. A letter from Babu Gajja Singh also came at
the same time, saying that the printing of the book has been completed. He has asked for the introduction. So please send the introduction page immediately to Babu Gajja Singh at Rawalpindi. And please do not write in it that Hazur Soami Ji had no
Guru. Also let me know at the earliest whether you are well now.
Radha Soami from Bibi Ji; Radha Soami also from all the residents of the Dera. Radha Soami to Bachint Singh, Narain
Singh, Khushal Singh, Babu Gulab Singh, and Nanak Singh.

2 December 1902

～ 129 ～

[Dictated]

Radha Soami. Radha Soami Ji is the Comforter.

Radha Soami greetings from Jaimal Singh to my obedient son,
Babu Sawan Singh. My dear son, you have not written a letter
since the day you left here. Even if you are unwell, at least you
should have written a postcard to let me know whether you had
arrived, or were ill, or had recovered. A letter [of safe arrival]
should always be written. No information has come about the

girders either. A letter from your grandfather came from your home; it has been forwarded to you. You should never write such angry letters home. Now write a letter home that you will send whatever they ask, that you have nowhere else to go but home.

Hazur Soami Ji's verse *Sar Bachan* has been printed. At Christmas, even if you get leave for only one day, you must come to the Dera, even if only for a night or half a day. You must come but you will also have to go home for a day because everyone there is perplexed. Their letters should not come to me—why should they have to write to me?

Regarding *Ghat Ramayan*, please let Gajja Singh know soon if it is going to be printed; also write to him if it is not to be printed. Gajja Singh has written to me that he never receives a letter from Babu Sahib. You should definitely write to him as well. I will go to Rawalpindi for four days in connection with the introduction. I will leave here by the mail train on Monday evening or on Tuesday, and reach Rawalpindi on Tuesday or Wednesday. From there, I will leave by the evening mail train on Saturday, 20 December, arriving at Beas at eleven o'clock on Sunday, in time to attend the satsang. Only the introduction is to be added to the verse edition of Hazur Soami Ji's book; not a single extra word, except the table of contents, is to be included. The text should contain only what was said by the gracious Hazur Soami Ji himself. This is why I want to go to Rawalpindi: to inform the printer of all this. They are also asking me to put a price on the verse edition, but I do not know anything about it. Please figure it out and write to me by 18 December, in a letter addressed to Gajja Singh. You are urgently reminded to please write about the printing of either *Anurag Sagar* or *Ghat Ramayan*, and also about the price of Hazur Soami Ji's verse edition, by 18 December in a letter care of Gajja Singh.

Radha Soami to Narain Singh, Chanan Singh, Basant Singh, Nanak Singh, Khushal Singh, Babu Gulab Singh, and to all the other satsangis. A letter from Chanan Singh and Narain Singh was received. After reading it, a reply was sent that they should keep doing bhajan and simran. That is the message: keep doing bhajan and simran every day.

And you, Babu Ji, are also urged to keep doing bhajan and simran every day. If sitting is not possible, then do it lying down. But for whatever time it is done, even if only for a quarter-hour, it will be as good as doing it for twenty-four hours. Keep your attention focused in it even while walking about, and hold satsang daily for one hour. You should not worry unduly that you will have difficulty sitting for two or three hours. No! You just be attentive and stay within the will, that is, remain within the directives of the Satguru, and make your faith and refuge in him absolute. Keep listening to the sound of the Shabd while walking about, then you are always in his presence. It is the Shabd-dhun alone that sustains all activities. Other than the Shabd-dhun, who else is there to do the work? You should merely remain ready to serve. Consider the Shabd to be your only form, and realize that your form is Satguru's Shabd form, too. Have faith, do not worry, and remain even-tempered in pain or pleasure.

Please write your letters promptly; that is, you should write four letters a month, or at least three. When you visit me at Christmas or some other time, I will explain everything about the inner condition, even if you stay here for only an hour. I cannot write about it but will explain it in person. On behalf of Bibi Ji, Radha Soami greetings to you, her true brother. And Radha Soami greetings from all the sadhus at the Dera. Bibi Ji had fallen ill in my absence, but she is fully recovered now. Please have no worry.

14 December 1902

∼ 130 ∼

[Dictated]

Radha Soami. Radha Soami Ji is the Comforter.

From Jaimal Singh: Radha Soami greetings to my obedient son, Babu Sawan Singh. This is to let you know that I have been to Rawalpindi. I went there on Tuesday, and returned on Saturday and attended the satsang on Sunday. Soami Ji's verse edition is being printed. The account of Hazur Soami Ji's life history that was to go into the introduction will not be put in it now, because it did not come from the gracious Hazur himself. So it has not been included. In this book, only the words that were voiced by the compassionate Hazur Radha Soami Ji himself are going to be printed. Other than that, not a single word or letter or diacritic will be added. I have arranged for all this there. I went to Rawalpindi especially for this purpose and explained everything to Lala Buta Mal and Babu Gajja Singh. Sixty-four or sixty-five copies of the prose *Sar Bachan* have also been printed. The quality of printing is now much better. Please write and let me know if you want to get *Ghat Ramayan* printed, and write also if you would rather not have it printed. Actually, it won't look nice now if it is not printed, as it has become generally known that we are having *Ghat Ramayan* printed as well. For the rest, as you wish. No doubt it will cost about 500 rupees. Write to me about this and also about how much Babu Gajja Singh has taken for all his previous expenses. The cheque for 100 rupees that you sent was not cashed; he has still got it. I gave a little money to him, as he would not take more. He will be happy if you call him for employment; on the other hand, he is happy also if he is kept for the printing of the books. Do what you think is proper.

The situation at the Dera now is that the main satsang hall has been completed up to a height of fourteen feet. Within a week it will be completely finished, because eleven masons are now working on the building. But the iron girders have not yet arrived. The wood for the cross-ties is being kept aside, but they cannot be made in case they get damaged. The girders are late in arriving. Please inform us about the girders so that upon their arrival at Beas railway station we can fetch them in a bullock cart. Do arrange to send them soon and pay their freight up to Beas railway station. Please let me know soon when they can be expected so that we may continue with the construction or suspend it. This is a matter of great urgency as the weather right now is very good. Later, in the rainy season, we will face difficulties, so this matter needs to be taken care of expeditiously.

You should send a postcard or letter of your well-being more frequently, because now they come after a considerable lapse. Please convey Radha Soami greetings to Basant Singh, Chanan Singh, Narain Singh, Babu Gulab Singh, Khushal Singh, Nanak Singh, and all the other satsangis—grace and mercy upon them all. And you should always keep doing your bhajan and simran. If a long sitting is not possible, do it while lying down, but do it you must. Worldly work also has to be carried on. Keep the surat, nirat and the mind, with the inherent yearning, that is, love, of the higher mind, always attached to the Shabd-dhun. The actions of walking, moving, sitting or sleeping, and other worldly affairs, are performed by the body and the vital energy (pran). The soul and mind do not perform them. Hold your mind and the soul's attentive faculties always in the sound of the Shabd-dhun, and keep on with your worldly work. Please reply soon. On behalf of Bibi Ji, Radha Soami greetings to you, her true brother. Radha Soami also from all the satsangis at the Dera.

27 December 1902

～ 131 ～

[Dictated]

Radha Soami. Radha Soami Ji is the Comforter.

From Jaimal Singh: Radha Soami greetings to Babu Sawan Singh, and to Babu Gulab Singh, Basant Singh, Nanak Singh, Narain Singh, Chanan Singh, and all the other satsangis. I received your letter and was happy to read the news. It was a well-written letter. You write that the money for the girders has been dispatched. It is good that this has been taken care of. It would be good if the girders were to arrive soon, because the work is now in full swing and only the girders are not yet here. The sawing of timber is continuing. Earlier also a letter was written to you about the need for money. It is difficult to carry on with the work without money in hand, so whichever way you can, please send money soon. If it cannot be done, then let me know: just drop me a line whether or not money will be coming.

I am also very worried about your illness. May Hazur Maharaj soon grant you health, and may he bless you very soon with his special grace. My thoughts remain with you day and night. If you are unable to write a postcard in Gurmukhi yourself, you should ask Narain Singh to send me the news of your well-being. May the compassionate Radha Soami Ji himself be merciful to you. If you feel discomfort, please have Narain Singh do the writing—because these are his instructions. Soami Ji Maharaj himself will shower his mercy, and indeed is doing so. Look upon it all as his grace.

You are urged repeatedly to continue doing bhajan and simran. Hazur Soami Ji is always with and within you. In pain, too, you should continue doing bhajan, and not forget it, because pain and pleasure are both the same. In pleasure, the mind keeps wandering; but when it is in pain, it does not go anywhere. It does not then wish for any worldly, sensual, or wicked desires. At such a time it prays to the Lord only that it may get better. So please think about this: one does not gain anything in having physical health so long as surat, nirat and the higher mind do not devoutly love the Dhun of the Shabd. Were one to immerse oneself in the Dhun, such love and devotion for the Satguru's Holy Feet and form would arise in the mind that it would remove the suffering of the past twenty-one births. Only through such effort, and through such love and devotion day and night, can the karmas from millions of past lives be erased. And when ... with the Satguru's will and a tranquil mind, the disciple grows in love and devotion for the Shabd-dhun and obtains its bliss, that love and devotion will merge surat, nirat and the higher mind into the Shabd-dhun, and it will feel as if the Supreme Lord, Radha Soami Dayal, is showering his mercy upon us. However much pain the body might feel, even then consider it to be his grace and mercy. Always remember this: that you are to give your whole love and affection to the sound of the Shabd-dhun, then grace and mercy will reach you in every way. So do not be perturbed.

Radha Soami greetings from Bibi to you, her true brother. And Radha Soami greetings from everyone at the Dera. Please accept respectful greetings from the postman, Ganda Ram. Do not think yourself to be in pain; think that it is his grace and mercy. Reply by return post, even if it is a postcard.

[Baba Ji's writing:] My son, this letter has been written in Urdu. Please read it carefully and consider everything to be his grace and mercy. This is the suffering that could lead to a rebirth. Therefore let it work itself out at this very point. Guru's grace is with you, so the suffering will soon come to an end— please treat all pain as pleasure.

[January 1903]

∼ 132 ∼

Radha Soami. Radha Soami Ji is the Comforter.

Radha Soami greetings from Jaimal Singh to my obedient son, Babu Sawan Singh, and to Basant Singh, the little boy, Narain Singh, Babu Gulab Singh, Nanak Singh, and all the other satsangis. Dear son, I received 200 rupees through Chanan Singh on 24 January. From these, 100 were spent on timber, and the rest on the masons' wages. This has helped us to continue the work. Had the girders arrived by 1 December, the roof would have been constructed and all the work finished by this time. But even now, with Hazur's grace, it will be done. Only the girders are being awaited. Chanan Singh stayed here for a day. He left today, 26 January, by the 12:30 mail train, and will reach your place tomorrow, 27 January. I am concerned about your illness, my son. No doubt it will disappear after the karmas have worked themselves out. So please do not worry, because both good and bad karmas are like debts that must be cleared. For a satsangi, there is no rebirth; right now, in this very body, all karmas are to be paid off. So do not worry—this is the way the Lord tests our faith and patience. When the Lord sends us pain, it is for our own good. So look upon pain as pleasure, my son—and this pain is now about to end.

Please do not forget your bhajan and simran. Do not indulge in useless talk at night-time—night is for rest and for bhajan and simran. Any work you have to do is to be done during the day. I advised you about this in Rawalpindi. But did you follow the advice? At night, no one should come to you with an errand. Do you go to the officers' bungalows at night to talk with them? If they do not allow it—and you work for them—then why should you do so? My son, why do you spend your time uselessly? If you talk, say, for four hours at night, how much does that help in constructing a building? If that work is done during the day, then what is gained by idle talk at night-time? Enough! I have counselled you sufficiently; it is up to you now. Every evening, if you are able to sit, you should definitely hold satsang for an hour between 7:30 and 9:00. But if your body is weak, then read for half an hour while lying down. Read five shabds from Hazur Soami Ji's book every day. And make a two-ounce pudding with cream of wheat and eat it daily.

A letter in Urdu was written to you earlier; it has probably reached you by now. Please settle the matter of Buta Mal when you go to Rawalpindi. It is fine if he prints *Ghat Ramayan*; otherwise, Gajja Singh should have it printed when he again becomes free. The gum is good; be sure to eat as much of it as suits you. And do your bhajan and simran every day.

Radha Soami greetings from Bibi and all the sadhus at the Dera. When the girders arrive, we will hurry up with the construction of the roof. Two men are now engaged in sawing the timber, and five in making the ties, planks, and doors.

26 January 1903

～ 133 ～

[Dictated]

Radha Soami. Radha Soami Ji is the Comforter.

From Jaimal Singh: Radha Soami to Babu Sawan Singh, Babu Gulab Singh, Basant Singh, Chanan Singh, Nanak Singh, the young boy and all the other satsangis with you. Your letter arrived and I was happy to read it. You have written about your illness. Please have no worry; you will get well shortly. Don't become perturbed; be optimistic. Two letters have already been sent to you. It is urgent that the girders arrive here soon. They are very late; the hot weather will be here before long. An urgent letter has been written to Babu Gajja Singh and Nabi Bakhsh the painter that they should reach Rawalpindi by 31 [January] 1903. I expect they will do so. Have no worry about your illness. You are going to recover from it very soon. Rather, make it a point to keep doing bhajan and simran and to look upon pain as pleasure. This postcard has been written to you because we have already sent two letters. Radha Soami from Bibi Ji to you, her true brother. Your official work will not be affected; do it slowly.

30 [January] 1903

∽ 134 ∽

[Dictated]

Radha Soami. Radha Soami Ji is the Comforter.

Radha Soami greetings from Jaimal Singh to my obedient son, Babu Sawan Singh, and to Basant Singh, Babu Gulab Singh, Chanan Singh, Narain Singh, Nanak Singh, and the little boy. May the grace and mercy of Hazur be upon everyone. Your letter was received and I was very happy to read it and learn your news. In the letter you have asked for the craftsman Nabi Bakhsh and Babu Gajja Singh to come there, but both are in Rawalpindi. I immediately wrote a postcard to them, that they should go to your place, so they may have already reached there. Therefore please let me know whether or not they have come. Secondly, the girder dealer is taking a long time. Send him an urgent telegram to ask why the girders have not yet been dispatched. It would have been nice if the girders had arrived by now because the weather is good. Later, the hot weather will come and cause much difficulty. Write about your illness, whether you have recovered by now. Always let me know immediately whenever you are ill. You should not become perturbed by illness; rather, consider the soul, body, and vital energy (*jio, pind,* and *pran*) all to

be the Satguru's—and indeed they all do belong to the Satguru.
Pain or pleasure that has been planted in the body will surely
bear fruit, but a satsangi will go through only a sixth part of it—
he is let off the other five. Look upon pain as pleasure and learn
to endure it. As the hymn from *Sri Guru Granth Sahib* says:

> You give me joy, it is you I worship;
> in hardship too I think of you.
> You give me hunger, still I am sated;
> the pain you send is the pleasure true.
> *Je sukh dehi ta tujhahi araadhee,*
> *dukh bhee tujhai dhiaaee.*
> *Je bhukh dehi ta itahee raajaa,*
> *dukh vich sookh manaaee.*[18]

Remember these words and fix your mind in them. The
words of the compassionate Hazur are: "Look upon the hour of
pain as a blessing" *(Dukh kee gharee ganeemat jaano),*[19] because
the moment of suffering is always welcome as it reminds you of
the Lord. It comes through his grace, not by itself. So do not
worry in suffering for it will come to an end shortly. Keep your
thoughts towards the Lord, and also do your official work. Just
be there as an observer—the Lord will do the work himself. I
had conveyed through Chanan Singh that you should eat a small
amount of wheat pudding regularly. So prepare it like this: take
ghee worth five rupees, sugar or crystallized sugar worth six, and
cream of wheat worth five. Mix them together to make the pudding and eat as much as you can; that is, eat what you can digest
daily. Also, soak chickpeas in water and make a curry dish with
that water. Eating that every day will improve your digestion and
gradually make it normal. The physical hardships that you are
experiencing are like the onset of a storm when the force of the

wind tears off the branches of many trees and even rips out some whole trees by their very roots. Suffering of this kind similarly debilitates the body. Indeed, such an attack enervates the whole body, but one should not worry—you will get well soon. Rather, make sure to keep me informed of your condition. When you feel that the pain is unbearable, put your mind in bhajan or simran and you will be all right.

Radha Soami greetings from Bibi Ji to you, her true brother. Radha Soami greetings also from all the residents of the Dera. We have now less than half a canister of coal tar left. You should definitely send two canisters of coal tar. If two are not possible, at least one is definitely needed. We also need twenty blocks of stone to support the girder-ends. Please write in case they are not available from your place; we will then get them from Amritsar. So please send them soon, or reply by return post so that other arrangements can be made—whatever you do, please do it soon. But the coal tar, at least, must come in time. Do dispatch it soon. After arranging all these things please reply by return post. If your body is still weak and you are unable to function properly, even then you should write and we will stop the work. The work can be started again later when you are physically fit, but send the reply promptly; do not delay.

We have nine men working as carpenters. For stoppers and ventilator-frames, wide planks of deodar costing 30 rupees will come from Amritsar. Double sets of cross-ties and boards are to be prepared, as we would like to put up a box ceiling. For the rest, write soon what would suit you in this. Your postcard has also arrived. I am delighted to know that your illness is gone. You will regain full health. Hazur himself will be graciously merciful; he is always by your side. Please do not feel perturbed. He will bless you with grace and mercy.

3 February 1903

∾ 135 ∾

[Dictated]

Radha Soami. Radha Soami Ji is the Comforter.

Radha Soami greetings from Jaimal Singh to my obedient son, Babu Sawan Singh. Your letter came and I was very happy to read it; the invoice for the girders has also been received. We will go and check at the railway station whether they have arrived. Immediately upon receiving them we will inform you, with a detailed letter to follow later. In the meantime, please let me know from where the stone has been arranged. It should arrive soon because the stone blocks are to be placed under the girders. Could you also write why eleven girders are being sent? You had already determined that the land measured fifty-five feet, and required ten girders. So why have eleven been sent? There is an extra girder, but it is nothing to worry about. Please reply soon if the stone is not available; we can then arrange to buy iron plates from here. Nihal Singh the carpenter has gone mad, and new carpenters have come and constructed a box ceiling. I was busy with these concerns. Iron plates, one-half inch thick, six inches long, and five inches wide, are available at 5 rupees per 36 kilograms. However, the stone would be better, if it could be obtained. Please convey my Radha Soami greetings to everybody. Radha Soami from Bibi Ji to you, her true brother. And the scribe of this letter [Pandit Ganda Ram] is a very incompetent fellow! He also sends you his Radha Soami.* Keep doing your bhajan and simran. Radha Soami to everybody.

7 February 1903

---

* The two preceding sentences are an interpolation by the scribe, Ganda Ram. *See also* Glossary.

~ 136 ~

[Dictated]

Radha Soami. Radha Soami Ji is the Comforter.

Radha Soami from Jaimal Singh to Babu Sawan Singh, and
Babu Gulab Singh, Gajja Singh, Basant Singh, Sunder Singh,
Chanan Singh, Nanak Singh and the other satsangis with you;
also, to Nabi Bakhsh the craftsman, to the masons and to all
others, Radha Soami greetings. I received your letter and was
pleased to know of your well-being. The invoice for the girders
has been received, but not the girders. It is hoped they will arrive
in a day or two. Ten girders were expected but the invoice shows
that eleven have been dispatched; that is, there is one extra
girder. Write to me by return post about the stone: will you be
sending it or should it be bought in Amritsar? Please reply urgently as the stone has to be placed under the girders. We did
not purchase it in Amritsar in case you have bought it. We shall
do as you write. Stone from Amritsar will cost about 20 rupees,
including freight. It would be good if you could send it. Again, I
repeat: please write soon what should be done about the stone
for the girders. A box ceiling is now being put on the building.
Nihal Singh the carpenter became sick and went mad, so we replaced him with another carpenter. He has constructed the frame
for the exposed deck roof. One hundred cross-ties had already
been prepared by the time your letter arrived. A total of 140
cross-ties will be needed for the roof, including the 100 that are
ready. We are now waiting for the girders to arrive. The invoice
has come, so the girders also should be on the way. You have already written about the coal tar; that too should arrive here soon.

Radha Soami greetings to Babu Gajja Singh. A letter has
been received from you along with the copies of the book. The
other letter that you wrote from Fakiran Headworks has also

been received. However, the letter with the books arrived after some delay as the railway people misdirected the package. Five copies and the index have been received. Let me remind you to please continue doing your bhajan and simran. The compassionate Hazur Radha Soami, the merciful, is always with you, and will bestow his mercy. If you feel weak, it is all right to do bhajan and simran, and to listen to the melody of the Shabd-dhun, while lying down—there is no harm if sitting is not possible. As much attention as you can give will be to the good. But pay attention wholeheartedly, and keep your longing in that direction. And as regards the government work, the compassionate Lord, Radha Soami himself, will do it all, and indeed is already doing so. You should not become perturbed. In illness, it is good to keep up one's spirits. His grace and mercy will be upon you, and indeed it is already so.

Please accept Radha Soami greetings from Hakim Singh the mason. He is a satsangi and a relative of Sunder Singh of Battery No. 1. He would like to come to you if there is any skilled work for him; or if there is some other work, such as on contract, etc., then, too, please write. In case you wish to write to him directly, the address is: Hakim Singh, Mason, c/o Babu Sher Singh, Supervisor, Lahore City Railway Station. He will wait for your letter for four days. This mason has now come here with Jawahar Singh of Amritsar, who constructed the durbar hall.

Day and night there was much concern here about your illness. It is good that you have now received Hazur's grace and mercy. He is merciful and will shower his mercy upon you. You write that from time to time you keep getting letters from people at home in which they sometimes write one thing and sometimes another. Do not feel disturbed; when you feel strong we will look into it. This is the householder's lot; many such problems arise in family life. If you think it appropriate, write to them that you will inform them before you come home on leave. Please continue with your bhajan and simran every day; the compassionate Hazur is always with you. You wrote that you were holding satsang. This is very good. It is important to do bhajan without fail—there is no real work other than bhajan. Reply to this letter by return post because day and night my thoughts remain with you.

Radha Soami from Bibi to you, her true dear brother. Please also accept Radha Soami greetings from all the residents of the Dera.

[February 1903]

～ 137 ～

Radha Soami. Radha Soami Ji is the Comforter.

Radha Soami greetings from Jaimal Singh to my obedient son, Babu Sawan Singh. Dear son, we have obtained the building stone from Amritsar. Each stone measures 18 inches long, 12 inches wide, and 3¼ inches high. There are twenty in all. So now do not send any, but if you have bought them, try to use them elsewhere. However, it does not matter if you have already dispatched them, they will be used somewhere. Someone was sent to inquire about them, and he ended up buying them instead. The girders have not yet arrived; they should be coming any day now. Should we use these stones, which are 18 inches long, 12 inches wide, and 3¼ inches high, or should we use wider ones than these? If these seem all right, then please do not send any yourself, because we should not duplicate the expense. But please send your replies promptly.

The divider boards for the doors should be 17 inches wide, but wood of that width is not available. We could not find such timber in Amritsar; we inquired at Phillaur too—finished wood that wide is not available. For this purpose, a log could be purchased for 50 or 60 rupees, but who knows what it might be like on the inside? So we will make the dividers by joining two pieces in the middle. All this is for your information. We went to Amritsar and had a log sawn, which turned out to be worthless on the inside. Send a reply soon about this.

Please write to me about your condition, my son. If you are unable to sit for bhajan and simran, then do it while lying down, even if only for ten or fifteen minutes, or for half an hour. Even that much will be very good. Keep your love in the mind's *(chitt)* inner yearning all the time. Look upon pain as pleasure and do not worry. Do not consider anything except Shabd-dhun Nam to be yours. That is our Lord, protector, life and breath, my son. Only for that should we feel true, heartfelt love. May the grace and mercy of the compassionate Lord, Radha Soami Ji, always be upon you.

Radha Soami to Basant Singh, Harwant Singh, Chanan Singh, Babu Gulab Singh, Narain Singh, and Nanak Singh. All are reminded to do their bhajan and simran every day, because other than bhajan nothing is our own. Do not let the attraction of any worldly thing make you forget it. This opportunity will not come our way again. Do not listen to the mind's counsel; remain singularly within the Satguru's will. Do not follow what the mind says. Attend to all your worldly duties but keep your love and faith in the Satguru's Lotus Feet, because our breaths and morsels of food are all numbered. Worldly work is for our livelihood, meditation for our salvation—attend to both. As for the rest, tell your mind that you will not obey its behests—keep the Satguru's teachings always alive in the mind. What more can I write to you, my son? If you obey, you will go directly to Sach Khand.

Has Babu Gajja Singh found a job yet? Write about him. Radha Soami to Babu Gajja Singh. He should do his bhajan and simran every day.

Radha Soami from Bibi Ji to you, her true brother. And Radha Soami to everybody from the sadhus at the Dera. Write frequently about how you are doing, my son; and upon reading this letter reply immediately, even if only by a postcard. Nihal Singh the carpenter has gone mad. He is now somewhat better than before, but is still unable to do his work.

10 February 1903

∼ 138 ∼

[Dictated]

Radha Soami. Radha Soami Ji is the Comforter.

Radha Soami greetings from Jaimal Singh to my obedient son, Babu Sawan Singh, and to Basant Singh, Babu Gulab Singh, Chanan Singh, Sunder Singh, Nanak Singh, Babu Gajja Singh, the little boy and the other satsangis, and to Nabi Bakhsh the craftsman. The girders have arrived and have been set in place. Also, 60 rupees were received in two money orders of 50 and 10 rupees respectively. Today, we also received a postcard informing us that the building stone would be sent in two or three days. Earlier I wrote that the stone had arrived here, that is, it had been purchased. I hope that the letter about this has reached you; there is now no need for the stone here because of the local purchase. The ten girders have been set in place; an extra, thirteen-foot girder is left over. Stone is no more needed here now— you may please use it if something needs to be built there.

Continue with your bhajan and simran every day. The compassionate Lord, Radha Soami Ji, is always with you—keep your trust in him. Please do not exert yourself too much, because you have gone through a serious illness. The compassionate Hazur Radha Soami Ji will do all your work. About this you should have no worry. Be concerned only with your meditation. The affairs of the world will take their own course; they just go on and never come to an end. What is needed more than anything is meditation.

Radha Soami on behalf of Bibi Ji to you, her true brother. Radha Soami also to Babu Gajja Singh and Gulab Singh. Radha Soami greetings from all the residents of the Dera.

[February 1903]

∽ 139 ∽

[Dictated]

Radha Soami. Radha Soami Ji is the Comforter.

From Jaimal Singh: Radha Soami greetings to my obedient son, Babu Sawan Singh. The stone for the building has been received and set in place, though it was rather late in arriving. The old ones were pulled out and replaced by the new. Also, ten girders have been installed, and one set aside. Railway freight charges of 17 rupees and 13 annas for the stone have also been paid. The girders are now in place, the frames are ready, and construction of the roof will start in eight days—we think we have enough bricks on hand and won't run short.

Keep doing bhajan and simran every day. If you cannot sit, you must still do it lying down. While walking or moving around, continue to listen to the Shabd-dhun. The inner attention *(chitt)* should be in it all the time, as whatever work you then undertake will be done at once. It is through the effulgence of Nam that the earth, the sky, and everything else in the universe have originated. Nam is primal, all else is secondary. Where Nam is present, everything is present. That is why Nam should be grasped first, for when Nam is attained, everything is attained. Therefore never ever forget Nam.

Your cooking pot has been received. If possible, you should come on leave soon because we should decide about Hazur

Soami Ji's books, as many people are asking for them. You also need to come to see the girders installed in the building. If you cannot get leave to come, then send Chanan Singh immediately with 200 or 300 rupees. A money order will take time: the money should reach here definitely by Friday or Saturday at the latest. Be sure to send at least 200 rupees, if more is not available. Send Chanan Singh as soon as you receive this letter. He can stay at the Dera for a day and then return to your place the next day. He should come to Beas quickly by the mail train.

Of the workers here, nine are carpenters, four masons, and seven labourers. They are all to be paid wages for one month, so send the money as soon as possible. Chanan Singh will bring you a full account.

Please convey Radha Soami greetings to the satsangis Basant Singh, Babu Gulab Singh, Chanan Singh, Narain Singh, and Nanak Singh. All are urged to do their bhajan and simran every day. They will all receive grace and mercy. Radha Soami from Bibi Ji to you, her true brother. Also Radha Soami from everyone else at the Dera. The consignment of coal tar was received on 23 February.

I urge you to keep meditation specifically in your mind— with an attitude of deep devotion. Since all worldly activities are false, keep doing them with that in mind. Heartfelt love is to be given only to meditation.

Written: [23 February 1903]

∼ 140 ∼

Radha Soami. Radha Soami Ji is the Comforter.

Radha Soami greetings from Jaimal Singh to my obedient son, Babu Sawan Singh. Dear son, your letter has been received and I was delighted to read your news. I had earlier written a letter about how things were over here, which has probably reached you by now. Since your new house is now ready, you should move into it. Before moving in, all the satsangis should recite five shabds from Hazur Soami Ji's book, and then say out aloud, "Radha Soami, Radha Soami," for five minutes. In your heart, picture Hazur Soami Ji to be sitting on a seat or a charpoy. Then sit in bhajan for a quarter-hour. If sitting is not possible, do simran instead, and afterwards pick up the charpoy and enter the house. Regard this as very important. You should definitely move into your house because my coming now is doubtful. In the Shabd form, I am with you in every respect. Of course, if you get leave for four days, by all means please do come yourself.

The news from here is that the construction of the roof is to start on 27 February, so now it will be finished soon. All the large and small doors are now ready. Also the ten girders have been set in the walls at a height of seventeen feet and three inches. Each girder is twenty-two feet long, six inches wide, and twelve inches high. There was an extra twenty-three-foot long girder which was not used but set aside. In my previous letter I had asked you to send 200 or 300 rupees through Chanan Singh—the money is definitely needed here. I had 400 rupees that were left with me by some satsangis—that has been spent. An extra 200 rupees were spent by borrowing from Parmanand. Additionally, ten or twelve beams, at 4 or 4½ rupees each, will soon be needed. The work will now proceed only when the money is received. We have four carpenters who work at 7 annas each per day, three at 6 annas each, and one at 5—a total of eight carpenters. Of the masons, three work at 7 annas each per day, and two at 5 annas each. Eight labourers work at 3 annas per day. The carpenters and masons take all their meals at the Dera, while the labourers eat one meal a day on their own. On Sundays, the labourers also take all their meals at the Dera. So now I have described to you the whole situation. The cross-ties for the roof have been placed at a height of eighteen feet and three inches—that is the height at which the roof is being constructed. Three brick projections for beams have been constructed at the level of the cross-ties. So if the roof for a veranda is constructed later on, the two roofs will be at the same level, allowing many satsangis to sit upstairs.

Please do your bhajan and simran every day, my son. Always keep in mind that the world is unreal, and unreal also are all its kingships, goods and services. From our body on, everything is unreal. All your work is to be done with that realization in mind. Just as in a dream everything is done as if it were real, but on awakening it is found to be unreal, so also the whole business of the world is unreal. You are never to give it your true, deep love. True love is to be given to the sound of the Shabd-dhun. Have firm faith in the Satguru's instructions, that his words are true. While doing your official work, moving around, sitting up or lying down, always mentally continue with your simran. All worldly and spiritual work will be done by the compassionate Anami Lord, Radha Soami Ji.

Radha Soami greetings to Basant Singh, Chanan Singh, Babu Gulab Singh, Narain Singh, and Nanak Singh. All are reminded to do bhajan and simran every day. Radha Soami from Bibi Ji to you, her true brother. Radha Soami also to all the others from Bibi and all the sadhus at the Dera.

My son, the fruit of inner darshan has now reached you. I will explain it when you come to visit me. Briefly: when you sit in meditation, be by yourself and remind yourself of the Satguru's instructions; then start the simran, and keep the inner attention on the Satguru's form—you will receive darshan. Then firmly fix your inner hearing and seeing faculties into the music of the Shabd-dhun—you will receive darshan. But your love and devotion must be full and complete. Send a reply soon.

28 February 1903

~ 141 ~

[Dictated]

Radha Soami. Radha Soami Ji is the Comforter.

Radha Soami greetings from Jaimal Singh to my obedient son, Babu Sawan Singh. This is to let you know that a sum of 300 rupees was received through Chanan Singh, and it has been used for the construction work. Also, on 9 March 1903, I received a money order for 10 rupees. This information is being sent so that you may rest assured. On 27th of Phagun, i.e., 10 March, a hardwood box ceiling, with one set of planks below the cross-ties and another above them, was constructed on the main satsang hall. Coal tar was coated on the top set of planks, over which a double row of brick tiles was laid and grouted with lime. A layer of clay was then spread over it all. The frames are all ready, except for two or three. The plastering of the walls with lime will start on 13 March. Some bricks will still be left over. The two canisters of coal tar that you sent here were less than half full. Both did arrive, but one was three-quarters full and the other even less than half. So please do not pay for full canisters. All the girders still to be painted have become rusted. It is urgent that you find a painter and send him here. As an alternative, there are painters here, too, from among whom we could engage someone. I do not know how good they are, but they claim that they can do the job. It would be better if you could send a good painter; also write what kind of paint should be used. It would be preferable to do the painting quickly, otherwise the ceiling will become damaged. The canister of red paint which was used for the frames is still one-third full and could be used too. But whatever you write will be done.

Buta Mal has written from Rawalpindi to inform us that Hazur Soami Ji's books are ready. Many servicemen from the batteries are asking for them. I have written to Buta Mal that I have no idea about their price or if they have to be hardbound. So please let me know the price to be charged for Hazur's books and also whether they are to be hardbound. I will then inform him accordingly. And have you settled the charges for labour, etc., with him? You have not sent me any information through a letter, nor has any other mail come from you. Please let me know why there has been a delay in writing. Perhaps you have too much work to do, but still the information should have been sent. Anyway, nothing is lost if it hasn't been done. Please do your bhajan and simran every day, and always feel a mental yearning within, an eagerness in the mind, to listen to the Shabd-dhun. Everyday work also has to be done, but the craving to hear the Shabd-dhun must always remain uppermost in the mind. If you have time, an hour or two of satsang should also be done. It would be desirable, if you can get leave for two, three, or even up to four or five days, to come and see the construction for yourself, because whatever is lacking could then be taken care of after your inspection. Later on that won't be possible. Therefore, it is urgent that you take leave to come and see the construction.

Radha Soami to Chanan Singh, Basant Singh, Babu Gulab Singh, Narain Singh, Nanak Singh, and all the others. All are urged to do their bhajan and simran every day. On behalf of Bibi Ji, Radha Soami to you, her true brother. And Radha Soami from all the residents of the Dera. You should definitely get leave and come to the Dera without fail. The registers of those on the Radha Soami path have arrived from Allahabad, but they have come per Chacha Ji's command. When you come, one will be given to you as well—Chacha Ji's directive is that one is to be given to Babu Sawan Singh. So please come and take it with you. Radha Soami from everybody here to everyone there. Convey my Radha Soami greetings to Babu Gajja Singh as well, and also let him know about this letter. Keep doing your bhajan

and simran every day. I have written to Nabi Bakhsh the painter,
of Sri Hargobindpur, but so far no reply has come. You will be
informed when he arrives. Please give my love to the little boy,
Balwant Singh. Reply by return post as to when you are coming. Inform me without fail.

12 March 1903

~ 142 ~

Radha Soami. Radha Soami Ji is the Comforter.

Radha Soami greetings from Jaimal Singh to my obedient son,
Babu Sawan Singh, and to Babu Gulab Singh, Basant Singh,
Chanan Singh, Narain Singh, and any other satsangis who may
be there with you. May the grace and mercy of the compassionate Anami Lord, Radha Soami Ji, always be upon you. Dear
son, I have received no news from you since the day you left here.
You should definitely keep up with the correspondence. The
news from here is that the building is now ready and being
painted: a worker is busy painting it an almond colour—he has
finished one coat and will put on one or two more. We are also
having an outer gate made. Three thousand bricks were purchased for 11½ rupees per thousand, plus 3 rupees per thousand for cartage. The total expenditure came to 44 rupees.

Postcards have come from Chacha Ji in Agra, and 100 rupees are now to be sent there for Hazur's bhandara. Also 100
rupees' worth of wheat is to be purchased for the year. Then
there is an expense of 80 or 90 rupees for the masons and
labourers as well. For the rest, do as you think proper, but the
money is needed soon. Either send it in instalments of 50 each,
or send the whole amount with Chanan Singh, because then it
will arrive here sooner. He will return in two days. If Chanan

Singh cannot come, then send the amount in money orders of 50 each. For the rest, do as you think proper.

The other news is that a man by the name of 'Ganga', who used to work at Buta Mal's printing press, is asking me for his wages. Please ask Babu Gajja Singh what is all this. Did you have him employed with an understanding to pay his wages? He has written three or four letters, so please inquire and let me know. Buta Mal is refusing to pay his wages.

Lots of satsangis are now asking for the books. I have written to Buta Mal to send fifty copies of the verse edition and fifty of the prose one, that is, a total of one hundred copies. I have asked him to pack them in a box and send them in the railway brakevan to Beas railway station, where I will pay the freight. So far there has been no reply. Please resolve these matters with him and let me know, because I do not think we should ever again have printing done through Buta Mal—no work is to be done through him. If at some point we want to have *Ghat Ramayan* printed, we will have it done at some other press.

Do your bhajan and simran every day and also arrange to hold satsang. Do your official duty also, and while doing it, find time for bhajan and simran as well. Keep death in your mind all the time. Always remember the words of the Satguru. Our home is beyond the Alakh and Agam regions; we are going there with the help of the Shabd-dhun—that is our guiding light. The whole business of the world is going on because of its radiance. God, soul, maya, the subtle, the gross, the body, that is, the physical frame, and the universe—the Dhun is the light and creator of all. So hold fast to its sound at every moment. Concentrating and blending together all three inner faculties, the mind, surat and nirat, and driving out all worldly attractions, listen devotedly to the Shabd-dhun. Whether for fifteen minutes or half an hour, listen to it every day. Have full faith, my son, that the

Shabd-dhun will make the soul pure and take it to the land of Radha Soami.

Radha Soami greetings from Bibi to you, her true brother. Radha Soami greetings also from the sadhus at the Dera to you and to all the others. Your money order for 10 rupees arrived here on 20 April 1903. The money has been spent on general expenses. Do keep me informed, my son.

21 April 1903

～ 143 ～

[Dictated]

Radha Soami. Radha Soami Ji is the Comforter.

From Jaimal Singh: Radha Soami greetings to my obedient son, Babu Sawan Singh, and to Babu Gulab Singh, Chanan Singh, Narain Singh, Basant Singh and all the other satsangis. A long time has passed since a letter came from your side and this has me quite worried. Please write to me about your health as soon as you receive this letter. The main satsang hall has been painted; all the work on it is now finished. I am of the mind that the small rooms, the durbar hall, and the upper-storey rooms should all be painted white. The ceilings too should be painted white, and the doors and windows, brown. Immediately upon receiving this letter, please send me four brushes and two canisters of Bolander's linseed oil. Send two canisters of brown paint as well, the proviso being that you are to send them soon if the three buildings are to be painted.

Please call Fazal Din the painter if you have found some work for him. He is capable of doing very good work—his work is flawless. Radha Soami on behalf of Bibi Ji. Keep doing your bhajan and simran. Convey my Radha Soami to Nanak Singh.

1 May 1903

∼ 144 ∼

Radha Soami. Radha Soami Ji is the Comforter.

Radha Soami greetings from Jaimal Singh to my obedient son, Babu Sawan Singh, and to Babu Gulab Singh, Narain Singh, Diwan Singh, Babu Gajja Singh, Aya Singh, and young Harwant Singh. Dear son, Chanan Singh has arrived here and from him I have received 300 rupees on 4 May. All the work has now been completed.

When you take the ten days' leave, go directly home first; then come to the Dera on the way back at five o'clock on Saturday evening and, after the Sunday satsang here, resume your official duties the following day. You must go home because there are many matters awaiting your attention there for the last two to three years. So go straight home: I will be greatly pleased at your going home and coming here upon your return.

You have written that your mind feels sad, that it does not wish to do any work, that it has become tired. Definitely the mind should remain detached from the world, my son. Don't worry; keep your mind in the Shabd-dhun, and firmly fix your attention in simran all the time, and listen to the Shabd with love and devotion—then the physical tiredness will go away. You also write that the officer who has now come is very strict. So what if he is strict? You have to do your official duty, and it will do you good when your mind, nervous and worried, turns towards bhajan and simran. So the news is good. Whatever has to be done, my son, is going to be done by the compassionate Lord, Radha Soami Ji. So have no fear. Remain dauntless in your heart—nothing can happen without his command. Whatever has to happen has already happened. We are going to do only that which has already been done—the true Lord, Radha Soami Ji, is doing it. Continue to work fearlessly; the compassionate Guru is always your protector. Since we have been granted the true wealth, why should we care about the false one? Rather, the mind is not to be attached to the unreal. Whenever you are free, listen to the Shabd-dhun by fixing the mind and soul in it.

Radha Soami from Bibi to you, her true brother. May grace and mercy be upon everyone. Please accept Radha Soami from all the sadhus at the Dera.

[Postscript:] Radha Soami greetings from Jaimal Singh to Narain Singh. Your letter has been received, and I am very happy to read it. Your description of the mind is true; the mind is definitely like that. There is, however, a means to control the mind: always remember the Satguru's words, and whenever the mind begins to ruminate, immediately start doing your simran. Do not yield to its reasonings. Remember the Satguru's words, and know that death is hovering over our head. Understand that you will have to pay for every violation of the Satguru's words. Once you understand this, my son, then the mind will shrink. So do your simran and listen to the sound of the Shabd-dhun. Practise this every day and the mind will become still. You are never to ask for worldly things nor ever to indulge in them. Then the mind will become weak. Have faith in the Satguru's words— they will all be fulfilled.

4 May 1903

~ 145 ~

[Partially dictated]

Radha Soami. Radha Soami Ji is the Comforter.

Radha Soami greetings from Jaimal Singh to my obedient son, Babu Sawan Singh, and to Basant Singh, Chanan Singh, Narain Singh, Babu Gulab Singh, Diwan Singh, Harwant Singh, and the satsangi sisters. Some parshad from Hazur's bhandara has been sent to you by railway delivery. Please receive it from Mone-ke-Thaon [Mona Remount Depot] railway station. If it is not enough, add some extra to make it sufficient.

[Dictated, written in Urdu:] I would like my son, Babu Sawan Singh, to know that I had started to write this letter in Gurmukhi, but due to lack of time had to dictate it in Urdu. The parshad from Hazur's bhandara is being sent to you. Twelve or thirteen people went to Agra for the bhandara, which was well attended. I was also directed to send in the names of all the satsangis, so I will do that. For your information, a membership committee has already been appointed. Chacha Ji will write a letter to you asking you to send him the satsangis' names. Chacha Ji also repeatedly stresses that satsangis should cooperate harmoniously. So I said "yes," but I am not particularly keen to associate with them since their teachings are not like those of Hazur Soami Ji Maharaj, nor do they follow his method of sitting in bhajan—no one even remembers Soami Ji's technique. Because of this, we cannot join them in fellowship. Consequently, the connection is to be superficial. Whenever we meet them, we will greet one another with "Radha Soami, Radha Soami." You are being informed so that when Chacha Ji writes, you should reply that you know nothing about it, as it concerns Baba Jaimal Singh. I will then reply myself. We will send them the names if they satisfy my three objections. These are:

First: The teachings should be those of Hazur Soami Ji, as he used to impart them; the technique and tradition also should be that which he practised. The whole way of _____ is wrong; it is not according to Soami Ji.

Second: There should be three members from among our satsangis since we do not fully understand their language. In brief, you and I should not become members; the members should be selected from among the others.

Third: As to donations and contributions, our satsangis will not give them anything, because all our satsangis are poor, and we do not wish to take anything from them. It is only for bhajan and simran that this teaching is imparted to them.

Please note down all these points in your journal, so that they can be used in your reply. When Chacha Ji writes to you again for the names of the satsangis, reply to him with these three points. If they accept all three points, we have no objection to sending in the satsangis' names. But please do not be in a hurry, wait until they write two or three times.

All of you are reminded to keep doing your bhajan and simran. Do it every day and also read from Hazur's writings. Always remember that we do not belong to this world. Let me give you an example. First, when you were in the area of Murree Hills, you worked very hard at Khairagali. Then you moved on to Rawalpindi, and now you have come to a third place. Similarly, we are going to be transferred from this world. We have no affiliation with this body. If we live within the Satguru's will, do our bhajan and simran every day, drive out worldly desires from the mind, and fix—and continue to fix—the longing of the surat, nirat and the higher mind, all three, into the inner music of the Shabd-dhun, we will keep on filling our hearts and minds with its true love, and will merge into it by listening repeatedly with devotion every day. Always remember these words. Reply soon, my son. This is to be impressed upon all the satsangis: you may read it to them.

Radha Soami from Bibi Ji and all the sadhus at the Dera. Radha Soami from Bibi Ji to you, her true brother. At Agra, both the estate and the arrangements for the bhandara have been placed under the charge of committee members; no one from Soami Ji's family has any authority over them. This is being written solely for your information.

Radha Soami from Milkhi Ram and Moti Ram. I went to

the bhandara at Agra. Soami Ji's teaching is contained singularly in the twenty-sixth hymn:

> Then the Lord revealed his Word,
> and secret of the path uncovered:
> Meditate on the fivefold Nam;
> point the surat in dark into light.
> *Tab swaamee ne bachan sunaayaa,*
> *maarg ṭaa yoṇ bhed laṭhaayaa.*
> *Paanch naam ṭaa sumiran ṭaro,*
> *shyaam set meṇ soorat dharo.*[20]

19 June 1903

∾ 146 ∾

Radha Soami. Radha Soami Ji is the Comforter.

Radha Soami from Jaimal Singh to my obedient son, Babu Sawan Singh, and to Basant Singh and all the family members and satsangis. This is to let you know that both Ma Ji and Bachint Singh left here today, Monday, to go home. A 100-rupee note, number 27-97561, was found on the floor near your bedding. Also, four gold sovereigns, worth 15 rupees each, as well as some single rupees—I am not sure how many—were found tied up in a handkerchief in the almirah. If they are yours, don't worry, I have them with me—I have not sent them with Diwan Singh.

Dear son, please do not worry about any work, including that for the government. Whatever is to happen has already happened. The compassionate Radha Soami Ji always works for our good. He will do whatever is for our benefit. He is ever merciful and gracious. Do your bhajan and simran every day, have complete love and faith within, and continue to listen to the Shabd-dhun.

Radha Soami from Bibi and all the sadhus here.

13 July [1903]

~ 147 ~

Radha Soami. Radha Soami Ji is the Comforter.

Radha Soami from Jaimal Singh to my obedient son, Babu Sawan Singh, and to Basant Singh, Harwant Singh, Babu Gulab Singh, Babu Gajja Singh, Chanan Singh, Narain Singh, Diwan Singh, Aya Singh, Dr Ishar Das Ji, and all the others. Dear son, your letter was received, and I was very happy to read it. I fully appreciate your situation. The corrugated iron sheets used for the roof should have been tightly fixed with strong, heavy iron bolts. Have such work done under your personal supervision. The work on the iron sheets should be done while you oversee it yourself, my son.

Whatever is to happen, happens according to the will of the Supreme Lord, Radha Soami. Without him no one can do anything. Have firm faith in this, my son. Man can do nothing: he can neither increase nor decrease anything. Anami Radha Soami, the Supreme Lord, has assumed the human form to direct worldly affairs on the material plane. This is the divine law. Whatever good is in one's karma, or is to be given to an individual, comes through the human form. Just as whatever is lost due to karma, that is, when something is to be taken away from an individual—more than what the karmas allow is not to be given—that, too, is snatched away through the human form. So do not have any apprehension, my son, no one can ever erase what is in our destiny. Remain happy with your destiny: neither

will you receive more, nor will less be given to you. You will receive only as much as is the will of the compassionate Anami
Lord, Radha Soami. So remain happy within that.

Bhajan and simran is our real work, my son. This will always remain with us, as it is the Satguru's gift. This gift will
grow, and never diminish. Every other honour, right up to the
gods' abode or paradise, is unreal. It is subject to destruction and
also to creation again. So to gain or not to gain it is the same,
because an honour which is first given and then snatched away
means nothing. But this is how the affairs of the world go on. So
what is there in high distinction? If received, it is good, and if
not, still better. There is nothing in this to be sorry about.
Through his grace and mercy, the Lord himself has shown you
the way to his real home. You have found the Anami Radha
Soami's home, which is beyond everything. So now work to
achieve it and remain firm in your love and devotion. Have firm
faith that one day, in this very body, he will take you to the
real home. Listen to the sound of the Shabd-dhun with love
and devotion, and with the pull of the higher mind focus the
surat and nirat into it. Discarding the desires of the gross mind,
listen to the Shabd-dhun every day, even if you do so only for a
short while. Everyone there is urged to do his bhajan and simran
every day.

Gajja Singh has written a letter inquiring when he should
send the books. I have told him to send them in Asuj so that the
box or the bags they are in may not get wet lying outside in the
rain. For the rest, we will do as you write.

Radha Soami to Chanan Singh. Your postcard arrived, and
I was happy to read it. Continue with your bhajan and simran
every day. If you want leave, ask Babu Sawan Singh Ji. Take the
leave if there is little to do at present. Write again, my son, and
let me know if the leave you request is for fifteen days, or more,

or less. Make a request to Babu Ji and tell him what is really on your mind. He will himself then let you know. As for me, you are always by my side, my son, because the Satguru, by assuming the Shabd form, is always with every disciple. But he remains hidden, though always by the side of his loving devotee. So have no worry, stay within the will of the Satguru, and do your work. Grace and mercy will always be upon you.

Radha Soami from Bibi to you, her true brother. Radha Soami to all and everybody from Bibi and from all the sadhus and everyone else at the Dera.

31 July 1903

Note: I had supervised the construction of the artillery barracks at Rawalpindi. Due to a hurricane, two or three corrugated iron sheets were blown away. An antagonistic English Sub-Divisional Officer complained to the C.R.S., so I made my plea to Hazur, to which this was the reply.

—*Sawan Singh*

∼ 148 ∼

[Dictated]

Radha Soami. Radha Soami Ji is the Comforter.

Radha Soami greetings from Jaimal Singh to my obedient son, Babu Sawan Singh. A letter was sent to you earlier, in which two points were left out. First of all, have the two pairs of shoes been sent to Maharaj Sujan Singh at Lucknow? Please let me know soon. If the shoes have not yet been sent, please do so soon. Secondly, keep me informed about whatever happens at your end. Keep studying Hazur Soami Ji's books. Whenever you are free from official work, be sure to read five shabds from the books, and sit in bhajan and simran every day. Remove worldly desires and speculations from your mind and remain happy in his will. Radha Soami from Bibi Ji and from all the residents of the Dera.

2 August 1903

～ 149 ～

Radha Soami. Radha Soami Ji is the Comforter.

Radha Soami greetings from Jaimal Singh to my obedient son, Babu Sawan Singh. May the grace and mercy of the compassionate Anami Hazur Radha Soami Ji always be upon you all. Dear son, a letter from you was given to me by hand. I was happy to read and note its contents. Your 10 rupees have also arrived. I will be sending Narain Singh any time now. You had written that when you find time you would be coming to the Dera on a one-day leave. So the time has not yet been found!

The stone for the main satsang hall has been prepared and has arrived in the Dera. Babu Mohan Singh sent it by railway delivery from Sialkot. Please let me know how much it has cost. Do your bhajan and simran every day; also read selections from Hazur's books daily. Hold satsang every day, whether for an hour or an hour and a half. The true status, my son, belongs to Nam, the Shabd-dhun; every other status is false. So attach your surat, nirat, and the higher mind, with love, to the sound of the Shabd-dhun. When the soul, with loving devotion, will listen to it for a minute or two, or four, five, or ten minutes, innumerable sins and transgressions will be set aside, and that soul, becoming pure, will recognize the sound of the Shabd and merge within it to obtain the bliss of the Shabd-dhun. Then during this very lifetime it will certainly reach Sach Khand. But do not be in a hurry, my son. Always hold love for the Shabd-dhun within your mind. Do not waste any time when you are free from official

work. Not a minute of this time will be had again. You and I
are to make our home in the Shabd-dhun while still in the body.
The love and devotion of the inner attentive faculties and the
inclination of the higher mind should never be neglected.
Everyday affairs, in fact, do not stand in our way. There is ample
time to do our spiritual work, and it has to be done. Nothing
worldly will serve us at the final hour; only the Satguru's Word
and Nam-dhun will protect us at that time.

Radha Soami from Bibi to you, her true brother. Radha
Soami from Bibi, the sadhus at the Dera, and Narain Singh to
everybody and to Babu Ji.

25 August 1903

～ 150 ～

Radha Soami. Radha Soami Ji is the Comforter.

Radha Soami greetings from Jaimal Singh to my obedient son,
Babu Sawan Singh Ji, and to Basant Singh Ji, Harwant Singh
Ji, Babu Gulab Singh Ji, Dr Ishar Das Ji, and Chanan Singh Ji.
Dear son, I have given Nam to Rajinder Singh whom you had
sent here. He has taken a copy of *Anurag Sagar* with him. Today, 31 August, Narain Singh has been sent by train from here
to your place. He will arrive there on 1 September. I had asked
Narain Singh to stay on to do some work at the Dera. The rains
have been heavy, and the houses needed to be repaired every
day. Narain Singh did very good seva, but now I have sent him
to you. The stone has been set in the main satsang hall today.
With the grace of the compassionate Hazur, all is well here. One
Natha Singh has departed from this world.

You are all reminded to do your bhajan and simran every
day, because only now, in the human form alone, can the work
of bhajan and simran be done. It cannot be done in the forms of

any other species, because we can find the Lord only in the human form. Only through finding the perfect path, meeting the perfect Satguru, and generating a complete love and devotion within—never should any disrespect or negative tendency enter the mind—can the goal be attained. There is no honour higher than Nam, my son. You have found the perfect way and also found its whole secret. Protect yourself from the illusions of this enemy, the mind, because its desires are all false. The power of the mind's desires and illusions has tied up the whole universe within the walls of pain and pleasure. Stay within the Satguru's will, my son, and listen to the Shabd-dhun with love and devotion. By listening to it again and again, getting purified, and holding fast to the Dhun, you will reach the very home of Radha Soami Ji. Have firm faith in this, my son.

Radha Soami from Bibi to you, her true brother. Radha Soami also to all the other satsangis from Bibi and the sadhus at the Dera. May the grace and mercy of the compassionate Hazur be upon all of you.

Listen to the Shabd-dhun with love and devotion because it is the creator and destroyer of the entire universe. Unlimited powers and miracles are vested in the Shabd-dhun. With grace and compassion, it reverberates day and night as an unbroken melody. When you focus on it, it pulls up the attention immediately. What a pity, then, that one would leave aside such a bounty, such true bliss, for the artificial and useless allurements of the self-conceited mind! To follow the illusions of the enemy, the mind, is a grave, senseless, careless, and foolish act. Never have we given a thought to restraining the mind. So think now, and hold fast to the Shabd-dhun. The affairs of the world will never end—why do you then waste time in the musings and agitations of the mind?

31 August 1903

∼ 151 ∼

[Dictated]

Radha Soami. Radha Soami Ji is the Comforter.

Radha Soami from Jaimal Singh to my obedient son, Babu
Sawan Singh, and all the other satsangis. This is to remind you
about that work. Do not say later that you forgot about it. Bring
a canister full of coal tar with you when you come, or send it by
railway delivery now—personally check it during the packing to
see that it does not come short, because the ones that arrived earlier were only half-full. If it is to be sent by railway delivery,
please do so at the earliest. If you are coming soon, then bring it
with you. The point is that the coal tar should reach here quickly.
Continue doing bhajan and simran every day. Do not waste any
time which is free from official work, because it is all recorded in
your account. It is imperative to do bhajan and simran with every
breath and every morsel of food. Once again you are urged that
no time should remain devoid of bhajan and simran.

Radha Soami from Bibi Ji and all the residents of the Dera.
Keep me informed of your welfare and write a letter soon when
you decide upon Aya Singh's salary.

28 September 1903

∼ 152 ∼

[Dictated]

Radha Soami. Radha Soami Ji is the Comforter.

From Jaimal Singh: Radha Soami greetings to Babu Sawan
Singh, Babu Gulab Singh, Babu Gajja Singh, Doctor Issar
Das, Narain Singh, Basant Singh, Harbans, Diwan Singh,
Puran Singh, and all the other satsangis. My son, I am writing

this letter to find out the appropriate pay for Aya Singh: at what monthly rate should his salary be paid? Please write after deciding about it. Also inform me by return post for how many months he should be paid, so that his arrears may be cleared. You have written asking me to pay Aya Singh's wages: what should I give to him? I have not settled any wages with him. You should please let me know how many months Aya Singh stayed at Rawalpindi and how much he should be paid. Write to me and I will pay him. At this time the poor man is down with fever. He has no money or anything else with him, and he has received a letter from his home. I do not know whether or not he will go home. Please reply by return post as to how much he should be paid; write and let me know the amount you have settled upon.

This is to let you know again that the Sunday after you left, Bibi Kishen Kaur,* accompanied by Chanan Singh, came here from her home. She arrived on Saturday and left on Tuesday. She was expecting that you would come again on Sunday, but you did not come. Chanan Singh then returned with her.

It was stressed earlier that whenever you are free from official work, you should engage yourself in bhajan and simran without fail. Instead, when free, you not only do no bhajan and simran, but rather keep talking ill or well of others. This is not good; uselessly you are wasting time. What can you say to this? What good is it if that which is within your power is not realized? The attitude of a satsangi should be to observe his own faults and see the virtues of others. Admonishing your mind in this way, attach with love the surat, nirat, and the higher mind to the Shabd-dhun every day. This is the way of satsangis. This is how we should live daily so that at the time of death our mind and soul are not misled, so that the soul gets out of the jurisdiction of Kal and reaches its real home, Sach Khand, the land of Alakh,

---

* Wife of Maharaj Sawan Singh.

Agam, and Anami Radha Soami. This is how we should live.
Please do not worry about any worldly work, leave the self out
and continue doing the work. The Satguru will let you act as he
thinks proper, and indeed it has already been done. Whatever he
had to do has already been accomplished. Keep him in your
mind and remain happy. In his Shabd form, he is looking after
you from within. All the body forms that exist, their activities, life
and senses, and the intellect and consciousness, everything is
created by the Satguru—he is the Shabd, which is the real form
of the Satguru. And Shabd is with you all the time, so why
forget it?

Babu Sawan Singh is to please note that Babu Sujan Singh
has received the pair of shoes. He is asking how much he should
send in payment for them. Please let me know their price by return post, so that he may be informed accordingly. Radha Soami
on behalf of Bibi Ji to you, her true brother. And Radha Soami
to all the satsangis from all the residents of the Dera. Please
reply by return post.

October [1903]

∼ 153 ∼

Radha Soami. Radha Soami Ji is the Comforter.

Radha Soami greetings from Jaimal Singh to my obedient son,
Babu Sawan Singh, and to Babu Gajja Singh, Babu Gulab
Singh, Basant Singh, Narain Singh, Doctor Ishar Das, Diwan
Singh, Puran Singh, and the young boy. Earlier, I wrote a post-
card in which all the news from here was given. I am now writing
again: please let Babu Sawan Singh know that his letter was
received and I was happy to read it and learn of its contents.
A letter from Babu Gajja Singh was also received. I have read

its contents, but the letter does not respond to my inquiry as to why the money was sent. Doctor Ishar Das has also not sent a reply. I have been pleased to read the other letters as well.

May the grace and mercy of Hazur Radha Soami Ji always be upon you all. You are all reminded to do bhajan and simran every day. Babu Sawan Singh is to bear in mind that if he gets leave, he should first go directly home, because his going there is important. Take the time to do your work, my son: stay there for four, five, or even six days, so long as you are free. You should definitely go if you get leave. From there you should go straight to your duty. Afterwards, if you get two or three days' leave, write to me and we will go together to Tarn Taran. At this time I, too, am busy, because my mother has passed away, and her last rites are to be performed. Aya Singh has been paid 37 rupees for all of his work for twelve months and ten days at the rate of 3 rupees per month. From this, 7½ rupees were deducted. He has been paid for the six months' work he did at Rawalpindi, and for his six months and ten days with Babu Gajja Singh, a total of twelve months, ten days. He has now gone to his brother at Lahore. Chanan Singh is now at the Dera. He will go home after ten days to be treated for an enlarged spleen. The treatment will last for a month. He was saying that he would then return to the Dera and wait to hear from you before coming to you.

My son, I now write to you briefly on matters that are spiritual. When you find time from work, that is, when you are free, bring the mind to the state it is in during deep sleep, at which time no worldly desires exist. Then do simran of the names, and keep deepening the concentration of surat and nirat into the Dhun. Listen to the sound of the Dhun with the loving devotion of the higher mind, touched with love and the anguish of separation—the mind will then become still and the Dhun will yield its bliss. The concentration may last for only a short while, but you will receive a full measure of the bliss of the Sound. Do this practice daily or whenever you find time. Work that is useless, that does not produce worldly or spiritual fruit, is not to be done, my son. Time that is free is not to be lost needlessly, because our time has all been measured out. Twenty-four thousand breaths a day have been allotted to us: they are to be spent in worldly affairs or in spiritual practice. The mind is to be kept within the Satguru's will, my son. Then your worldly and spiritual tasks will all continue to be done by themselves.

Radha Soami from Bibi to you, her true brother. Radha Soami also to all the satsangis there from Bibi Ji and from all the sadhus at the Dera.

20 October 1903

∼ 154 ∼

Radha Soami. Radha Soami Ji is the Comforter.

Radha Soami from Jaimal Singh to my obedient son, Babu Sawan Singh. Your letter has been received, my son; it was addressed to Nihal Singh the baker. I have followed its contents. Please do not worry, I am all right now. Do not send a telegram, nor will I reply through one, because I am now quite well. Keep doing your bhajan and simran every day. I am all right, my son. Whenever you send a message, do so through the post. All the Dera residents are quite well. Radha Soami from Bibi Ji and from all the residents of the Dera. Radha Soami also to all the satsangis with you. This letter, that is, this postcard, has been personally written by me. Therefore understand the contents carefully. It is in reply to your letter.

30 October 1903

~ 155 ~

[Dictated]

Radha Soami. Radha Soami Ji is the Comforter.

From Jaimal Singh: Radha Soami greetings to my obedient
sons, Narain Singh, Babu Sawan Singh, Babu Gulab Singh,
Gajja Singh, Harbans Singh, and Basant Singh. Your postcard
came and I was glad to read the news in it. I am now doing well.
You should please continue doing your bhajan and simran. The
compassionate Lord Radha Soami Ji is always with you; his
grace and mercy will be upon you. Babu Sawan Singh should
be informed that a letter full of blessings came from Chacha Ji in
which he asked about him and sent him his grace and mercy.
When I get better, I will come, and will inform you beforehand.
Radha Soami on behalf of Bibi Ji. Radha Soami also from all
the residents of the Dera.

6 November 1903

Additional Letters

Letters to the Sangat of Bhandal

∼ 1 ∼

Radha Soami. Radha Soami Ji is the Comforter.

Sri Wahiguru Ji ki Fateh from Jaimal Singh to my obedient sangat of Bhandal: to Inder Singh, Dargah Singh, Sardar Bela Singh, Nihal Singh, Naurang Singh, Nand Singh, Ganda Singh, Deva Singh, and all the other satsangis. This is to let you know that I was planning to leave on 27th Phagun for your place but on the 26th I became ill. Nobody could say whether I would survive, but I did recover on 12th Chet. That is why I have not been able to come. I will now come to Bhandal later, when the Lord wishes to bring me there. You should all continue doing bhajan and simran every day. Radha Soami to all the satsangi sisters. Whenever you are free, study Hazur Soami Ji's book, because listening to the saints' words and precepts purifies the mind. It strengthens the love in our Satguru and inclines the mind towards bhajan. Radha Soami from Bibi to everybody and to the satsangi sisters.

April 1897

∼ 2 ∼

Radha Soami. Radha Soami Ji is the Comforter.

From Jaimal Singh to the sangat of Bhandal: may the grace and mercy of the compassionate Lord be upon you all the time. I

245

have received your letter and read its contents. I am happy and
pleased to learn of your well-being. I feel sorry to learn about the
hardship that you are going through. This must be his will; think
of it as a blessing. May the bounty of grace and mercy always be
upon Inder Singh, Dargah Singh, and upon each and every
satsangi and satsangi sister of Bhandal. You write that Mangal
Singh of Maddar has passed away, yet no ceremonial rites, such
as the burning of lamps, incense, etc., were performed. My sons,
if such penalties were still to be paid, then why would we have
accepted a perfect Satguru? Everything was done the day you
found the Guru. Now no superstition should remain. Please
accept Radha Soami from Bibi.

24 August 1897

~ 3 ~

Ik Onkaar Satgur Parsaad.[*]
"There is but one God. By the True Guru's Grace He is obtained."

Radha Soami. Radha Soami Ji is the Comforter.

Radha Soami greetings from Jaimal Singh to the whole sangat
of Bhandal: Radha Soami with lots of grace and mercy to Inder
Singh, Dargah Singh, Sunder Singh, Sardar Bela Singh, Nand
Singh, Naurang Singh, Ram Singh, Nihal Singh, Deva Singh,
and to the other satsangis and satsangi sisters. This is to let you
know that I arrived at the Dera that very night at ten o'clock. I
am very pleased with all of you. Do your bhajan and simran every
day and also hold satsang. Consider it your great good fortune
that the Lord has granted you such a great opportunity. Listen
to the Shabd-dhun every day—becoming pure through listening,

---

[*] Traditional Sikh invocation. *See also* footnote to letter 1.

one day you will reach Sach Khand. All satsangis should maintain deep fellowship with one another, because you are all one and the same. Have firm faith in the Satguru, that one day he will take you along with him. If someone speaks ill of me, you should not get perturbed. Such is the saints' grace: they have already liberated those whom they have initiated; and those whom they have not initiated, they will liberate through such criticism. There is no other way. This is how those without Nam will be liberated. Only the saints know the saints' will—everyone to whom the saints have given Nam will be taken to Sach Khand. I am very pleased with you. Radha Soami from Bibi to all of you.

[No date]

~ 4 ~

Sri Wahiguru Ji ki Fateh to my son, Ganga Singh. Your postcard has been received, and I am glad to read its contents. Do your meditation with every breath so that the soul and mind may remain attached to the sound of the Shabd. Then every breath you take is bhajan. Continue mentally with simran all the time. It purifies the mind and does not let it collect any dross. Becoming pure, the mind then listens to the Shabd-dhun.

Bad deeds are: not to accept the Guru's will but to follow what the mind says. The moment the individual follows the mind, my son, it takes him towards evil deeds. And good deeds are: to hold the mind within the Satguru's will, to accept whatever the Satguru says, and not to step outside his words. Bad deeds are vices, regardless of whether they are called bad deeds or vices.

You have written that you are unable to do bhajan, that you are helpless. This is your negligence and carelessness, my son. Twice a day, whenever your mind desires, you eat nice food and dishes that you like. But bhajan and simran that give everything, the work for which you received the human form—the priceless body in which alone the Supreme Lord can be found—this precious gift is wasted for nothing. You say your job is hard. In the villages, the ploughing goes on all night, the wells are run, and the sugarcane presses are worked throughout the night. All through the night such work continues. Worldly activities and whatever needs to be done are all carried out during the night as well. Who sits around idly? Your life, my son, is meaningful because you have a perfect Satguru and have found the perfect way. Why don't you use in meditation the time that you waste in worrying so that your life can continue to be meaningful? Read this postcard every day.

6 May 1899

～ 5 ～

Radha Soami. Radha Soami Ji is the Comforter.

Radha Soami greetings from Jaimal Singh to the whole sangat of Bhandal. May the grace and mercy of the compassionate Anami Lord always be upon everyone. Your letter informing me of your well-being has been received and I am happy to read it. I was thinking of writing to you about Dharam Singh's illness. I did not mention in the previous postcard that one does not become free without paying for past karmas. Even if a god or the Supreme Lord himself were to assume a human body, he too would be subject to the law of karma. So please do not worry about it; pain and pleasure disappear after being gone through. The span of life given to the individual on the day of his birth does not increase or decrease. There is, however, a means to reduce the penalty. If the individual finds a perfect Satguru and lives within his will, then, by his grace, there is some decrease in penalty through the firm refuge at the saint's Holy Feet.

Do construct a dharmsala and have it fitted with doors. I will come when it is completed. Everyone is urged to do his bhajan and simran every day. Radha Soami from Bibi.

10 July 1899

∼ 6 ∼

Radha Soami. Radha Soami Ji is the Comforter.

Radha Soami greetings from Jaimal Singh to the whole sangat of Bhandal. May the grace and mercy of the compassionate Hazur be upon everyone all the time. You have written that you have constructed new houses. The sister from Valtoha says that she will reside in her house only if I visit it. I am very pleased with this. In accordance with your means, invite two or three devotees and sadhus to a meal in your new homes and start living in them, because it is uncertain when I can come. The Satguru is fully with you in his Shabd form. The moment you put your attention in the Shabd, the Satguru is right there: I myself will be there. You have written that a baby boy was born on Saturday around midnight, and you ask what name should be given to him. You have not written to whom he was born. So write to me again about his parentage. Do not write the letter in the month of Kartik, write in Maghar. I did not go to Musarhi; I stayed at the Dera and did not go anywhere. A gentleman had arrived here on leave, so I could not go. Now I intend to visit you, but it is not definite when I will do so. You are never to come to the railway station to receive me, because you are not to allow your work to suffer. Whenever you appeal inwardly with a true heart, it will be heard instantly. The Satguru will then be with you. All of you should do your bhajan and simran every day, so that you make your home in the Shabd-dhun. Listen to the Dhun whenever you are free. Listening repeatedly to it will purify you. Nothing in the world is our own except bhajan. Bhajan and simran are the work of our own home, but the every-day tasks also have to be done. Continue doing simran mentally. In every task, walking about, sitting up, or lying down, remember bhajan and simran all the time. "Where lies our hope, there we will reside" *(Jahaaŋ aasaa tahaaŋ baasaa).** Then you will merge into the Word itself.

Bibi's Radha Soami to everybody, and also to all the satsangi sisters. May grace and mercy be upon everyone. It is my firm intention to come in the month of Kartik. The rest is up to Hazur's will. I am very pleased with you.

In all our worldly activities, please understand that it is not we who do anything; all good work is done by the Satguru him-self. Bad deeds are done by the mind, but we should not do them—we are not to act according to the dictates of the mind.

September 1899

---

* Proverb.

Letters from Soami Bagh, Agra

SERIES 1: FROM SETH PRATAP SINGH JI

≈ 1 ≈

Grace of the merciful Radha Soami; Radha Soami is the Comforter.

Satguru's beloved son, Shabd-adorned lover of Nam, dear Sawan Singh Sahib: Radha Soami and good wishes. This to let you know that all is well at this end and that we always wish for your health and happiness from the Satguru's abode. Your loving letter regarding the building was received and I was very happy to read its contents and to learn of your well-being. You are especially blessed with grace and mercy that Baba Jaimal Singh Ji has set you on this peaceful path.

The condition of the mind is indeed as you have written. It is now desirable that after finishing your official work you take out a couple of hours from worldly activities for doing bhajan so that those low karmas that interfere with your objective, i.e., meditation, begin to get excised. Bhajan is such an activity that it immediately detaches the heart's inclination from low activities or desires and attaches it to the true Shabd to obtain the peace therein. The reason for the rise of worldly ideas is that as you continue with government work the whole day, your attention settles down in those activities and the accompanying thoughts become ingrained in the mind. During meditation those thoughts invariably arise in the consciousness as the attention becomes one-pointed. Similarly, however, as your meditation grows steadfast, the surat will become so constant in focusing on the Shabd that it will stay there all the time. So as the duration of your

251

meditation increases, it will start producing sweetness. Then this complaint about worldly thoughts will also be taken care of. In short, when you do this practice daily for two, three, or four hours, within a month or two you will yourself see its affect. Topic concluded *(faqat)*. Warm Radha Soami greetings and good wishes. Please also accept Radha Soami from the sadhus and satsangis here. This time I had little leisure to write but in the future I shall reply in full as I come to know more about the condition of your meditation.

The money order for the construction of the rooms has been received. Materials are being bought and the construction of the rooms is going on. End of writing.

Writer and well-wisher, Pratap Singh Seth, pensioner
26 August 1901

PS: A postcard was mailed to you yesterday. The address on it was not properly written. At the time I had not received your letter. End of writing.

Pratap Singh Seth

≈ 2 ≈

Grace of the merciful Radha Soami; Radha Soami is the Comforter.

Satguru's beloved, Shabd-adorned blessed sight, noble-minded Babu Sawan Singh Ji: Radha Soami greetings and good wishes. This is to let you know that I received your loving letter of 5 November, which informed me about your well-being. I was extremely happy to read its contents. The 100 rupees that you sent me were duly received—a receipt for that was sent earlier and I trust it has reached you by now. In all I received 850 rupees. Regarding the construction, what remains to be done are the following: a tiled roof over the rooms and the veranda, a finishing coat of plaster on all the surfaces, and the flooring of the rooms. Should the floor of the verandah be made with bricks or with stone? A letter about this matter has been sent to Baba Jaimal Singh as well. I still have 100 rupees left with me. The stone slabs for the floor will be bought with these. Some lime and gravel also need to be bought. Help from about twenty workers will be required so that the work can be finished in a month. For this I will need 100 rupees after ten or twelve days. I think all the work will be completed within the estimate given by the builder. For the rest, we shall let you know whatever eventuates from the will of the merciful Radha Soami. Warm Radha Soami greetings to you and to all others. End of writing.

Writer, *Pratap Singh Seth*
13 November 1901

~ 3 ~

Satguru's beloved son, Shabd-adorned blessed sight, noble-minded Babu Sawan Singh Ji: Radha Soami and good wishes. I received your loving letter and was very happy to read it. As regards the rooms, I wrote to Baba Ji Maharaj about a month and a half ago that they were completely ready. The floors of the rooms have been finished with the square stone slabs, and that of the outer veranda with bricks and plaster of lime. Also, eight strong Aligarh-made locks have been placed on the doors and almirahs. Only the punkahs remain to be made and I am trying to get them ready. Also, two additional sheets to cover the durries will be made. I am sending you a detailed account of all this in a packet per registered post for your review. There is now no need for more money. Rather, from the previous money, after spending 972 rupees 7 annas and 9 pies, rupees 27 annas 6 and 3 pies are still in trust with me.

Earlier, Bibi Rukko had asked me to send her 5 rupees for rail fare. I had thought that she was planning to come here due to some disagreement with Baba Ji, and for that reason I had put her off. Now a letter from Milkhi Ram informs me that she has come to Milkhi Ram's house and has asked for my permission to stay there for twenty days and then come to Agra. I have written to them that she is welcome to stay over at Milkhi Ram's house and then, if she does not feel at home, to come to Agra for three or four months.

If you have not yet sent a money order to pay for the books, please do not do so now. The books will be bought out of your money that is left with me. You may send the receipt for the registered packet and the reply to this letter at your convenience. If you like, the account book may be passed on to Baba Ji Sahib for his review as well.

I, too, shall make a request to Hazur Soami Ji Maharaj that your visit here should happen soon. Firstly, you should think of coming here at the main bhandara of Soami Ji Maharaj on 22 June. But if for some reason you are unable to be here on that occasion, then please come before or after it—indeed it would be all right to come anytime you can find the occasion. My heart is also very desirous that we should meet. End of writing.

Writer and well-wisher, *Pratap Singh Seth*
22 February 1902

∼ 4 ∼

Radha Soami is the Comforter.

Satguru's beloved son, Shabd-adorned blessed sight, noble-minded Baba Jaimal Singh Ji: heartfelt Radha Soami greetings from Chacha Ji. Your kind letter was received and I was very happy to learn of your well-being. The stone about which you have written will be put in—please be assured. And dear Suchet Singh has come on pension.

I find that division and groupism have made their appearance in the Radha Soami Satsang, and that not all satsangis get on well with each other or treat each other well. For this reason I came to Allahabad to talk things over with Pandit Ji in order to get his advice and counsel as to how this problem could be managed. After discussing the matter we have come to the conclusion that a central organization of Radha Soami Satsang should be set up, of which Pandit Ji is adamant upon making me the president. He will become its vice-president. Hazur Sahib's son, Lala Ayodhya Prasad, and eight other persons and you will be its members, according to how the people choose. The total number of members will be ten—those who receive the majority vote. For this reason, I am sending you a detailed account of the organization in this letter. We will send you as many copies as you request. Please order all your satsangis to choose from the following names; they should indicate their selections by signing on one or more sheets. If your satsangis are living far apart, they should sign and send separate sheets with the same ten names. These ten names are:

1. Lala Ayodhya Prasad Sahib
2. Pandit Brahm Shankar Misra Sahib, M.A.
3. Lala Balishar Prasad Sahib
4. Lala Madho Prasad Sahib
5. Rai Ishwar Sahai, alias Raja Sahib
6. Lala Suchet Singh
7. Baba Jaimal Singh Ji Sahib
8. Lala Sudarshan Singh
9. Munshi Hargobind Dayal Sahib
10. Mr. Bol Chand Sahib

I hope the divisions will disappear after this organization comes into being and that satsangis will begin to treat each other with love and affection like brothers.

Please convey my Radha Soami greetings to Rukko Bibi and tell her that someone has grossly misinformed her that ——— , etc., wants to have it. He is truly a spiritual person of honest inclination who has wholly surrendered and sacrificed his body, mind, and wealth in the name of Radha Soami and continues to do so. He is extremely pleased when others take the name of Radha Soami. She should have full assurance that nothing improper will ever happen from his side.

Heartfelt Radha Soami to all of you from Pandit Sahib and from me. Radha Soami also to Rukko Bibi. Brother Sudarshan Singh, Soami Das, Waryam Singh, and others also wish to convey their Radha Soami greetings to you, to all the other satsangis, and to Babu and Rukko Bibi. After reading this letter please pass it on to Babu Sawan Singh for information. End of writing.

Allahabad: Radha Soami Satsang
Writer and well-wisher, *Pratap Singh Seth*
6 August 1902

~ 5 ~

Grace of the merciful Radha Soami; Radha Soami is the Comforter.

From: Seth Pratap Singh, Agra
To: Hazur Baba Ji Maharaj, Waraich

Satguru's beloved Baba Jaimal Singh Ji and Rukko Bibi Ji: Radha Soami and good wishes. Your letter was received and I learnt your news. We have decided today to send Moti Ram Sadhu and he is ready to leave. Please write to me at once about how Baba Ji is doing now. On hearing from you we will dispatch

Moti Ram at once from here. Do not delay in replying, and please tell Baba Ji from me that Soami Ji Maharaj had always commanded the taking of medicine. He would say that, in illness, prayer and medicine are both of use. Baba Ji must take the medicine whose prescription we have sent. Deeply felt Radha Soami.

Writer and well-wisher, *Pratap Singh Seth*
30 December 1903

P.S.: Please send your reply on the attached postcard.

∽ 6 ∽

Grace of the merciful Radha Soami; Radha Soami is the Comforter.

Radha Soami Bagh, Agra
5 January 1904

From: Seth Pratap Singh, Soami Bagh, Agra
To: Bibi Rukko, Waraich

Hazur Radha Soami's beloved Bibi Rukko: Radha Soami. Your postcard arrived and gave me the news of the passing away of Baba Jaimal Singh Sahib. I feel extremely sorry and pained because a great service for humanity was being performed by him. Still, whatever is the will of the Lord, we have no option in that, so it is imperative that in every situation we show patience and gratefulness. Have faith in Radha Soami. With his grace and his mercy, he will look after you as before in every way. One should not get perturbed; such is the way of this world, everything here is perishable. If the Lord has taken back what he had entrusted, then we should remain content in his will—that is the way of his devotees.

Writer and well-wisher: *Pratap Singh Seth*

∼ 7 ∼

Grace of the merciful Radha Soami; Radha Soami is the Comforter.

Radha Soami Bagh, Agra
7 January 1904

Hazur Radha Soami's beloved Babu Sawan Singh Ji Sahib:
Radha Soami greetings. Your letter was received and I came to
know of your situation. I am very sorry and pained at the passing
away of Baba Jaimal Singh Ji Sahib. Through him a great service
was being performed for humankind. But the Lord's will was
like this, no one has a say in that. That is why there is no other
way but to accept his will and be thankful. The merciful Radha
Soami is all-powerful and omniscient. His will is not without
purpose. He undertakes to shelter and protect the beings who
have come under his refuge, and one day through his darshan he
will definitely bring contentment to every one of them. But until
such a time it is desirable that in accord with his command we
increase our love and devotion for his Holy Feet by regularly
doing simran, dhyan and bhajan inside with feeling, because he is
present within each one of us. He is all the time looking after and
protecting everyone who has love and devotion for his Holy Feet.
Therefore, one should not become perturbed. Have implicit faith
in his grace and mercy in your heart and never despair of it.

    If the merciful Radha Soami so wishes, the satsang will also
continue there as before since two or three lovers of satsang like
you can always set it up wherever they like—the grace of the
merciful Radha Soami is always helpful in such projects. But the
individual's resolve must be absolute. It is appropriate that you
give solace to everyone—to Rukko Ji especially such a counsel is
necessary. I have also sent a postcard to Rukko Bibi. Deep-felt
Radha Soami and good wishes to you and to all others.

                                                Pratap Singh Seth

∼ 8 ∼

Grace of the merciful Radha Soami; Radha Soami is the Comforter.

Radha Soami Bagh, Agra
18 January 1904

From: Seth Pratap Singh, Agra
To: Bibi Rukko, Waraich

Hazur Radha Soami's beloved Bibi Rukko: Radha Soami greetings. Your letter arrived and informed me of your news. A money order of 1 ¼ rupees was also received; its parshad will be distributed in the satsang. I am very sorry at the passing away of Baba Jaimal Singh. No doubt because of him everyone was greatly benefitting from satsang and now there will be some abeyance. But one should not get perturbed. With trust in the merciful Radha Soami, it is imperative to continue the daily routine of satsang and meditation. Thus if satsang continues to be held every day, with the merciful Radha Soami's grace it will certainly flourish, and the protection and looking after of everyone will also continue. Regarding satsang, what has Babu Sawan Singh Ji proposed for holding it daily?

Writer and well-wisher, *Pratap Singh Seth*

∼ 9 ∼

Grace of the merciful Radha Soami.

Hazur Radha Soami's beloved Babu Sawan Singh Sahib: Radha Soami greetings. This is to let you know that a letter was received from Milkhi Ram and Rukko Bibi. From it I learnt about your spiritual practice of not coming out of the house for four days on end, and also about Bibi Rukko going away after

creating a scene. A considered and appropriate response to that
was written, a copy of which is given below for your review.
Hereunder is the copy:

I am informed that Babu Sawan Singh's interest and
exertions in bhajan and meditation are such that he does
not come out of the house for four days on end. I am very
happy to know this. And indeed when he decides to retire
from service it would not seem suitable for him to attend to
anything other than meditation. But in this connection
whatever duties he has assigned, and to whomsoever he has
assigned them, should be carried out by them cheerfully. It
is completely out of order to hamper him in any way. The
bliss of satsang and meditation will disappear if you quar-
rel with one another. If you see that someone is engaged in
an untoward activity, inform Babu Sahib and he will take
care of it as he thinks proper. But to force him to do something is not right. The violence and fighting that Rukko
Bibi has indulged in are absolutely out of order. To attack
one's brothers with a staff after becoming a sadhu or satsangi is a shameful act. I was very sorry and sad to learn
this. If Rukko Bibi writes, I can send 50 rupees for her
train fare. But I will send nothing if she wants to come after
quarrelling and breaking off with others. Therefore, it is
proper for Rukko to apologize to them for the excesses that
she has committed. I would not be pleased if I find out that
it was her fault. No householder gives up his home or family for praying and meditation, and Babu Sawan Singh has
shown great courage in giving up all worldly business for
prayer and meditation.

It is my singular wish that after Baba Ji and myself there
should be three or four such devoted disciples who would
spread the Word and illuminate the Radha Soami path.

Do not get any worldly work from Babu Sawan Singh; let him continue with his meditational devotions. He should definitely not get into work that involves handling money and keeping accounts. Such matters will interfere with bhajan and simran. You should look upon him as a sadhu and an elder of yours, and let him continue with his spiritual work. The whole business of the world is no better than dirt, while the spiritual work is like searching for diamonds. So to detach a person from diamonds and to force him towards dirt is a grave, foolish mistake. Topic concluded. Deep-felt Radha Soami.

Radha Soami to you, to Rukko Bibi, and to all the other satsangis. Please read this letter well and also read it word for word to Rukko Bibi. Copy of the writing ends here.

Babu Sawan Singh Ji: in your meditation please be careful not to exert so much all at once that through the creation of heat some difficulty is caused. That is to say, it is proper to do as much meditation as the body can stand and the sweetness keeps coming. When the body gets tired, rest it awhile and begin again. End of writing. Heartfelt Radha Soami and good wishes.

Writer and well-wisher, *Pratap Singh Seth*
1904

~ 10 ~

Grace of the merciful Radha Soami.

Radha Soami Bagh, Agra
13 February 1904

Hazur Radha Soami's beloved Babu Sawan Singh Sahib: Radha Soami greetings. Your loving letter was received, and I felt reassured after reading it. It is a very good idea that you intend coming here for a while for satsang. The merciful Radha Soami will shower his grace in fulfilling your wish. It would be better to plan on first taking three months' leave on compassionate grounds, hold satsangs, and then get leave on half-pay after sometime. I have noted that 21st February is the date of the bhandara for Baba Jaimal Singh Ji Maharaj. Your asking me to join the bhandara there shows your love and affection—may the merciful Hazur Radha Soami show his grace and continue to bless you with love, devotion and attachment for meditation. As for my coming and joining the bhandara, I also feel that it would be appropriate and desirable, and my heart wants it too, but I am helpless due to old age and the weakness of the body. Also, I cannot now withstand the hardship of travel, and my health as well is not good these days, that is, at times I get pain in the feet and at other times in the back, or some other major or minor ailment keeps bothering my body.

I wanted dear Suchet Singh to join the bhandara—Rukko Bibi has also written about it. But the fact of the matter is that about two months ago he took service with Raja Maur Sen at 75 rupees per month. I have written to him that it would be very important to join the bhandara if he can get fifteen days' leave. However, he has been in service for only two months, and there is a wedding before Holi at Raja Sahib's, so his chances of getting leave are not good. However, I will know for sure only when his reply comes.

If the date of the bhandara had been set so as to let us know a month or two earlier, then perhaps dear Sudarshan Singh could have come, since in that duration there was scope for him to get leave. Now I intend to send Sadhu Waryam Singh. I have sent a money order for 50 rupees towards the expenses of the bhandara in Rukko Bibi's name. I expect it has reached there. I have also received 25 rupees from Rukko Bibi for rail fare, etc.

A sadhu by the name of Nihal Das has been here for some

days. He belongs to Karnal and presents himself as a disciple of Baba Jaimal Singh Ji Sahib. Previously, he worked as a syce. Please inform me if you know anything about his character so that we may keep him here if he is fit, or tell him otherwise—he is of a mind to stay here. All is well otherwise. Please convey my Radha Soami to everyone.

Writer and well-wisher, *Pratap Singh Seth*

~ 11 ~

Grace of the merciful Radha Soami.

Radha Soami Bagh, Agra
13 May 1904

Hazur Radha Soami's beloved Babu Sawan Singh Ji Sahib: Radha Soami greetings. This is to let you know that I received your letter informing me of your well-being.

In fact the mind's condition is like you have written. But the merciful Radha Soami is the all-powerful Lord of everything. Whosoever detaches himself from the world to take refuge at his Feet with a true heart, on him He will definitely shower his grace and one day bless him with perfect love. It is therefore imperative to exert as much as you can in the practice of simran, dhyan and bhajan that he graciously established, and to trust absolutely in his grace and mercy. It is not right to ever feel disheartened and disenchanted with his mercy. So long as the heart is not completely purified and cleansed of worldly pollution, his mercy will not be visible, but slowly and steadily cleanliness will come through labour in the practice he has ordained, and his mercy also will become apparent. This is work that should not be done in a hurry. Therefore continue the effort with patience, gaining strength from his grace and mercy, and you will surely succeed one day.

The bhandara of Soami Ji Maharaj will be held on Tuesday,

the first day of the moon in Asarh, Samvat 1961, that is 28 June 1904. It would be good if before the bhandara you could arrange leave that allows you to come here on that occasion—my heart also desires it.

News of the Dera has been received in person from Waryam Singh, who has arrived here in the last three or four days. Radha Soami to everyone from me and from all the sadhus and satsangis.

Writer and well-wisher, *Pratap Singh Seth*

~ 12 ~

Grace of the merciful Radha Soami.

11 August 1905
Radha Soami's beloved Bibi Rukko Ji:

Radha Soami greetings. This is to let you know that I received your letter, which informed me about your and Manna Singh's well-being. The payment of 3 rupees and 13 annas that you have made for the parcel is correct. No other payment now remains to be made. I also received four stamps worth 2 annas for the par-shad of melons. But it could not be ascertained on whose behalf this money was sent. It was also written that selected bachans should be sent, but we could not understand whether the selec-tions are to be from the saints or some other bachans, and in whose name we should send them. We will send them as soon as a clarifying reply is received.

Manna Singh should know that he who takes the refuge of the merciful Radha Soami with a true heart will definitely be protected. The merciful Radha Soami by his grace will definitely give him darshan as well. But he should continue to follow his command to the best of his ability and unfailingly continue to do his daily simran, dhyan and bhajan, and at the same time reflect upon his infractions and feel shame and repentance. Above all, he should have faith in his grace and mercy. Then undoubtedly by his grace and mercy he will ferry him across—a firm resolve of this should be kept in the heart.

Subsequently, your second letter containing a *rakhi* was also received. The 10 rupees that you sent by money order have also been received. This money will be spent at the Janam Ashtami. All is well otherwise. Please convey my Radha Soami to everyone.

You should now be careful in incurring expenses. The seva was sufficient during Baba Ji's time, but I have no idea what the situation is now. No doubt with his grace Radha Soami carries on the activities of all his children, but you should certainly not think that after Baba Ji it should continue as it had previously. At this time whatever can be done without problems is the proper thing to do. Radha Soami is taking care of all the expenses here. Send only whatever you are left with after all the expenses have been settled. Do not think about it being more or less. Topic concluded.

Please convey my Radha Soami to Milkhi Ram and inform him that he is to keep busy with his simran, dhyan, bhajan, etc. This practice is to be done every day. It benefits both the spiritual and the temporal life. End of writing.

Writer and well-wisher, *Pratap Singh Seth*
11 August 1905

~ 13 ~

Grace of the merciful Radha Soami.

Radha Soami Bagh, Agra
23 August 1905

Hazur Radha Soami's beloved Bibi Rukko Ji:

Radha Soami greetings. This is to let you know that your letter and postcard were received and informed me of your situation.

Five copies of saints' writings (selections) have been sent to you by V.P.P. parcel post. Please get the parcel released on payment of 1 rupee and 7 annas. The money that has come from Babu Sawan Singh for the bhog ceremony will be used only for that purpose. There is no urgency about the sheets, furnishings, soap, etc., that the elder daughter-in-law has asked you to send. Please bring them with you when you come, or send them with someone coming from there.

Whosoever has taken refuge in the merciful Radha Soami, has love and devotion for his Holy Feet, does simran, dhyan and bhajan according to his command, and other than the merciful Radha Soami does not believe in any other deity, etc., and, looking upon the merciful Radha Soami as the all-powerful saviour, has taken refuge in him with a true heart—he and all individuals like him will definitely be saved one day. No matter from whom such individuals may have received the initiation, the merciful Radha Soami himself will ferry them across—in this there should be no doubt.

Whatever Bir Bhan has said purporting to come from me is absolutely wrong. Perhaps he misunderstood or misapprehended the matter. Radha Soami to Bhai Manna Singh Ji, Milkhi Ram Ji, to you, and to all the satsangis. Radha Soami from Dayal Saran.

Writer and well-wisher, *Pratap Singh Seth*

~ 14 ~

Grace of the merciful Radha Soami.

Soami Bagh, Agra

Hazur Radha Soami's beloved Babu Sawan Singh Ji Sahib: Radha Soami greetings. This is to let you know that your letter was received and I came to know of your situation. The teaching can be given through some educated satsangi, if someone is at hand there, by sending him a paper with instructions from here. So if such a person is available, please designate him for this work for a few days. At the time of Hazuri bhandara, that is in the month of December, Waryam Singh also will arrive from Hoshangabad. He will then be sent there. Later on, when you start residing there after retiring on pension, there will be no special need for such an individual.

A note has been sent to Lala Tara Chand to send *Prem Patra*, volumes one, two, and three, by railway parcel. So they should reach you soon. All is well here. Radha Soami and good wishes to all of you.

Writer and well-wisher, *Pratap Singh Seth*
1906

~ 15 ~

Grace of the merciful Radha Soami.

Soami Bagh, Agra
16 November 1906

Hazur Radha Soami's beloved Babu Sawan Singh Ji Sahib:

Radha Soami greetings. This is to let you know that I received your letter which apprised me of your situation. In the Radha Soami path the praise of the Sant-Satguru has been given a very high place. The designation Sant-Satguru is only for those refined souls who have reached the stage of Sat Lok and Radha Soami and become one with the form of Sat Purush and Radha Soami. Even the highest praise given to such individuals is too little. Such Satgurus, however, are rare. Even if somebody were to meet such a Satguru, he would not recognize him because there is a plethora of gurus in this world who are all aspiring to wealth and fame. From among them, to recognize and select *the*

true and perfect Guru is very difficult. If someone by reading
books and deducing the attributes of refined souls from them
were to try to identify the true ones through his intellect and education, he could never succeed in doing so. But the Sant-Satguru
or the Sadh-Satguru invariably helps true spiritual seekers. So
anyone who will do meditation of the Surat-Shabd honestly, according to the instructions, will slowly and gradually begin to recognize the Guru as well. It is therefore imperative that so long as
the seeker is not completely satisfied, he should look upon them
with the feelings of respect accorded to sadhus, and not with the
devotion offered to a Sant-Satguru. That devotion he should
place at the Holy Feet of the merciful Radha Soami, the Lord
of everything, and keep on increasing it, while all the time asking
for his grace and mercy. Then He himself with his grace day by
day will keep on transforming the nature of such a true devotee—
making him appropriately feel love and respect for the Holy Feet
and for the Guru and the sadhus—and also gradually open up
his inner vision. The individual will then automatically continue
to correctly understand the nature of the merciful Radha Soami
and the Guru. At this time he will be able to deal honestly with
the merciful Radha Soami and the Guru with the right attitude
of a devotee—and day by day his love and devotion for the Holy
Feet will keep on increasing.

My health is better than before, but once in a while it gets
bad as well so that I am unable to be regularly present at the
satsang each day. But I definitely attend satsang on the days I
feel better. Of course I will take out an hour for you when you
arrive here. So by all means do come when you find time. If you
feel a great yearning to be here, then I would not discourage you
from coming for a whole week. Even otherwise you yourself write
that the construction work will be over by the end of December.

Rukko Bibi has not written anything to consult me regarding
the building, otherwise I would never have written to you for the

construction of the house. In the future, except for bhajan and satsang, do not engage at all in such activities that would interfere with your spiritual work. Henceforth, if Rukko Bibi writes to me about buildings, etc., I will certainly not agree to anything. The delay in replying to your letter occurred because I kept waiting for the money order. It has not reached me so far. Radha Soami to you, to Rukko Bibi, Manna Singh, and to all others. End of writing.

Writer and well-wisher, *Pratap Singh Seth*

SERIES 2: FROM SETH SUDARSHAN SINGH JI

~ 1 ~

Radha Soami is the Comforter.

Allahabad
7 April 1914

Satguru's beloved, Shabd-perfected, Radha Soami's redeemed Babu Ji Sahib—may your courtesies abide and endure.* Please accept Radha Soami greetings with folded hands at your Feet. Your affectionate letter was received. I was very pleased to know that dear Basant Singh's attention stayed at the Holy Feet right till the end and he remained constant in his love for Radha Soami and suffered from no perturbation or worldly thoughts. Along with this I was also very gratified that you were able to bear this great loss, rather you did not feel it at all. A special

---

* Sudarshan Singh prefaces his letters with formal expressions traditional in classical Urdu writing.

grace of Radha Soami is visible in all this. For this we all must offer thanks at the Feet of the supreme Father, the all-giving, merciful Radha Soami. I have come to Allahabad these days for a change of air. At Agra, I was unwell all the time, so I thought it best to affect this change of air. I will go back to Agra after fifteen days; that is to say, I will leave here by the 16th instant. My residence is still in Agra.

Supplicant,
Sudarshan Singh Seth

~ 2 ~

Radha Soami is the Comforter.

Soami Bagh, Agra
4 December 1933
Hazur Maharaj Ji Sahib:

The well-spring of grace and liberality, most perfect refuge of kindness—may you always remain prosperous. Please accept Radha Soami with folded hands and bowed head at your chaste Lotus Feet. The auspicious arrival of your loving letter obliged and exalted me and I thank you from the bottom of my heart for this special favour. After thinking further about it, my request about the land seems to be superfluous. Since to get a residence ready may take up to two years and I will have to wait out that time anyway, I might as well endure it for two or three years more. So please do not exert any further in this matter. My wife is saying that if the difficulties become unbearable, we will also move to the Dera to live at Hazur's Feet. We will then get a house built and stay under your refuge.

Please find out from Dr Prem Nath Ji that since the moon is visible in my left eye only from a bit of the lower corner and the light is just enough for everything to appear foggy, should the operation on the eye be done now or when it has completely closed up? And also, in which season should it be performed: beginning or end of March, or in April or some other month? The doctors are giving conflicting advice: apparently some prefer to operate while a little bit of light is still there, while others do it when the eye has completely closed up. In which district is this place, and how far is it from your residence? Please write when you are free as there is no hurry. Heartfelt Radha Soami from both of us at your Feet, and also to Rai Harnarayan Sahib and to all the satsangis and lady satsangis. Topic concluded.

It is seen that often people claiming to be satsangis from Beas come and are given accommodation here. There is no way to find out if they are telling the truth. Please announce in the general satsang that those who wish to come here should bring with them a note with a few words of introduction from someone designated by you. We will be thankful for this because we have already been deceived two or three times. Servant of your servants,

Most humble of the servants,

Sudarshan Singh

~ 3 ~

Radha Soami Satsang
Soami Bagh, Agra
13 January 1935

Venerable Master, Eminent Soul, Gracious Being, Generous Spirit of the Times, Bearer of the Exalted of Titles, Sri Hazur, Guide of the Lost Souls—may you continue to prosper.

Please accept Radha Soami greetings with folded hands and bowed head at your feet from both of us. I have already directed a humble letter to your kind attention; I hope it has arrived there. Because of the excessively low temperature here, a bad cold and cough have been bothering me for the last fifteen days. For this reason, my wife is of the opinion that the bhandara of Hazur Chacha Ji Maharaj should be held in mid-Phagun. It is hoped that by that time my health will be all right. So it will not be possible to hold it at Basant. I would like your noble self to oblige me by coming here when you can do so with ease and comfort. Please inform me a day or two beforehand about the day, the station, and the train that will be graced with your presence, so that a motor car can be sent to await your arrival. If you come in the middle of the second half of January, or the beginning of February, I too probably will be all right by then.

Radha Soami with folded hands from both of us to Rai Harnarayan Sahib and to all others.

Lowliest and most humble of your servants,
Sudarshan Singh Seth

∽ 4 ∽

Radha Soami Satsang
Soami Bagh, Agra
8 January 1936

Venerable Master, Eminent Soul, Sri Hazur Sardar Sahib: may you continue to prosper.

Radha Soami greetings with bowed head and folded hands at Hazur's chaste Lotus Feet; please accept our Radha Soami offered with hundredfold humble supplications and deep-felt humility and submission. Your very gracious letter arrived and made us extremely happy. More than your kind self, this slave yearns beyond measure for Hazur's darshan. If this being had been fit to travel, he would have presented himself before you. But alas, my weakness is extreme, and because of this constraint I am helpless from being there. You are a generous soul; please shower your grace and give darshan to make this being's life a success.

The bhandara of the pious and blessed Hazur Chacha Ji Maharaj is set for 28 January, the day of Basant. If you could grace the occasion here that day you will bestow kindness upon kindness on your servant and make him extremely obliged and thankful.

Please let me know a day beforehand about the date, the time, the train, and the station in Agra of your arrival—a motor car will then be there at your service. To use the words "supreme being, all-giving" for this silly nothing of dust does not seem right; this honour belongs only to the radiant, holy and blessed Hazur Soami Ji Maharaj.

My wife bows at Hazur's feet and the feet of Rai Harnarayan Sahib; please also convey my Radha Soami with folded hands to Rai Sahib. Radha Soami also with folded hands and bowed head to Bibi Ji and Ma Ji Sahiba from both of us.

Most humble of your servants,
Sudarshan Singh Seth

Endnotes

1 Kabir, *Kabir Saheb ki Akhravati.*
2 Soami Ji, *Sar Bachan,* p. 122:15:14.
3 *Sri Guru Granth Sahib,* M5, p. 608.
4 *Sri Guru Granth Sahib,* M1, p. 903.
5 Kabir, *Kabir Saheb ki Akhravati.*
6 *Sri Guru Granth Sahib,* M4, p. 1422.
7 *Sri Guru Granth Sahib,* M5, p. 265.
8 Soami Ji, *Sar Bachan,* p. 122:15:14.
9 Kabir, *Kabir Saheb ki Akhravati.*
10 *Sri Guru Granth Sahib,* M4, p. 305.
11 *Sri Guru Granth Sahib,* M3, p. 509.
12 *Sri Guru Granth Sahib,* M3, p. 394.
13 Soami Ji, *Sar Bachan,* p. 42:4:8.
14 *Sri Guru Granth Sahib,* M5, p. 290.
15 *Ratan Mala, Ramkali,* M1, p. 627.
16 Soami Ji, *Sar Bachan,* p. 122:15:14.
17 *Sri Guru Granth Sahib,* M1, p. 469.
18 *Sri Guru Granth Sahib,* M4, p. 757.
19 Soami Ji, *Sar Bachan,* p. 122:15:14.
20 Soami Ji, *Sar Bachan,* p. 222:26:4.

Appendix

BIOGRAPHICAL DATA OF THE MASTERS

Seth Shiv Dayal Singh (known as Soami Ji)

Born:	25 August 1818 in Agra, Uttar Pradesh
Father:	Seth Dilwali Singh
Mother:	Maha Maya
Wife:	Narain Devi (known as Mata Radha Ji)
Summary:	Soami Ji meditated in a dark, back room in his house for seventeen years prior to holding public satsang in January 1861 (Basant Panchami Day). However, he held private satsangs in his courtyard and also gave a few initiations prior to this date (including the initiation of seventeen-year-old Baba Jaimal Singh in 1856).
Passed away:	15 June 1878

Baba Jaimal Singh (known as Baba Ji)

Born:	July 1839 in village Ghoman, District Gurdaspur, Panjab
Father:	Sardar Jodh Singh
Mother:	Daya Kaur
Brothers:	Dan Singh and Jeevan Singh
Sisters:	Bibi Tabo and Bibi Rajo

Summary: Initiated by Soami Ji in 1856 at the age of seventeen; then joined the Twenty-Fourth Sikh Regiment as a sepoy in the same year. Retired from military service on 7 June 1889, after over thirty-two years of active service.

                  Began initiations at Soami Ji Maharaj's instructions when he was still in active service. Early records establish that his first initiations took place at Jhansi in the late 1870s. His first initiate is thought to be Amir Singh of Jhelum. Once he retired to the Dera, he kept a record of his initiates in a diary, which includes various undated names before the first recorded dates in July 1884. Last person initiated by him: Mangat Rai of Lohari village, district Muzaffarnagar, Uttar Pradesh, on 26 December 1903. (Lala Mangat Rai was the first to serve as secretary with Hazur Maharaj Sawan Singh.) Initiated a total of 2,343 people.

Passed away: 29 December 1903

Maharaj Sawan Singh (known as the Great Master)

Born: 20 July 1858 in village Jatana (his mother's home), near Mehmansinghwala, District Ludhiana, Panjab

Father: Sardar Kabal Singh, who died when Maharaj Sawan Singh was still very young

Mother: Jivani Kaur

Grandfather: Sher Singh

Wife: Kishen Kaur

Summary: Served in Military Works Services (now called Military Engineering Services) as a sub-divisional officer for 28 years. Retired on premature pension in 1911.

Initiated by Baba Jaimal Singh on 15 October 1894 in Murree Hills (now Pakistan). First person to be initiated by him: Hira Singh of Miyan Vind, district Amritsar, on 26 July 1904. Last person to be initiated personally by him: S. S. Padki of Bangalore on 20 May 1947; some applicants abroad were accepted by him and initiated by representatives at a later date. Initiated a total of 125,375 people.

Passed away: 2 April 1948

Maharaj Jagat Singh (known as Sardar Bahadur Ji)

Born:	27 July 1884 in village Nussi, District Jalandhar, Panjab
Father:	Sardar Bhola Singh
Mother:	Died when Maharaj Jagat Singh was very young
Wife:	Sada Kaur
Cousin-brother:	Sardar Bhagat Singh
Summary:	Served in Govt. Agricultural College, Lyallpur (now Pakistan) as a professor of chemistry. Retired from service as vice-principal in July 1943 and came to live at the Dera.

Initiated by the Great Master in 1910 in Abbotabad. First person to be initiated by him: Dr (Miss) Sinha, on 30 December 1948. Last person to be initiated: Mr Jerry Seffens of the American Consulate in Bombay, on 15 October 1951. Initiated a total of 18,111 people.

Passed away: 23 October 1951

Maharaj Charan Singh (known as Hazur Maharaj Ji)

Born:	12 December 1916 in Moga (his mother's home), Panjab
Father:	Sardar Harbans Singh
Mother:	Sham Kaur
Grandfather:	Maharaj Sawan Singh (the Great Master)
Brothers:	Capt. Purushottam Singh and Sardar Jagjit Singh
Sisters:	Satnam Kaur, Gurnam Kaur, Mohinder Kaur and Baljinder Kaur
Wife:	Harjeet Kaur
Summary:	Practised law at Sirsa and Hissar, Haryana.

Initiated by the Great Master on 30 January 1933 at the Dera. First person to be initiated by him: Mrs Kinzinger of USA, on 10 April 1953 at the Dera. Last initiation: 20 April 1990 at the Dera; some applicants abroad were accepted by him and initiated by representatives at a later date. Initiated a total of 1,438,498 people.

Passed away: 1 June 1990

EARLY CONSTRUCTION
AND PUBLICATION LANDMARKS

1891 Baba Jaimal Singh's single-room meditation hut built
of brick set in mud with mud plastering inside and out
and a thatched roof. This was gradually made more permanent by Maharaj Sawan Singh when he started to
visit the Dera after his initiation in 1894. In these early
days there were two such huts, one used by Baba Ji and
one used by Bibi Rukko. They were so small that when
Maharaj Sawan Singh visited, he used to sleep under
Baba Ji's charpoy (bed).

18 May 1897 Baba Ji started the first brick-kiln on 5th Jeth
[Letters 7, 8].

8 December 1897 Soami Sagar (the first well inside the
colony) was begun in September 1897; water was first
drawn in November; the well was completed in December, 24th Maghar [Letters 23-24, 27, 29].

7 May 1898 Durbar Hall (the first satsang hall, 30' x 15')
begun in January 1898 and completed in May, 26th
Vaisakh [Letters 30, 37].

February 1901 Nine small rooms built (at the back of what
later became the Great Master's house), five on the
ground floor, four on the first floor; the work was begun
in September 1900 and completed in February 1901
[Letters 69-79]. The rooms are now used as residential
quarters for sevadars.

1901 The rooms mentioned in Seth Pratap Singh's letters to

Babu Sawan Singh are the two rooms and verandah constructed by Seth Pratap Singh in Soami Bagh, Agra, at the request and expense of Baba Jaimal Singh and Maharaj Sawan Singh for the use of Beas satsangis [Seth Pratap Singh letters 1-3].

1902 Seth Pratap Singh sent his copy of Soami Ji's *Sar Bachan* (prose and poetry) to Baba Jaimal Singh and gave his permission to have it printed in Gurmukhi (Panjabi) script, and wrote an introduction for it [Letters 112, 119, 125].

December 1902 First edition of Soami Ji's *Sar Bachan Prose* and *Sar Bachan Poetry* (Panjabi) [Letters 129-130].

April 1903 Nam Ghar (the second satsang hall, 55' x 20') begun on 10 November 1902 and completed by the end of April 1903 [Letters 126, 142, 143]. It is recorded in *Sant Britant*, a booklet written by Bhishen Das Puri in the time of the Great Master, that Baba Ji gave only one satsang in the hall and intimated to the sangat that he would be leaving them soon. In reply to a request to give further satsangs there, he is reported to have said: "In future the one destined to give satsang here will do so."

1923/24 Maharaj Sawan Singh's residence, which incorporates Baba Jaimal Singh's room, was constructed.

1937 The main Satsang Ghar completed (a spacious hall that seats several thousand people, used regularly for initiation).

Glossary

Adi Granth. Primal *(adi)* scripture *(granth);* also called the *(Sri Guru) Granth Sahib;* the scripture containing writings of the first five and the ninth Gurus in the line of Guru Nanak and many other saints of India; adopted by the Sikhs as their most sacred scripture.

Agam. Inaccessible. Alakh, Agam and Anami (the Unseen, the Inaccessible and the Nameless) are stages within the realm of pure spirit or attributes of the one Supreme Being. *See also* **Sach Khand.**

Agra. City in north India, birthplace of Soami Ji Maharaj, the spiritual Master of Baba Jaimal Singh Ji.

Alakh. Invisible or indescribable. *See also* **Agam.**

almirah. Cupboard, closet.

Ambala. City halfway between Beas and Delhi.

Amritsar. Situated in Panjab, it is the most sacred city for the Sikhs.

Anami. Nameless; the Supreme Being, referred to also as Radha Soami in the letters. *See also* **Agam.**

And. Egg *(andaa);* the astral region, the grand division of the creation lying immediately above the physical realm.

anna. A unit of Indian currency no longer in use; sixteen annas equals one rupee.

Anurag Sagar. A book attributed to the fifteenth-century saint, Kabir Sahib, set in the frame of a dialogue between Kabir and his disciple Dharam Das speaking about the creation.

Asarh. Indian month, equivalent to mid-June to mid-July.

astral body. Subtle body through which the consciousness functions in the first region above the physical, Sahansdal Kanwal.

Asuj.   Indian month, equivalent to mid-September to mid-October.

Attock.   Town in the north-western area of the subcontinent (now Pakistan).

baaraa.   A large leather container for drawing water from a well; ordinarily pulled by oxen; also called *charas*.

Baba Ji.   A term of respect and/or endearment for an older man, a grandfather, a holy man.

Babu Ji.   A term of respect for a person working professionally in an office or business. Before he became the Master at Beas, Maharaj Sawan Singh was known as Babu Ji or Babu Sawan Singh Ji.

bachan.   Speech, word, teachings; in *Sar Bachan Poetry*, denotes the chapters or sections of the book.

Bachint Singh.   Eldest son of Maharaj Sawan Singh; he passed away in 1952.

Baisakhi.   First day of the month of Baisakh or Vaisakh falling in mid-April.

Banta Singh   A distant relative of the Great Master, he worked as the Master's cook in Murree Hills. After retirement he settled in Sikanderpur where he served on the Master's lands under his youngest son, Sardar Harbans Singh, looking after the cows and bringing the mail to Sirsa each day.

Bapu Ji.   A term of endearment for a father, grandfather, or older male family member.

Basant.   The spring season of the Indian calendar, starting with a spring festival (Basant Panchmi).

Basant Singh.   Maharaj Sawan Singh's second son, mentioned regularly in the letters. He died in his early thirties.

battery.   Artillery unit.

Beas.   The name of an important river in Panjab; also the
  name of a small village near Amritsar, on the banks of the
  Beas river, the closest sizeable settlement to Dera Baba
  Jaimal Singh.

bhajan.   Worship; listening to the inner Sound or Shabd;
  meditation. *See also* **Shabd.**

bhandara.   Popular usage denotes a religious feast where free
  food is distributed on a large scale; at the Dera, the large
  monthly satsang gatherings are called bhandaras.

Bhandal.   A village southeast of the Dera, across the river Beas.

Bibi.   Sister, woman; conventional Panjabi way of referring to
  or addressing a woman, rather than using her name, which
  would be discourteous; in the letters refers to Bibi Rukko.

Bibi Ji.   *See* (Bibi) **Rukko.**

Bibi Jis.   In the letters, Maharaj Sawan Singh's wife and
  daughter-in-law are referred to as "the older Bibi and the
  younger Bibi".

Brahm Shankar Misra.   Known as Pandit Ji, he was a disciple
  of Rai Saligram and was his successor in Agra.

Brahmand.   The causal realm (*Pind* being the gross or physical
  realm, *And* being the astral).

causal body.   The subtle form through which the mind and
  soul function in the causal realm; it registers the root or seed
  karmas which keep the soul bound to the creation.

causal maya.   The most subtle form of maya (illusion).

Chacha Ji (Sahib).   Seth Pratap Singh Ji, youngest brother
  of Soami Ji Maharaj (Baba Jaimal Singh Ji's Master).

Chanan Singh.   Maharaj Sawan Singh's cook during his service
  days; disciple of Baba Jaimal Singh. He came to live at the
  Dera when Maharaj Sawan Singh retired in 1911.

charas.   *See* **baaraa.**

charpoy. Four *(chaar)* legs *(paaee)*; a lightweight traditional bedstead made from interlacing strings woven onto a wooden frame; moved around in the daytime for use as a seat.

Chet. Indian month, equivalent to mid-March to mid-April.

Chibbar. A gherkin-like vegetable used for pickling.

chitt. Consciousness; reflective aspect of the mind, the faculty of remembering and discerning beauty, form and colour; one of the four aspects of mind.

cycle of eighty-four. *See* **eighty-four.**

darshan. Beholding, seeing; used for seeing the Master either in his inner Radiant Form (inner darshan) or on the physical level (outer darshan) when the disciple is so absorbed as to be unaware of anything.

Dassam Granth. Literally, "the book of the Tenth Guru"; a scriptural text that for the Sikhs is next in importance to *Sri Guru Granth Sahib.*

Daswan Dwar. Tenth door; the third of five spiritual regions above the physical; also referred to as Sunn.

Dera. Tent, camp, colony; here refers to Dera Baba Jaimal Singh, the Radha Soami colony on the west bank of the river Beas, in Panjab.

Devnagri. Script traditonally used for writing Sanskrit and Hindi.

Dhaliwal. A village near the Dera. The inhabitants entreated Baba Jaimal Singh to make Dhaliwal his permanent residence. However, Baba Ji chose the wasteland that is now the site of the Dera.

dharmsala. A hostel or rest-house, often managed by a charitable institution.

Dhun. Inner sound or melody. *See* **Shabd, Shabd-dhun.**

dhyan. Attention, concentration, contemplation; beholding the Radiant Form of the Master within.

Diwali. The most important festival of the Hindu calendar, Diwali takes place in October/November and is celebrated as the festival of lights.

drishti. Look or glance; the Lord's abundant grace and mercy bestowed through the Master.

durbar hall. Royal court, hall of audience. Here refers to the small meeting hall adjoining Maharaj Sawan Singh's house (and originally right next to Baba Jaimal Singh's room); it was completed in 1898 and is the first of three satsang halls built at the Dera.

durries. Hand-woven cotton rugs.

ego. One of the four aspects of mind creating the sense of separate identity; the chief barrier between the soul and the Lord. It is depicted as one of the five passions (lust, anger, greed, attachment, ego).

eighty-four. From the Hindi word *chauraasee*. Refers to the eighty-four lakh (eight million four hundred thousand) species into which the soul may have to incarnate, conveying life's endless cycle of death and rebirth; also called the wheel of eighty-four and the wheel of transmigration.

elements. *See* **tattva**.

faqat. End; used at the end of a letter or document to signal its completion.

fateh. Victory. *See* **Wahiguru Ji ki Fateh**.

five names. *See* **simran**.

five shabds. The five-part Nam, or the five names of the simran, that the Master imparts at the time of initiation, and which is liked with the five inner stages of the Shabd within the individual. *See also* **Shabd, Shabd-dhun**.

fivefold Nam. *See* **five shabds**.

Gajja Singh. One of the people regularly greeted in the letters, Babu Gajja Singh was initiated by Baba Jaimal Singh. A lifelong bachelor, he worked as an overseer in the Military Engineering Service under Maharaj Sawan Singh and later helped in the construction of the Satsang Ghar. He built a small room for himself at the original gateway to the Dera (the present location of the Nature Cure Hospital).

Ganda Ram. Postman of Sathiala, the nearest post office to Beas in Baba Ji's time. In villages, even until recently, the postman would often act as scribe and write out letters. Ganda Ram would thus write out letters on behalf of Baba Jaimal Singh.

Ganda Singh. Sevadar of Baba Jaimal Singh; one of the first people to settle at the Dera.

Gayatri Sandhya. Hindu evening prayer.

Ghat Ramayan. A book by the eighteenth-century saint, Tulsi Sahib of Hathras (the Master of Baba Jaimal Singh Ji's Master, Soami Ji Maharaj); it is a series of discussions on the teachings of the saints (Sant Mat) with followers of different religions.

ghee. Clarified butter.

Ghuman. Baba Jaimal Singh's village, 16-18 miles from the Dera, in District Gurdaspur, Panjab.

Granth. A book of scriptural writings, as in: Tulsi Sahib's *Granth*; the Tenth Guru's *Granth (Dassam Granth)*; the *Adi Granth*.

Granth Sahib. *See* **Adi Granth.**

gross body. The physical body; the most coarse of the three coverings (gross, astral and causal) over the pure consciousness of the soul.

Gulab Singh. Greeted frequently in the letters, Babu Gulab Singh was a devoted satsangi of Baba Jaimal Singh. He was associated with Maharaj Sawan Singh while in service, and gave satsang regularly at the Dera. He was the first chairperson of the Radha Soami Satsang Beas society. He passed away in 1959.

gurmukh. One whose face *(mukh)* is turned towards the Guru; a devotee who has completely surrendered to the Master. Used frequently to refer to the saints since only they embody total surrender.

Gurmukhi. Panjabi script in which the Adi Granth is written; the script Baba Jaimal Singh Ji used in writing to Maharaj Sawan Singh.

guru. Teacher, guide; a Master.

Guru Granth Sahib. *See* **Adi Granth.**

Guru Poornima. A full-moon festival in the summer, dedicated to the Guru.

Harbans Singh. The youngest son and devoted disciple of Maharaj Sawan Singh; father of Maharaj Charan Singh. He passed away in 1956.

haveli. In Panjab villages, while the male relatives of the lady of the house are accommodated in the main house itself, a separate building located away from the main house is used for other male guests. Sometimes a barn is also attached to it.

Hazur. Presence; a respectful form of address that avoids using the person's name and is equivalent to 'My Lord'. Used frequently by Baba Jaimal Singh Ji to refer to his own Master, Soami Ji Maharaj, and in Maharaj Sawan Singh Ji's notes, to refer to Baba Ji.

Hazur Sahib. Title by which Rai Saligram Ji, a devoted disciple of Soami Ji, was known in Agra; he was a contemporary and fellow disciple of Baba Jaimal Singh Ji.

higher mind. *See* **nij man.**

Holi. One of the major festivals of the Indian calendar, falling

in spring (March), when brightly coloured powders are
sprinkled and thrown amongst the family and community.

Holy Feet.   Translation of the word *charan*; refers to the inner
subtle form of the Master, known as the Radiant Form.

hukam.   Order, command; will of the Lord; used also for
Shabd, Nam or Word.

initiate.   Here refers to someone who has been given the inner
spiritual practice of the Word (Shabd or Nam) by the
Master.

Jaimal Singh (1839-1903).   Baba Jaimal Singh Ji, disciple
of Soami Ji Maharaj of Agra, was told by his Master to
spread the teachings of the Word in Panjab. After retirement, he settled in a deserted area on the banks of the river
Beas. In the late 1890s, at Babu Sawan Singh's request,
Baba Ji consented to sink a well and construct the first
buildings of what was later to become Dera Baba Jaimal
Singh, the modern colony that is named after him.

Jalandhar.   A city about twenty-five miles southeast of the
Dera.

Janam Ashtami.   A festival celebrating the birthday of Lord
Krishna falling sometimes on 25 August, Soami Ji's
birthday.

jeev.   A living being; the individual or unliberated soul; sometimes used to denote human beings generally.

jeevaatmaa.   Soul *(aatmaa)* embodied in a physical form.

Jhelum.   One of the five rivers of the province of Panjab.

Jeth.   Indian month, equivalent to mid-May to mid-June.

Kabir.   Fifteenth-century saint of Banaras (Kashi) whose writings are still widely quoted in daily life throughout India.
Like all saints, Kabir Sahib strongly condemned religious

rituals and external observances, emphasizing the inner practice of the Word as the only means to supreme realization.

Kal.   Time; the universal mind, the ruler of the three perishable worlds (physical, astral, causal); another name for Brahm. Kal personifies the negative power of the creation, known also as Dharam Rai (the lord of judgement) and Yama (the lord of death), in contrast to Anami Radha Soami or Dayal, the eternal positive power, the Supreme Being. *See also* **karma.**

Kaliyug.   The Dark Age; the present and fourth age, according to Hindu mythology which divides time into cycles of four great ages.

kareer.   The berries of capparis spinosa or caper, used as a condiment.

karma.   Action; the law of action and reaction that governs the three worlds (physical, astral, causal); the debits and credits resulting from our deeds, which bring us back to the world in future lives to face their consequences. There are three types of karma: *pralabdh karma,* the fate or destiny we experience in the present life as a result of some of our past actions; *kriyaman karma,* the action karmas, the debits and credits created by our actions in this life, to be settled in future lives; *sinchit karma,* the stored karmas, the balance or store of unpaid karmas from all our past lives.

Kartik.   Indian month, equivalent to mid-October to mid-November.

Kasur.   A town south of Lahore (now in Pakistan).

Khalsa Akhbar.   Early Sikh periodical published in Gurmukhi script.

Kishen Kaur.   Bibi Kishen Kaur was Maharaj Sawan Singh's wife and a disciple of Baba Ji.

kriyaman.   *See* **karma.**

lakh.   One hundred thousand.

Lotus Feet.   Translation of the phrase *charan kamal*, 'sacred feet'; refers to the inner subtle form of the Master, known as the Radiant Form.

Ma Ji.   Mother; in the letters, refers to Mata Jivani Ji, the mother of Maharaj Sawan Singh.

Machhar.   Devoted disciple of Baba Jaimal Singh; farmer by profession; mentioned in *Tales of the Mystic East* (Machhar and Ramditta).

Maddar.   A village a few kilometres north-east of Jalandhar City.

Madho Prasad.   Known as Babuji Maharaj, he was the disciple of Rai Saligram Ji and successor of Pandit Brahm Shankar Misra at Soami Bagh, Agra.

Maghar.   Indian month, equivalent to mid-November to mid-December.

Majha.   The Lahore-Amritsar region.

Manna Singh.   Served Baba Jaimal Singh as a sevadar in the early days at the Dera; is said to have built the first hut for Baba Ji when he came to live on the banks of the river Beas. From 1903 to 1911, he and Bibi Rukko looked after the day-to-day running of the Dera while Maharaj Sawan Singh was still in service; gave satsang in Sardar Bahadur Maharaj Ji's time.

Mata Ji.   Mother; here refers to Narain Devi Ji, also known as Mata Radha Ji, the wife of Soami Ji Maharaj. Soami Ji Maharaj indicated her spiritual power by the authority he gave her in his last recorded words. Hence the reference in letter 28 to her blessing Maharaj Sawan Singh on his journey through the inner regions.

mauj.   Divine will; the will and pleasure of the Satguru; sometimes has the sense of the overflowing of the Lord's grace.

maya.   Illusion, delusion; whatever comes and goes and is tran-

sient; the phenomenal worlds (physical, astral, causal); the
veil of illusion that conceals God. Sometimes personified in
Indian philosophy as Maya or Shakti.

meditation cell. In the early years of the Dera when there
were no houses or other buildings, it was a common practice for disciples to live in cave-like rooms, sometimes quite
spacious, that they carved out of the ravines. Some were fitted with doors and reinforced with brick, and most had
ventilation shafts, making them cool in summer and warm
in winter. As the colony developed, there was no longer any
need for the caves. Most were destroyed in a flood in the
1950s and the occupants were given accommodation in the
building known as Sadhu Ashram.

Mehmansinghwala. Ancestral village of Maharaj Sawan
Singh, near Ludhiana, Panjab.

Milkhi Ram. Sevadar of Baba Jaimal Singh, from the nearby
village of Mithapur; he used to write letters for Baba Ji. He
was the father of Bibi Ralli, who as a child widow was
taken in to the Great Master's home and devotedly served
the Dera Masters and their families from an early age till
the end of her life in 1983.

Mohan Singh. Babu Mohan Singh, as Baba Jaimal Singh
calls him, was a clerk in the Military Engineering Service
who worked with Maharaj Sawan Singh.

muklaavaa. In traditional India, since the bride and groom
were married at a young age, consummation of the mar-
riage came after a subsequent ceremony *(muklaavaa* in
Panjabi) a few months to some years later. Until then, the
bride would live with her parents.

Nam. Name; the Shabd, Logos or Word; the divine creative
power. *See also* **Shabd.**

Nam-dhun. *See* **Shabd-dhun.**

Narain Das. Originally from Quetta, Baluchistan, he served Maharaj Sawan Singh in the Military Engineering Service and came to Baba Jaimal Singh for initiation in spite of his scholarly and orthodox background in traditional Hindu worship and the Vedas in particular. He later retired to Delhi, where he devoted himself to meditation, and passed away in the time of Maharaj Charan Singh.

nij man. Real, innermost mind; the causal or higher mind.

nirat. The seeing faculty of the soul.

Nimani Kasti. Also called Nirjala Ekadashi; an annual event towards the end of June (the height of the hot season), an occasion for refraining from the use of water. No wedding or associated ceremony takes place on that day or the day after.

pandit. Scholar; learned in Hindu theology and religion; applied to the Hindu priestly class (brahmins) regardless of learning.

Pandit Ji. *See* Brahm Shankar Misra .

parshad. Grace, benediction; generally used to refer to something blessed by the Master, whether food or anything else.

Phagun. Indian month, equivalent to mid-February to mid-March.

pice. Coin of a very small denomination: 1/64th of a rupee until the introduction of decimal coinage in India.

pralabdh. *See* **karma**.

Pran Sangli. A book in verse form attributed to Guru Nanak but not accepted as authentic by most scholars. The book deals primarily with Yoga but a fair portion is also devoted to the practice of Shabd.

Pratap Singh (1830-1909). Youngest brother of Soami Ji Maharaj of Agra (the Master of Baba Jaimal Singh Ji),

Seth Pratap Singh Ji's letters to Baba Ji are included at the end of this volume.

pukka bricks. Kiln-fired bricks, as opposed to unbaked, sun-dried mud bricks, which were also commonly used.

punkah. A *pankhaa* is a ceiling fan made of canvas or strong material stretched on a frame and swung by pulling a rope or cord.

Radha Soami. Lord or Master (swami) of the soul; a name for the Supreme Lord; also used as a greeting among the followers of Soami Ji and his successors.

rakhi. A cotton or wool bracelet that is tied by sisters on their brothers' wrists to signify the annual renewing of the bond between brother and sister. Brothers usually reciprocate by a gift of money or clothing.

Ram-Ram. A Hindu greeting invoking the Lord's name.

Ratan Mala. The final section in what is known as *Bhai Banno's Beed* (Bhai Banno's copy of *Sri Guru Granth Sahib)*; not included in the authorized edition published by the Shiromani Gurdwara Parbandhak Committee, Amritsar.

Ratan Sagar. A book by the eighteenth-century saint, Tulsi Sahib of Hathras; it takes the form of replies to disciples' questions on the principles of Sant Mat or the teachings of the saints.

Roor Singh Employed by Maharaj Sawan Singh during his service days to look after his horses. When Maharaj Sawan Singh retired, he gave him a small shop at the Dera for selling milk and sweets. At his death, he gave the milk-and-sweet shop to his assistant, Mangal Singh. Until the day of his death, he remained busy with seva and meditation.

Rukko. Bibi Rukko was in the service of Mata Radha Ji

(Soami Ji Maharaj's wife) and was sent by her to serve Baba Jaimal Singh in Panjab. As the Dera developed, she took care of the day-to-day administration along with Bhai Manna Singh, seeing to the langar and the other needs of the sangat. She passed away in 1934.

saag.   Cooked greens (spinach, mustard leaves and others)— a favourite Panjabi dish.

Sach Khand.   True *(sach)* realm *(khand)*, the fifth of five spiritual regions above the physical; the eternal, imperishable realm of pure spirit, unalloyed by matter, by change, transience or death. This realm or level of being, also referred to as Sat Lok (the true realm), is subdivided into three stages: the Invisible (Alakh), the Inaccessible (Agam), the Nameless (Anami, known also as Anami Radha Soami).

Sadar Bazaar.   Cantonment shopping centre in Murree.

sadhu.   Adept; a holy man following a path of spiritual discipline, usually a renunciate, an ascetic; may also be used to denote one who has crossed the three worlds, the sphere of mind.

Sahansdal Kanwal.   Thousand-petalled lotus; the astral region, the first spiritual region above the physical.

Saligram.   Rai Sahib Saligram Ji, who held the position of Post-Master General of U.P. was a disciple and sevadar of Soami Ji Maharaj and a contemporary of Baba Jaimal Singh Ji.

Samvat.   The Hindu calendar system, starting at 57 B.C., the era associated with Vikramaditya.

sangat.   Gathering, congregation; collectively refers to the seekers and disciples of a Master.

Sant Sangreh.   A compilation *(sangreh)* of compositions by different saints *(sant)*.

Sar Bachan.   Essential, true *(saar)* words *(bachan)*. The name of two key Sant Mat books by Soami Ji Maharaj, one in poetry and the other in prose.

Sat Lok. *See* Sach Khand.

Sat Nam. True *(sat)* Name *(naam);* a name for the Supreme Being.

Sat Purush. True *(sat)* Lord *(purush);* a name for the Supreme Being.

Satguru. True *(sat)* teacher *(guru);* a Master who has access to the fifth spiritual region, Sach Khand.

Sathiala. About four miles from the Dera, it was the nearest post office for the Dera in the days of Baba Jaimal Singh.

satsang. Association *(sang)* with truth *(sat);* the company of or association with a perfect Master; a congregation assembled to hear a spiritual discourse giving the teachings of Shabd, the Word.

satsangi. One who keeps the company *(sang)* of truth *(sat);* generally, one who has been initiated into the Sant Mat teachings. True satsangis are those who faithfully perform the spiritual practice, follow the instructions of the Master and conduct themselves accordingly in their daily lives.

Sawan. Indian month, equivalent to mid-July to mid-August.

Sawan Singh (1858-1948). Babu Sawan Singh Ji, as he was respectfully known to his fellow disciples, is the recipient of most of the letters in this book from Baba Jaimal Singh Ji. Before his death in 1903, Baba Jaimal Singh Ji named him as his successor. Gradually he came to be known as the Great Master, Maharaj Sawan Singh Ji.

seva. Service; serving the Supreme Being through voluntary service to the Master or his sangat. Meditation or spiritual service is the highest form of the four types of seva (monetary, physical, mental, spiritual).

Shabd. Word, Sound; audible life stream, sound current; the creative power, the source of all creation, manifesting as subtle sound and light in the spiritual regions. It is the Word or Logos of the Bible; Kalma, Ism-e-A'zam, Bang-e-Asmani, Kalam-e-Ilahi of the Qur'an; the Nad of the Vedas; Nam, Ram Nam, Gurbani, Bani and Dhun of the Adi Granth; the Tao of the Chinese; Vadan and Saut-e-Surmad of the Sufis; the Sharosha of the Zoroastrians. The secret of contacting the Shabd within the human form is imparted by a perfect Master. *See also* **five shabds.**

Shabd-dhun. The melody *(dhun)* of the Word *(shabd)*. Baba Jaimal Singh uses the compound term Shabd-dhun more frequently in the letters than Shabd, emphasizing the melodious nature of the Shabd through which the disciple makes actual contact with the supreme creative power.

Shabd Guru. The spiritual form of the Master merged with the Shabd that is encountered as the Radiant Form once the disciple crosses into the first spiritual region.

Shabd stages. The inner regions. Refers to the five regions the soul passes through on its inner journey; the practice of simran consists in repeating the five names associated with these regions.

shabds. Verses or hymns from spiritual texts; *see also* **Shabd, Shabd-dhun.**

sharan. Refuge, protection, unqualified surrender to the will of the Satguru.

simran. Remembrance, repetition. In Sant Mat, refers to the repetition of the five names given by the Master at the time of initiation, names that are associated with the five stages or regions of the inner journey; simran is a key aspect of the meditation process, designed to focus the mind at the eye centre.

sinchit. *See* **karma.**

Shiv Dayal Singh (1818-1878). Seth Shiv Dayal Singh Ji

was later known as Soami Ji Maharaj. See introductory
section of the book for biographical information.

sthool. Gross (of matter) or physical form.

Suchet Singh. One of the sons of Seth Pratap Singh Ji
(youngest brother of Soami Ji Maharaj).

Sudarshan Singh (1858-1936). Youngest son of Seth
Pratap Singh Ji (youngest brother of Soami Ji Maharaj).

Sound. *See* **Shabd.**

Sri Guru Granth Sahib. *See* **Adi Granth.**

square. A 25-acre section of arable land.

stage(s). *See* **Shabd stages.**

subedar. A non-commissioned officer in the army.

sub-tehsildar. A middle-rank rural administrator.

suksham. Subtle; fine; astral.

Surain Singh. With Magar Singh, he was among the last to
be initiated by Baba Jaimal Singh. They both served as
pathis *(paathee)* or chanters for Maharaj Sawan Singh for
several years in the early 1900s. Surain Singh died in the
late fifties.

surat. Soul, attention, inner hearing faculty of the soul.

Tarn Taran. A town southwest of Amritsar.

tattva. Indian philosophy describes all life-forms in terms of
five life-giving 'elements' or tattvas.

Tenth Guru. Guru Gobind Singh Ji, the tenth Guru in the
line of Guru Nanak Dev; his writings are compiled in the
Dassam Granth, referred to in the letters as the Tenth
Guru's *Granth.*

tonga. A horse-drawn two-wheeled vehicle commonly used for
transportation in rural India.

Trikuti. Three *(tri)* peaks or prominences *(kuti);* the second
of five spiritual regions above the physical universe; the

causal region, the source of the three gunas; the seat of Brahm (Brahm Lok), the region of the universal mind.

Tulsi Sahib.   Saint from Maharashtra who settled in Hathras, Uttar Pradesh; spiritual Master of Soami Ji Maharaj (Baba Jaimal Singh Ji's Master). Author of *Ghat Ramayan* and *Ratan Sagar;* in the letters, Baba Jaimal Singh refers to these collectively as Tulsi Sahib's *Granth.*

Urdu.   One of the Indian languages, written in Persian script. Indian languages are traditionally associated with particular scripts, but may in fact be written in any script. Maharaj Sawan Singh used the Urdu script when he wrote in Panjabi to Baba Jaimal Singh, and Baba Ji, writing the same language, used the Gurmukhi script.

Vaisakh.   Indian month, equivalent to mid-April to mid-May.
Valtoha.   A village in Amritsar district.
vina.   A stringed musical instrument, perhaps the oldest of the classical musical instruments in India, said to be the forerunner of the sitar. Its sound is associated with the highest spiritual region, Sach Khand. The sound of Sach Khand cannot be accurately conveyed in terms of any physical sound since it defies description.

Wahiguru.   A Sikh name for the Supreme Being.
Wahiguru Ji ki Fateh.   Diminutive form of the traditional Sikh greeting, "Wahiguru Ji ka Khalsa, Wahiguru Ji ki Fateh"; literally, "Hail, or Victory, to the Lord", it connotes "Blessings of the Lord's peace" in common parlance.
Waraich.   A village on the south side of the Dera.
Word.   *See* **Shabd.**

Index

Entries are indexed according to letter numbers. Where a lower case 'b' follows a number, the entry refers to the letters to the Sangat of Bhandal. Where a lowercase 'p' follows a number, the entry refers to the letters from Seth Pratap Singh of Soami Bagh, Agra.

Addresses for Information and Books

INDIAN SUB-CONTINENT

INDIA
The Secretary
Radha Soami Satsang Beas
P.O. Dera Baba Jaimal Singh 143204
District Amritsar, Punjab

NEPAL
Mr. Prakash Gauchan
RSS(B)—Nepal
P.O. Box 1646
Sundarighat, Kirtipur, Kathmandu

SRI LANKA
Mr. D. H. Jiwat
c/o Geekay Ltd.
33 Bankshall Street, Colombo 11

SOUTHEAST ASIA

INDONESIA
Mr. Gope L. Nanwani
Yayasan Radha Soami Satsang Beas
Jl. Alternatif Cibubur, Desa Jatikarya
Pondok Gede 17435, Jawa Barat

MALAYSIA
Dr. Narjit Singh Dhaliwal
Kumpulan Perubatan SMP
18 Lorong Sempadan, Jalan 16/7
(or P.O. Box 7081)
Shah Alam 40702

SINGAPORE
Radha Soami Satsang Beas
19 Amber Road
Singapore 439 868

THAILAND
Mr. Harmahinder Singh Sethi
ASA International Ltd., Part.
43/17-18, SOI Sawasdee,
Sukhumvit SOI 31, Bangkok 10110

ASIA PACIFIC

AUSTRALIA
Mrs. Janet Bland
P.O. Box 3, Oaklands Park
Adelaide, S. Australia 5046

HONG KONG
Mrs. Cami Moss
T.S.T., P.O. Box 97739
Kowloon

JAPAN
Mr. Jani G. Mohinani
1-1-10 Akamatsu-cho, Nada-ku
Kobe 657

NEW ZEALAND
Mr. Tony Waddicor
10 Maxine Place, Tauranga

PHILIPPINES
Mr. Kay Sham
P.O. Box 2346
MCC Makati, Metro Manila

TAIWAN R.O.C.
Mr. Larry T. Nanwani
No. 57 Tun Hwa South Road Sec. 1
Room 808, Choo Woo House
(*or* P.O. Box 68-1414), Taipei

NORTH AMERICA

CANADA
Mr. John W. Abel
701-1012 Beach Ave.
Vancouver, B.C. V6E 1T7

Dr. Peter Grayson
177 Division Street South
Kingsville, Ontario N9Y 1R1

UNITED STATES
Dr. Eugene Ivash
4701 Shadow Lane
Austin, TX 78731

Dr. Vincent P. Savarese
3507 Saint Elizabeth Road
Glendale, CA 91206

Dr. John Templer
114 Verdier Road
Beaufort, SC 29902

Dr. Frank Vogel
7 Pelham Terrace
Arlington, MA 02174

Science of the Soul Study Center
4115 Gillespie Street
Fayetteville, NC 28306

CARIBBEAN ISLANDS

CARIBBEAN ISLANDS
Mr. Sean Finnigan
P.O. Box 2314
Port-au-Prince, Haiti

BARBADOS
Mr. Bhagwandas Kessaram Gopwani
c/o Kiddies Corner, 43 Swan Street
(*or* P.O. Box 603)
Bridgetown

TRINIDAD (WEST INDIES)
Mr. Sean Finnigan
See Caribbean Islands

CENTRAL AMERICA

MEXICO
Mr. Jorge Angel Santana
Cometa 2821, Jardines del Bosque
Guadalajara, JAL 44520

For the following countries, contact:
Mr. Jorge Angel Santana, MEXICO

BELIZE
COSTA RICA
GUATEMALA
HONDURAS
NICARAGUA
PANAMA
EL SALVADOR

SOUTH AMERICA

BRAZIL
Mr. Alberto Cancio Ferreira
See PORTUGAL.

COLOMBIA
Mr. Alberto Garcia Botero
Calle 147 #22-19, Bogota

ECUADOR
Mr. Gonzalo Vargas Noriega
Calle Montalvo No. 200, Oficina 201
Edificio Ponce Larrea
(or P.O. Box 17-21-1477)
Quito

GUYANA
Mrs. Rajni B. Manglani
c/o Bhagwan's Store
18 Water Street, Georgetown

PERU
Mr. Gonzalo Vargas Noriega
See ECUADOR.

VENEZUELA
Mr. Jose Antonio Penaherrera
Calle Mohedano Con Sucre
Edif. Don Jose, Local 2
Apartado Postal 63-436
Chacaito, Caracas 1.016

EUROPE

AUSTRIA
Mr. Hansjorg Hammerer
Sezenweingasse 10
Salzburg A-5020

BELGIUM
Mr. Jacob Hofstra
See NETHERLANDS.

BULGARIA
Mr. Emil Saev
P.O. Box 342, Sofia 1000

CYPRUS
Mr. Heraclis Achilleos
18 Kyriacou Matsi, Flat 101
(or P.O. Box 9077)
Pallouriotissa, Nicosia CY1035

CZECH REPUBLIC
Mr. Vladimir Skalsky
Maratkova 916, Prague 4, 142 00

DENMARK
Mr. Rudolf Walberg
See GERMANY.

FRANCE
Mr. Pierre de Proyart
7 Quai Voltaire
Paris 75007

GERMANY
Mr. Rudolf Walberg
P.O. Box 1544
D-65800 Bad Soden/Taunus

GIBRALTAR
Mr. Sunder T. Mahtani
Radha Soami Satsang Beas
401 Ocean Heights, 4th floor

GREECE
Mr. Dimitrios Sotiriou
4 Moschoula & Apollonos St.
152-36 Penteli, Athens

ITALY
Mrs. Wilma Salvatori Torri
Via Bacchiglione 3
00199 Rome

NETHERLANDS, THE (HOLLAND)

Mr. Jacob Hofstra
Geulwijk 6, Leusden 3831 LM

NORWAY

Mr. Rudolf Walberg
See GERMANY.

PORTUGAL

Mr. Alberto Cancio Ferreira
Urb. do Buzano
Av. Comandante Gilberto
Duarte e Duarte, Lote 2, 3° Esq.
S. Domingos de Rana 2775

SLOVENIA

Mr. Marko Bedina
Brezje PRI, Trzicu 68, 4290 Trzic

SPAIN

Mr. Hiro W. Balani
Radha Soami Satsang Beas
Loma Del Valle, Cruce del Pinon
Alhaurin de la Torre
(or P.O. Box 486)
Malaga 29012

SWEDEN

Mr. Lennart Zachen
Norra Sonnarpsvagen 29
S-286 72 Asljunga

SWITZERLAND

Mr. Olivier de Coulon
Rue du Centre
Tolochenaz (VD) CH-1131

UNITED KINGDOM

Mrs. Flora E. Wood
Haynes Park
Haynes, Bedford MK45 3BL

AFRICA

BENIN

Mr. Jaikumar Vaswani
B.P. 951, Cotonou

CAMEROON

Mr. Nanik N. Balani
See NIGERIA

GHANA

Mr. Nanik N. Balani
See NIGERIA

IVORY COAST

Mr. Nanik N. Balani
See NIGERIA

KENYA

Mr. Surinder Singh Ghir
P.O. Box 39993, Nairobi

MAURITIUS

Mrs. Doolaree Nuckcheddy
17 Leconte de Lisle Ave.
Quatre Bornes

MOROCCO

Mr. Hiro W. Balani
See SPAIN.

NIGERIA

Mr. Nanik N. Balani
120 Awolowo Road
(or G.P.O. Box 10407)
Ikoyi, Lagos

SOUTH AFRICA

Mr. Sam Busa
P.O. Box 41355, Craighall 2024

TANZANIA
Mr. Diljeet Nath Pandit
83 Lugalo Rd., East Upanga
(*or* P.O. Box 1963)
Dar-es-Salaam

UGANDA
Mr. Sylvester Kakooza
Alanda Ltd., Plot 64, William Street
(*or* P.O. Box 31381)
Kampala

ZIMBABWE
Mrs. Dorothy Roodt
102 Suffolk Rd., Strathaven
(*or* P.O. Box 7095)
Harare

MIDDLE EAST

BAHRAIN, U.A.E.
Mrs. Shiela Chand
P.O. Box 3079

DUBAI, U.A.E
Mr. Chander Bhatia
Shabnam Trading Co.
P.O. Box 2296

ISRAEL
Mrs. H. Mandelbaum
P.O. Box 22121
Tel Aviv 61221

Books on this Science

SOAMI JI MAHARAJ
Sar Bachan

BABA JAIMAL SINGH
Spiritual Letters (to Hazur Maharaj Sawan Singh: 1896-1903)

MAHARAJ SAWAN SINGH
The Dawn of Light (letters to Western disciples: 1911-1934)
Discourses on Sant Mat
My Submission (introduction to *Philosophy of the Masters*)
Philosophy of the Masters (*Gurmat Sidhant*), in 5 volumes
    (an encyclopedia on the teachings of the Saints)
Philosophy of the Masters (abridged)
Spiritual Gems (letters to Western disciples: 1919-1948)
Tales of the Mystic East (as narrated in satsangs)

MAHARAJ JAGAT SINGH
The Science of the Soul (discourses and letters: 1948-1951)

MAHARAJ CHARAN SINGH
Die to Live (answers to questions on meditation)
Divine Light (discourses and letters: 1959-1964)
Light on Saint John
Light on Saint Matthew
Light on Sant Mat (discourses and letters: 1952-1958)
The Master Answers (to audiences in America: 1964)
The Path (first part of *Divine Light*)
Quest for Light (letters: 1965-1971)
Spiritual Discourses, in 2 volumes
Spiritual Heritage (from tape-recorded talks)
Thus Saith the Master (to audiences in America: 1970)

BOOKS ABOUT THE MASTERS

Call of the Great Master—Diwan Daryai Lal Kapur
Heaven on Earth—Diwan Daryai Lal Kapur
Treasure Beyond Measure—Shanti Sethi
With a Great Master in India—Julian P. Johnson
With the Three Masters, in 3 volumes—from the diary of
    Rai Sahib Munshi Ram

BOOKS ON SANT MAT IN GENERAL

A Spiritual Primer
The Holy Name—Miriam Bokser Caravella
Honest Living: A Means to an End
In Search of the Way—Flora E. Wood
The Inner Voice—Colonel C. W. Sanders
Liberation of the Soul—J. Stanley White
Message Divine—Shanti Sethi
Mystic Bible—Randolph Stone
The Mystic Philosophy of Sant Mat—Peter Fripp
Mysticism, The Spiritual Path, in 2 volumes—Lekh Raj Puri
The Path of the Masters—Julian P. Johnson
Radha Soami Teachings—Lekh Raj Puri
A Soul's Safari—Netta Pfeifer
Teachings of the Gurus—Lekh Raj Puri
Yoga and the Bible—Joseph Leeming

MYSTICS OF THE EAST SERIES

Bulleh Shah—J. R. Puri and T.R. Shangari
Dadu, The Compassionate Mystic—K. N. Upadhyaya
Dariya Sahib, Saint of Bihar—K. N. Upadhyaya
Guru Nanak, His Mystic Teachings—J. R. Puri
Guru Ravidas, Life and Teachings—K. N. Upadhyaya
Kabir, The Great Mystic—Isaac A. Ezekiel
Kabir, The Weaver of God's Name—V. K. Sethi
Mira, The Divine Lover—V. K. Sethi
Saint Namdev, His Life and Teachings—J. R. Puri and V. K. Sethi
Saint Paltu—Isaac A. Ezekiel
Sant Charan Das—T. R. Shangari
Sarmad, Jewish Saint of India—Isaac A. Ezekiel
Sultan Bahu—J. R. Puri and K. S. Khak
Tukaram, Saint of Maharashtra—C. Rajwade
Tulsi Sahib, Saint of Hathras—J. R. Puri and V. K. Sethi